Proposal Planning & Writing

Proposal Planning & Writing
Fourth Edition

Jeremy T. Miner and Lynn E. Miner

GREENWOOD PRESS
Westport, Connecticut • London

Library of Congress Cataloging-in-Publication Data

Miner, Jeremy T.
   Proposal planning & writing / Jeremy T. Miner and Lynn E. Miner. — 4th ed.
      p. cm.
   Lynn E. Miner's name appears first on the previous edition.
   Includes bibliographical references and index.
   ISBN: 978–0–313–35658–2 (alk. paper)
   ISBN: 978–0–313–35674–2 (pbk. : alk. paper)
1. Proposal writing for grants—United States. I. Miner, Lynn E. II. Title. III. Title: Proposal planning and writing.
HG177.5.U6M56   2008
658.15'224—dc22   2008013661

British Library Cataloguing in Publication Data is available.

Library of Congress Catalog Card Number: 2008013661
ISBN: 978–0–313–35658–2
        978–0–313–35674–2 (pbk.)

First published in 2008

Greenwood Press, 88 Post Road West, Westport, CT 06881
An imprint of Greenwood Publishing Group, Inc.
www.greenwood.com

Printed in the United States of America

The paper used in this book complies with the
Permanent Paper Standard issued by the National
Information Standards Organization (Z39.48–1984).

10 9 8 7 6 5 4 3 2 1

Contents

Preface

He from whose lips divine persuasion flows.
—*Alexander Pope*

WHY GRANTS FAIL

We begin the fourth edition of this book by posing a central question that every successful grantseeker must understand.

Why do some grant applications fail? What is the most common reason why proposals are turned down?

When we pose this question in grant writing workshops around the county, we hear these frequent answers:

1. Bad ideas
2. Good ideas poorly presented
3. No documented need statement
4. Lack of measurable objectives
5. Target population not clearly identified
6. Methods not well thought out
7. Weak evaluation approach
8. Inadequate dissemination strategy
9. Inexperienced project director
10. Failure to follow application guidelines
11. Insufficient preproposal contact
12. Poor budget justification

What do you think is the most common reason why grant proposals are not funded? Which one of these dozen possibilities would you pick as the top reason?

Our answer?

None of the above.

While all of these 12 reasons listed above certainly weaken a proposal and may result in its declination, the biggest reason that grants fail is lack of money.

That's right. Grantmakers simply receive more quality proposals than they are able to fund. Consequently, they have to turn down strong proposals simply due to insufficient funding.

In practical terms, this means that today, grantseeking is extremely competitive. Knowing that funds are limited, your responsibility, as a proposal writer, is to persuasively present great ideas that are well documented, whose objectives are expressed in measurable terms that implement innovative methods to targeted audiences, with the resulting outcomes rigorously evaluated and widely disseminated to other stakeholders. All of this will be done under the leadership of a strong project director who is well credentialed and has talked with program officers, past grant winners, and past grant reviewers prior to actual writing.

That's what this book is all about—leading you step-by-step through the process of planning and writing successful proposals.

The content of this book is based on our grantseeking experiences over the past four decades in writing successful proposals, conducting grant workshops nationwide, reviewing government and foundation proposals, and critiquing application guidelines for grantmakers. We don't just talk in abstract terms about grants; we share the practical tips that have enabled us to write winning grants for years.

We practice what we teach.

NEW TO THIS EDITION

While the fourth edition retains the crucial elements of previous editions for planning and writing proposals, the following additions are designed to better meet the emerging needs of today's grantseekers in an era of increased competition for limited resources.

Updated Web sites

Not only have Web addresses been updated in this fourth edition, but 25 percent more grantseeking sites have been added to put more useful tools at your disposal. These sites include information on public and private sponsors as well as information about writing all proposal elements and assembling budgets and budget narratives. An expanded presentation of

Grants.gov, your electronic "one-stop shopping" source for government grants, will help you to find and apply for billions of dollars awarded by 26 federal grantmaking agencies.

More Sample Proposals

The third edition contained two complete proposals and many samples from various proposal sections. Our book readers and workshop participants repeatedly tell us they want more examples of successful proposals—and we've listened. Sprinkled throughout this fourth edition, and especially in Chapter 6, you will find nine letter proposals, complete with annotations. With the exponential growth of family foundations, which typically require a short letter proposal, you will find value in examining requests for operating support, physical facilities renovation, capital campaign support, and programmatic support for training and service delivery projects. Readers wishing further model proposals along with paragraph-by-paragraph analyses of the key features that made them persuasive should consult our companion text, *Models of Proposal Planning & Writing* (Praeger Publishers, 2005).

Expanded Evaluation and Outcome Chapters

Most grant writers recognize that evaluation and outcome assessments are increasingly important proposal components. Accountability is the watchword as grantmakers want to know whether their funds are making a difference. New to this edition are evaluation and logic outcome models that can be easily adapted to most grant projects, merely by tweaking the examples presented.

Sustainability

One of the nagging questions with which proposal writers wrestle is: "What do we do when the grant funds run out?" That is to say, grantmakers usually want to know how you will sustain your project. While they don't expect guarantees, they at least want to know you have considered the issue of future funding and have a tentative plan in mind. In this edition, we've expanded our discussion of sustainability and included sample proposal language that can easily be adapted to multiple situations.

TARGET AUDIENCES

This fourth edition will be of value for grantseekers wishing a concrete guide through the fundamentals of proposal planning and writing. Based on our 15 years of experience with this text, users represent the following disciplines:

- **Economic Development:** City planning, land use, urban revitalization, workforce development, job creation.
- **Education:** Day care programs, adult education, public and private schools, special education departments, colleges and universities, English as foreign language programs, libraries.
- **First Responders:** Police, fire, emergency medical services.
- **Government:** Local, state, and federal agencies; courts, human services, parks and recreation.
- **Health Care:** Hospitals, nursing homes, public health organizations, Veterans Administration, International Health, families, maternal and child health.
- **Philanthropy:** Foundations, charitable organizations, service clubs.
- **Religions:** Churches, synagogues, mosques, and other houses of worship; faith-based organizations, religious education.
- **Social Services:** Community development, rehabilitation, mental health, welfare, senior citizens.

STRUCTURE AND CONTENT

This book discusses funding from government, foundation, and corporate sponsors. Sixteen chapters and a bibliography are arranged in logical order—developing proposal ideas, identifying and qualifying potential funding sources, setting up systems and procedures to support grantseeking activities for the present and future, developing the components of the proposal, budget forecasting, submission procedures, and follow-up techniques. You will find many specific examples, models, and step-by-step instructions throughout the text. Additionally, you will find many helpful Web site addresses that will simplify your proposal planning and writing.

Successful grantseekers are individuals who are so dedicated to their ideas that they will find the means to carry them out with or without outside support. Sponsors have clear objectives and expectations that they hope to realize by providing financial support to such dedicated persons. A persuasively written grant proposal is the link between them. This book helps you forge that link.

Let's begin planning your best grant ever!

PART I
Finding Sponsors and Planning Proposals

OVERVIEW OF PART I

Tens of thousands of grantmakers give away approximately $300 billion annually. How do you find those sponsors who would fund your projects?

Part I gives you the basic print and electronic information sources to identify a list of public and private sponsors who might fund your projects. With a little research time, you can narrow down that initial suspect list and identify those grantmakers who have a high probability of funding your organization.

Chapter 1 helps you get ready to begin your grantseeking journey. It examines the individual and organizational attitudes held by successful grantseekers. It offers an overview of the grantseeking process—from start to finish. It recognizes that you probably have other work responsibilities besides writing grants and suggests some effective time management strategies so you can write more grants in less time. Finally, it suggests some ways in which you can help build your own internal infrastructure for successful grantseeking.

In Chapter 2, the focus is on finding public grants from federal and state agencies. Most federal grantmaking agencies provide online information that is readily accessible, so much so, in fact, that the Internet search results can be overwhelming. We present some efficient ways of identifying federal grant dollars. State agencies, on the other hand, lag behind many federal agencies in making grant information available. Accordingly, we offer some strategies for ferreting out state-level grant funds.

With Chapter 3, our attention turns to finding private funds from foundations and corporations. We identify five different types of foundations and suggest how approaches to them might differ. Presently, there are more than 90,000 private foundations that award grants. Information about private foundation funding priorities and past grant support is generally accessible and we point to multiple print and electronic sources that will help you select likely sponsors of your projects. In contrast, information about corporations is less accessible and successful grantseekers must be especially resourceful in their quest for funding. We show you the tips that the professionals use when seeking corporate funding.

By the time you have completed your search of public and private funding sources, you have a list of potential "suspects" who might fund your proposal—but you don't know for sure. In Chapter 4, we prescribe a four-step process to convert these "suspects" to "prospects" by talking with program officers, past grant winners, and past grant reviewers **before** you start to write your next proposal. Engaging in preproposal contact substantially increases your likelihood of getting funded.

CHAPTER 1
Introduction to Grantseeking

There is nothing more uncertain in its success than to take
the lead in the introduction of a new order of things.
—Machiavelli

Grantseeking is a multibillion-dollar-a-year business—and growing annually!

Following a 500-year-old Machiavellian maxim, your challenge, as a grantseeker, is to introduce a new order of things without guarantees of outcomes. In Chapter 1, you will learn the following:

- The healthy attitudes necessary to be a successful grantseeker.
- How to start the grantseeking process.
- How to manage effectively your limited time to write grants.

ATTITUDES ABOUT GRANTSEEKING

"Is it really worthwhile to write grants?"

Yes, it is; and those organizations that receive grant dollars each year certainly think so. To find out how you can access those dollars and answer many questions along the way, we begin by looking at some attitudes—and misconceptions—about grants.

Individual Attitudes

What does the word "grants" mean to you? Frankly, for some people the term "grants" generates negative reactions such as "professional begging," "futility," "risk-taking," "mystique," "hustle," or "con job." To such people, pursuing grants is risky because positive outcomes aren't guaranteed. These people steer clear of grants for many negative reasons: lack of motivation, lack of skills, lack of confidence, fear of failure, fear of change, fear of success, lack of time, unrealistic expectations, and laziness. Such individuals, who are a

"quart low on attitude," are destined to fail if they pursue grants. Skeptics will say, "Grants, why bother?" Successful grant winners, on the other hand, will answer, "For many reasons." People write grants to

1. Earn money
2. Finance crucial projects
3. Gain job security
4. Achieve recognition
5. Break the regular job routine
6. Solve problems creatively
7. Have fun

What brings you job satisfaction? Certainly, money—a decent salary and the security it produces—is an extremely important factor on the job. More broadly, employee satisfaction fluctuates with the circumstances in each organization. Nevertheless, most job satisfaction studies show that employees desire (1) interesting work, (2) recognition for work performed, and (3) a feeling of being "in" on things. Grantseeking can satisfy all three components of a rewarding job. If you are responsible for mustering grant support from others on your staff, you must show how grants will meet these needs.

Perhaps the most critical element in your ability to pursue grants successfully is your sense of self-worth—the picture you have of yourself in your mental photo album, your self-esteem. Those with high self-esteem have a feeling of competence and believe in their ability to cope with the challenges of life. The value you place on yourself ultimately dictates your performance.

If you approach proposal planning and writing with a positive attitude and are willing to persist, you will succeed. If you doubt success from the start, you will fail. The applicable behavioral principle is the notion of the "self-fulfilling prophesy." In essence, it says, "What you believe will happen." Many like you have already mastered the grants process. We believe you too can be a successful grantseeker.

Organizational Attitudes

Grant Myths. Many nonprofit organizations harbor misconceptions about grantseeking that serve as formidable internal barriers to winning grants. Some common myths that need to be debunked include the following.

Myth: People will fund my needs. Sponsors fund their needs, not yours. When writing proposals, you must show you can become a change agent to solve a problem important to them. For example, as a school official you may want a new computer laboratory. Sponsors are apt to be much less interested in your perceived needs than an opportunity to support a project that will train computer-literate children in the new century. Put differently, sponsors care more about innovative ways to teach children than they do about buying computers.

Myth: You can run a program on grants forever. Sustained grant support over many years is difficult to obtain. Start-up project support is the easiest to find and operating support is the most difficult. While project support can be successfully parlayed over many years, it is usually segmented into different phases or is periodically redefined if it is to be sustained.

Myth: Use the weasel words that people want to hear. There are no magic buzzwords to sprinkle in your proposal. "In" words today go "out" tomorrow. Don't be concerned about using vogue words. The simple, honest, direct approach is best.

Organizational Benefits. Organizations pursue grants for many financial and administrative reasons. For instance, grants will provide budget relief through the direct and the indirect costs they provide. Often, grant money can be leveraged to attract additional funds from other sources. Beyond these fiscal considerations, receiving grants can have considerable public relations value for your organization. This, in turn, can bring zest to your recruitment program, making it easier to attract new talent to your organization.

Organizational Barriers. Agencies entering the grants arena must recognize and respond to one very

important principle of behavior, namely, *organization prevents reorganization*. This means the very fact that you are organized one way makes it difficult to organize another way. And yet, commitment to a successful grants program means that organizational priorities may need to change. Time and resources will be allocated differently. New systems and procedures will be implemented, as discussed below.

Resistance to change is natural and can be minimized by showing individuals how their job satisfaction will increase. Perhaps the best motivators for employees are the achievement, the recognition, the work itself, and the responsibility. One of people's greatest needs is the ability to achieve, and through achievement, experience psychological growth. Your task is to control and increase the effectiveness of the motivators within your organization that induce growth. Grants enable you to do things that you would not otherwise be able to do within your organization, or at least not as quickly.

Motivating Others within Your Organization. Work smarter, not harder. Encourage others to join your grantseeking activities. These suggestions will help you secure "buy-in" from your colleagues.

- Have a central administrator issue a policy memo indicating that grant writing is encouraged, indeed expected, within the organization.
- Give people time, resources, and training to write grants.
- Recognize and reward grant activities within the organization. For instance, writing grants should be one of the factors considered when awarding promotions and raises.
- Use the in-house newsletter or letters from a central administrator to praise grant writers on their efforts.
- Share your grant knowledge with others in your organization. Remember, enthusiasm is contagious.
- Start small and build. Pick a few people to become the in-house grant experts. As they develop and experience success, others will want to get involved also.

As you work with colleagues in your organization, help them build realistic expectations about grantseeking; otherwise, their false expectations will produce disappointments and disincentives for pursuing grants. For instance, supervisors must recognize that it takes approximately six to nine months to find out whether a federal grant has been funded. If bosses expect a decision soon after submitting a proposal, they will be needlessly disappointed.

Sponsor Attitudes

Grantmakers (sponsors) are vitally concerned about specific problems, injustices, or inequities they see in the world. They are so concerned, in fact, that they are willing to commit their money to solve these problems. In essence, they see a gap between what is and what ought to be. Their mission is to close this gap. Another name for "gap" in grant parlance is "need," perhaps the most crucial section of your proposal; see Chapter 7 for further details. The gap represents their view of the problems that interest them.

Successful grant writers understand the sponsor's view and express that view in proposals. Too often, proposal writers focus on their own need for funds instead of matching their project's goals with a sponsor's priorities. You should select sponsors that share your view of the world and tailor proposals to them. (See Chapter 4 for specifics.) Sponsors view grants as investments in an improved future. Proposals are funded when they express the priorities shared by the sponsor. Projects are rejected when they do not match a sponsor's priorities.

GETTING STARTED

Attitudes healthy? Ready to take the plunge? Great! We'll guide you through the five main steps to become a successful grantseeker.

1. **Select your grant ideas.** Look internally to your staff and volunteers for suggestions. Hold brainstorming sessions. Ask colleagues, "If we had a million dollars, what would we do with it?" Look externally to citizens, clients, and advisory boards. What suggestions would they have? For now, compile your list of grant ideas. Don't worry about which ones are the most fundable; that'll come later (Chapter 4).
2. **Identify possible funding sources.** Examine print and electronic funding sources for both public (Chapter 2) and private (Chapter 3) grants. When finished, you'll have a list of sponsors who *may* be interested in funding your projects.
3. **Conduct preproposal contacts.** Following the four-step process in Chapter 4, you will find out which sponsors are most likely to fund your proposals. Grantseeking is a contact sport. You will want to contact program officers, past grant winners, and past grant reviewers—all before you decide *if* and *what* you should write.

4. **Write your initial proposal draft.** Following the application guidelines and reviewer's evaluation form, quickly write your first draft. Remember: the first draft is for getting down, not for getting good. Experienced grantseekers spend approximately 25 percent of their time writing the first draft and 75 percent of their time rewriting and editing, your next step. (Chapters 5–14).
5. **Edit your initial proposal draft.** Cycle through your draft many times, continually looking for one feature to improve at a time (Chapter 15). Examples: make sure you provide all of the requested information, check for spelling and grammar errors, and design a visually appealing document.

Time Management: Writing More Proposals in Less Time with Greater Efficiency

Why do we all complain about the lack of that precious commodity—time? Effective time management enables you to feel in control, be productive, and enjoy what you do.

Very few people have grant writing as their only job responsibility. Usually it is one of many tasks that includes such things as project administration, training, research, advising, public relations, other fundraising, personnel management, budgeting, phone answering, envelope stuffing—and the list goes on.

We all know the basics of effective time management and we need periodic reminders about such things as the following:

1. Set priorities daily.
2. Do first things first.
3. Remember, you don't "find" time, you "make" time.
4. Recognize there is always time for important things.
5. Recall long-term goals while doing small tasks.
6. Eliminate unproductive activities quickly.
7. Focus on one thing at a time.
8. Establish deadlines for yourself and others.
9. Delegate whenever possible.
10. Handle each piece of paper only once.
11. Keep things organized.
12. Don't fret when time is spent on activities beyond your control.

Of the many good books on time management, our favorite is *How to Get Control of Your Time and Your Life* by Alan Lakein.

Beyond these common sense suggestions, successful grantseekers adhere closely to their "To Do" list, avoid a huge time robber—interruptions—and use efficient office procedures.

To Do List. Consider your "To Do" list inviolate. If you write it down, it shall get done. Examples:

- Identify possible federal and state funding sources.
- Review guidelines.
- Call program officer to get a copy of reviewer's evaluation form.
- Talk with past grant winner.
- Outline proposal.
- Draft three pages.
- Conduct a primary literature review.
- Use search engines to find documenting statistics.

Avoid Interruptions. Take control of your time. Examples:

- Tell colleagues that a closed door or a "Do Not Disturb" sign means business.
- Don't check your e-mail and voice mail frequently; schedule communications checks several times a day.
- Postpone the interrupters by asking them if you could talk later; then, set up a time.
- Jot down an agenda to use when you want to talk to them: it will hasten your meeting.

Using Efficient Procedures. Use your time effectively. Examples:

- Return calls during lunch hour that require only a short answer or when you're posing a simple question. Many people will be away from their desks and you'll reach voice mail. Be specific in your call. This way they can leave you a complete, detailed answer.
- "Power Block" your time in intervals where you do nothing except what you schedule yourself to do. Make appointments with yourself to work on your proposal.
- To get people off the phone, warn them your time is limited by saying, "It sounds interesting, but I've got to leave in five minutes," or "Since I really can't spend a lot of time on the phone, let's make plans to meet for lunch instead."
- Voice mail can receive calls while you're not there. Callers are now accustomed to it, but change your messages frequently to update callers on your schedule.
- When you leave a voice mail message for someone, say a time you will be available in order to avoid phone tag, e.g., "John, I'll be at my desk between 2:00 and 4:00 p.m. this afternoon," or "Sara, please call me tomorrow morning between 8:00 and 10:00 a.m."

- Leave some free time on your appointment calendar to provide you with the flexibility you need to deal with distractions, delays, and emergencies while avoiding stress.
- Sort the mail into six categories:
  1. To toss: go through the mail stack quickly, tossing things that aren't worth opening
  2. To ask about: attach sticky notes to remind yourself what to ask about
  3. To file: if you don't need it now, it can be filed
  4. To call: handle quicker than by letter
  5. To do: things that require action
  6. To read: be selective

Clip Files as a Premier Time Management Tool

Successful grantseekers have effective grant systems and procedures in place to save time when hunting for and organizing information. If you could cut down the amount of time you spend managing information, you could write more proposals or work on other responsibilities. We recommend using clip files to organize and manage grant information. With them, you "chunk" the grant process into small, manageable units and distribute your information into those categories.

The clip file theme runs throughout the book. We'll cite some examples below to get you started; additional tips are found at the end of each chapter. To begin, create a system of file folders, notebooks, or electronic files that contain the following labels.

Clip File Labels	Clip File Labels
Developing Grant Ideas (Chapter 1)	Goals, Objectives, and Outcomes (Chapter 8)
Refining Grant Ideas (Chapter 1)	Methods (Chapter 9)
Uniqueness (Chapter 1)	Evaluation (Chapter 10)
Advocates (Chapter 1)	Dissemination (Chapter 11)
Finding Public Funds (Chapter 2)	Budget (Chapter 12)
Finding Private Funds (Chapter 3)	Appendixes (Chapter 13)
Preproposal Contacts (Chapter 4)	Abstract/Summary (Chapter 14)
Statement of Problem (Chapter 7)	Grant Review and Funding Decisions (Chapter 16)

We'll give examples of the first four clip files here to familiarize you with the concept; the remaining topics are discussed in appropriate chapters as indicated in parentheses. Whenever you see the following symbol, get out your kitchen (or electronic) scissors, clip the action item, and add it to your *clip* file; you'll *save* time when you write your next grant. Just like people clip grocery coupons to save money, look for the *clip and save* symbol in this book to save you valuable grant writing time.

Clip File Action Item # 1
Developing Grant Ideas

Assemble your wish lists of organizational needs. Beyond the internal and external sources cited earlier, where else can you get grant ideas? Consider reports from commissions or government offices citing pertinent needs, consultant reports, grant idea worksheets, lists of recently funded grants, and lists of requests for proposals. Every time someone says "We ought to do this if we had the money," write "this" on a piece of paper and add it to your clip file. Experienced grantseekers have found they can sometimes combine ideas and craft them into a bigger—and more fundable—idea.

Clip File Action Item # 2
Developing Grant Ideas

To quickly build your clip files, search the larger regional and national newspapers for stories that pertain to your interest area. For instance, if you live in Atlanta, Georgia and you are seeking grant funds in the area of "school violence," electronically search your metropolitan newspaper for school violence-related stories and then, to see how Atlanta compares with other major cities, conduct similar searches in other city circulations as well. This information will help you document the frequency and severity of the problem (Chapter 7).

Clip File Action Item # 3
Refining Grant Ideas

The more ways you can describe your grant ideas, the better chance you have of getting funded. Why? Because different sponsors fund different types of projects serving different populations in different locations. You have four different options to redefine your project. You can identify alternative:

- Subject matter areas.
- Project locations.
- Constituency groups served.
- Types of grants.

Assume you work for an inner-city elementary school. How else might you describe your school? A model school for language immersion? A demonstration center for parental involvement in education? A cross-cultural community center? A school/industry partnership location? Each description presents your school in a different light and could attract different sponsors.

As another example, assume you work for a rural health care agency. How else might you describe yourself? A regional one-stop health shopping service? A countywide multispecialty health clinic? A rural life-care health center? A federal health demonstration center? Again, different focus points could appeal to different sponsors.

Each variable—subject matter, location, constituency, grant type—gives you some choices about the way you might describe your project. For example, suppose you wanted to create an information clearinghouse for the homeless. You might redefine your project as follows:

Subject Matter Area: In broad terms, your project might be described as one dealing with "education," "social welfare," or "social justice." In more narrow terms, keyword phraseology might include "low-cost housing," "information dissemination," or perhaps, "minority education." As further examples, keyword terms in the broad area of medical diseases might include the following: "accidents," "AIDS," "Alzheimer's Disease," "asthma," "breast cancer," "cardiovascular diseases," "cystic fibrosis," "diabetes," "mental health," "HIV infection," "Parkinson's Disease," and "Sudden Infant Death syndrome," among many.

Project Location: Your project impact area could range from the "neighborhood" to the "city," "region," "county," "state," "national," or even "international" level, depending upon the scope of your efforts.

Constituency Groups Served: While you might want to make your information clearinghouse available to all those who need its service, you might wish to specialize in serving the needs of one or more populations, e.g., "minorities," "aged," "disadvantaged," "single parents with low income," or "poor families." Other target groups might include the following: "children and youth," "handicapped," "refugees," "veterans," and "women."

Type of Grant: Keywords for different types of grants include the following: "service delivery," "capacity building," "research," "equipment," "exhibition," "workshops," and "travel." Because many different types of grants are available, you might choose to cast your information clearinghouse for the homeless project to emphasize any of these categories.

Putting some of these choices together, you might describe your project as follows:

- A low-cost housing dissemination project for minorities in your city.
- A housing demonstration information project for the disadvantaged poor in the Midwest.
- A housing training project for the aged in the state.
- A seed project for an information clearinghouse on housing in the region.

Use "out-of-the-box" thinking to identify different ways to appeal to potential sponsors. What can you adapt, modify, magnify, minify, substitute, rearrange, reverse, or combine to come up with a distinctive project?

Clip File Action Item # 4
Uniqueness

Include the following in your clip file: your mission statement, mission statements from other organizations like yours enabling you to identify your distinctive differences, endorsements from experts, bibliographies, resumes, and organizational self-assessment tools.

One starting point in identifying your uniqueness is to examine (or brush off the dust and reexamine) your organizational mission statement. It is a brief, clear summary of your organization's goals. Ideally, it contains no more than one hundred words. It provides a context for the specific grant activities that you will pursue.

One hospital identified its unique characteristics as follows: the only self-sufficient laboratory in the state with administrative support for the project, strong community reputation, centralized location, solid partnership program with physicians, open-heart surgery center, and active research program.

Consider this mission statement from an alcoholism rehabilitation agency named Return:

> The mission of Return is to help individuals regain an active, productive life without the use of alcohol. Recovery comes through rehabilitative support and a self-desired change

rather than from prescription. Return is a hospital-based program that emphasizes keeping the alcoholic in contact with family, employer, church, community, recreation, and cultural activities during the recovery process. (56 words)

Still having trouble determining your organizational uniqueness? Ask yourself and answer these questions.

1. What is your agency "known" for?
2. What are you recognized as being "the best" at?
3. What will make you more unique in the future?
4. What separates you from your grant competition in the eyes of grantmakers?
5. What do the leading grantmakers say about your agency?

Clip File Action Item # 5
Advocates

List the types of services that your organization needs but is unable to provide with internal staff (e.g., legal, financial, management, or personnel); contact external service providers who know your organization and may be able to advocate on your behalf. List specific services you might use but lack access to (e.g., telephone credit card, data entry, desktop publishing, and travel); perhaps your organizational friendraising can identify people who can assist with these services.

To help build your clip files, invoke the help of your colleagues. Have staff members, for example, bring one addition to your clip file at each staff meeting. Further, make full use of so-called idle moments. Whether you are reading the evening newspaper, waiting in a doctor's office, or scanning the in-flight magazine while flying, develop a habit of continually being on the lookout for printed ideas that may be useful someday in developing a proposal.

What about politicians? Are they good advocates? Should you use them to help get grants? The answer: like Thanksgiving Dinner, "Yes," but in moderation. Local, county, state, and federal government officials can be of some help in getting grants. Among the appropriate ways to network with politicians:

1. Keep them posted on your grant priorities.
2. Meet periodically with congressional staffers in charge of your specialty area: education, health, social services, environment.

3. Invite them to share new reports with you (for your clip file).
4. Write draft support letters you'd like to receive from them for major (not all) proposals you submit, if the sponsor would see value in it. Unsure? Ask as a part of your preproposal contact (Chapter 4).
5. Invite them to visit your organization and see for themselves the good work you are doing.

CHAPTER 2
Finding Public Funds

The art of government consists in taking as much money as
possible from one class of citizens to give to the other.
—*Voltaire*

OVERVIEW OF PUBLIC FUNDING

Consistent with the 200-year-old Voltaire observation, federal and state governments award billions of grant dollars each year. This chapter focuses on finding public grant funds at the national and state levels. Specifically, in Chapter 2, you will learn the following:

- The three different types of government funding.
- Basic reference tools for finding federal government funding.
- Basic reference tools for finding state government grants.
- Tips for conducting electronic grant information searches.

Although no one single source of information covers all government grants, many agencies have some type of grantmaking program, usually found on a World Wide Web site or in an agency publication. Because so much information is available on the Web, we begin by looking first at the interagency references and then focus on agency-specific print and electronic sources of information regarding federal and state government grants.

TYPES OF FEDERAL GOVERNMENT FUNDING

The federal government uses three different types of funding mechanisms to support or stimulate activities. Congress passed the Federal Grant and Cooperative Agreement Act of 1977 to distinguish between and establish criteria for using grants, cooperative agreements, and contracts. In practical terms:

1. A **grant** is a financial award from a federal sponsor that expects modest involvement from its program officers.
2. A **cooperative agreement** is awarded by a federal sponsor when it expects substantial involvement from its program officers.
3. A **contract** is a financial award from a federal sponsor wherein specific services are performed for a set fee.

The table on the following page highlights some of the differences among these three funding mechanisms.

FEDERAL GOVERNMENT INFORMATION SOURCES

The following section describes four global reference sources that transcend any individual agency: Grants.gov, the primary information source for grants and cooperative agreements, the *Catalog of Federal Domestic Assistance* and the *Federal Register*, two secondary information sources for grants and cooperative agreements, and FedBizOpps, the primary information source for government contracts. These sources disseminate information for all federal agencies in print and electronic formats.

Grants.gov

Grants.gov was created in 2002 to be your "one-stop shopping" source to find and apply for billions in federal government grants. Through the use of a common Web site, www.grants.gov, you can find and apply for grant funds online, thereby simplifying

Feature	Grants	Cooperative Agreements	Contracts
Funding idea initiated by...	Project Director	Project Director or Sponsor	Sponsor
Project announcement...	Unsolicited	Solicited	Competitive bidding
Project direction determined by...	Project Director	Project Director and Sponsor jointly	Sponsor
Level of oversight by sponsor...	Minimal	Substantial	Substantial
Payment plan...	Drawdown scheduled	Variable	Drawdown after expenditures
Purchased equipment belongs to...	Project Director	Project Director	Sponsor (sometimes)

grants management and eliminating redundancies. The 26 federal agencies that award grants and cooperative agreements have developed common data elements, electronic processes, and uniform administrative rules—all to be accessible through a single portal. Since November 7, 2003, all federal agencies have been required to post all competitive grant opportunities on this site.

While the idea of a common Web site is admirable, Grant.gov has not been without its share of challenges. Transitioning from a print to online process will, inevitably, produce growing pains. As much as Grants.gov attempted to account for unique cases, some processes can't be anticipated in full until they are implemented live. For instance, as a whole, Macintosh users have experienced more problems with the online system than PC users. And while Grants.gov does not identify a preferred Web browser, grantseekers using Internet Explorer experienced fewer difficulties than those using other browsers. The take home message: As Grants.gov continues to unfold, build time into your schedule to address the technological hiccups that will unavoidably occur, have patience, and be persistent.

Begin your search for funding opportunities by visiting the Grants.gov home page as illustrated in Exhibit 1.

Next, to find specific federal grants, you can search by keyword, funding opportunity number, Catalog of Federal Domestic Assistance Number, broad category designation (e.g., health, education, or environment), name of grantmaking agency (e.g., Department of Health and Human Services, Department of Education, or Environmental Protection Agency). Further, an Advanced Search feature enables you to combine individual search parameters. Exhibit 2 shows an example of a keyword search for "obesity" grants.

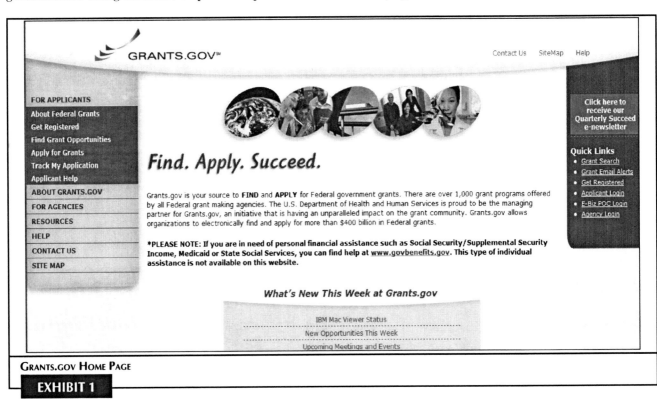

GRANTS.GOV HOME PAGE

EXHIBIT 1

EXHIBIT 2

Finally, once you have entered your search terms, you will be presented with a list of pertinent grant opportunities. The results of the keyword search for obesity grant opportunities are shown in Exhibit 3.

Each "hit" is a hot link that will open up information that can be viewed in either summary or detailed form.

Getting Started with Grants.gov. To use Grants.gov, you must register once before using. By registering once on this site, your organization can apply to more than 1,000 grant programs offered by 26 different federal agencies.

The Grants.gov registration process takes three to five business days to complete. You do not have to register with Grants.gov if you only want to find grant opportunities; however, if you plan to apply for a grant, you and your organization must complete the Grants.gov registration process listed below.

1. Your organization will need to obtain a DUNS Number, which is the unique identifier used by the government to track the distribution of federal grant money. If your organization doesn't have one, you will need to go to the Dun & Bradstreet Web site to obtain a DUNS Number; usually you can get it the same day. Visit http://fedgov.dnb.com/webform.

2. Ensure that your organization is registered with CCR (Central Contractor Registry) at

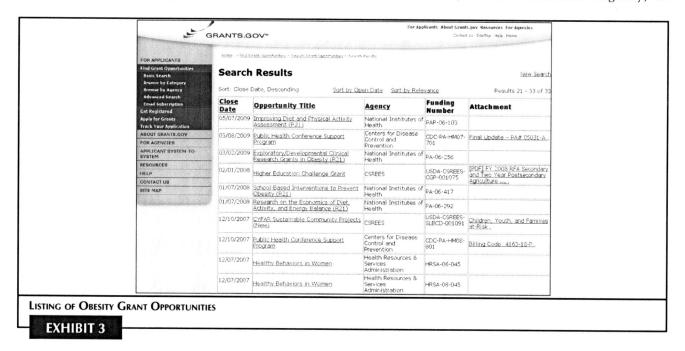

EXHIBIT 3

www.ccr.gov. If it is not, an authorizing official of your organization must register; this process takes about two days. You will not be able to move on to the next step until the CCR registration is completed.

3. Create a username and password with ORC (Operational Research Consultants), the Grants.gov credential service provider. Registration typically can be completed the same day; you will need to use your organization's DUNS Number to access the ORC Web site at http:// apply.grants.gov/OrcRegister.

4. Register with Grants.gov to open an account using the username and password you received from ORC. Grants.gov registration takes one day and can be done the same day as the ORC registration.

5. The E-Business Point of Contact at your organization must respond to the registration e-mail from Grants.gov and login at Grants.gov to approve you as an AOR (Authorized Organizational Representative). Authorization may take one to two days. Note that there can be more than one AOR for an organization.

6. At any time, you can track your AOR status at the Applicant Home Page of Grants.gov by logging in with your username and password.

You are now ready to upload and submit an application via Grants.gov.

Catalog of Federal Domestic Assistance

To many grantseekers, the *Catalog of Federal Domestic Assistance* (CFDA) represents a "Christmas Wish Book" of grant possibilities and includes more than 1,000 pages of federal grant programs. The CFDA is published annually in the spring with a fall supplement. It is available at a nominal charge from the Superintendent of Documents, Washington, DC 20402 or free at www.cfda.gov.

The CFDA contains useful browsing features that will save you time in identifying potential grant opportunities. Experienced grantseekers find four browsers particularly useful: Agency index, which lists grant opportunities by agency name; Applicant Eligibility index, which categorizes grant opportunities by type of applicant; Program Deadline index, which lists grants by their due dates; and Functional Area index, which classifies federal grant programs into broad categories ranging from agriculture, consumer protection, education, and health, to transportation. Many grant programs are cross-listed under multiple functional areas.

Following in Exhibit 4 you will find the home page for the CFDA. A click on the "Search for Assistance Programs" will lead you to the browsers cited above—and others too.

You have many search options to find federal grant programs. Besides using the browsers noted above, you can search by program number or key words or phrases. If you know the CFDA number, enter it in the "View Program" box. If you don't know it, you can enter an appropriate single keyword or phrase in the "Keyword Search" box. Sometimes beginning grantseekers get frustrated because their keywords yield no grant programs. Experienced grantseekers have learned several efficient search tips for the CFDA, as the following examples indicate.

CATALOG OF FEDERAL DOMESTIC ASSISTANCE (CFDA) HOME PAGE

EXHIBIT 4

CFDA Search Tips. Follow these tips when searching the CFDA.

1. Begin searching by using narrow terms, and broaden them on subsequent searches until acceptable "hits" are found. For example, if you are seeking funding for a youth violence prevention program, begin with narrow terms like "youth crimes" and, if that search is unsuccessful, use broader terms like "juvenile justice," "dispute resolution," "gangs," and "anti-crime."

2. Select some terms from the Functional Area browser to begin your search. More than likely, you'll come up with too many options, and some won't be relevant to your situation. It's time to narrow your search.

3. Skim read several relevant grant programs identified in step two. Look for the key words used in those grant descriptions and use them to search further. For example, we were once looking for funds for a "community development" project. Use of the phrase "community development" revealed very few hits. Conclusion: our search was too narrow. Looking for broader terminology, we read some grant descriptions and saw repeated use of the phrase "economic revitalization." When that phrase was entered into the search engine, it yielded the types of grant programs we were seeking.

4. When using phrases, enclose them in quotation marks; otherwise, the search engine might retrieve occurrences of each word singly rather than the literal string phrase.

5. To further narrow your search you can use Boolean Operators, words like AND, OR, NOT (all in capital letters). Named after a famous British mathematician, George Boole, these operators allow you to string words and phrases together. Examples follow:
   - "highway construction" AND noise
   - "drug abuse" AND "battered women"
   - "dispute resolution" NOT international
   - "community development" OR "economic revitalization"

   Phrases—but not single words—should be enclosed in quotation marks.

6. Use "wild cards," the asterisk symbol (*) or percent sign (%), for root words. For instance, *bio** or *bio%* will include search for such words as *bioenergy*, *bioinformatics*, *biological*, *biomedical*, and *bioterrorism*.

7. Remember, the CFDA is not only a source of information about federal funds, it also identifies state-level sources via flow-through dollars. Use the Applicant Eligibility browser to identify those grants that state governments are eligible to receive. Contact the federal program officer to identify precisely where those funds end up in the state government.

Sample CFDA Web Pages. Assume you want to find a grant program that dealt with the broad topic of "AIDS education." You would enter this phrase (in quotations) in the keyword box and click on "Search" as indicated in Exhibit 5.

The resulting search identifies several grant programs that match the search criteria, as shown in Exhibit 6.

A click on the hot links in the left-hand column will provide you with detailed program descriptions, including objectives, eligibility criteria, application procedure, deadlines, project duration, average grant size, contact information, and selection criteria.

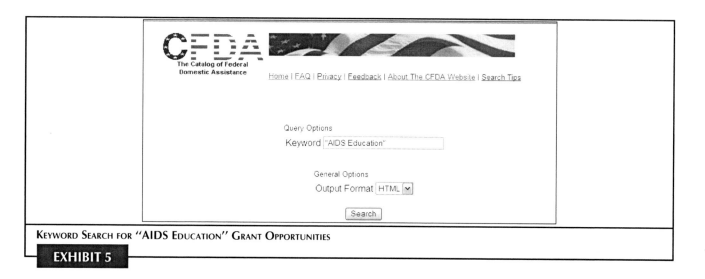

KEYWORD SEARCH FOR "AIDS EDUCATION" GRANT OPPORTUNITIES

EXHIBIT 5

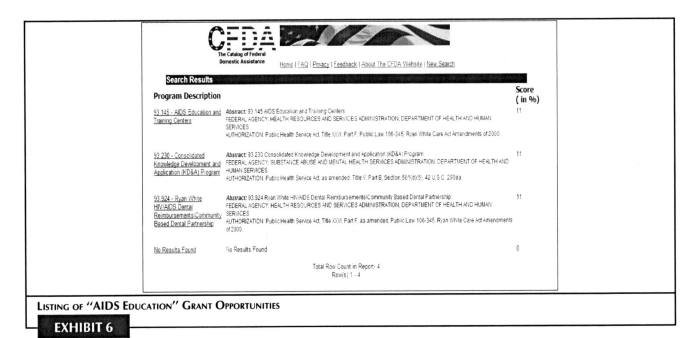

LISTING OF "AIDS EDUCATION" GRANT OPPORTUNITIES

EXHIBIT 6

Federal Register

The *Federal Register* is the government's "daily newspaper." Among other things, it lists rules, regulations, and application deadlines for new grant programs from federal agencies, although with the growing emphasis on Grants.gov as the primary information source, more federal grantmaking agencies are shifting away from the *Federal Register* to announce grant opportunities. Like the *Catalog of Federal Domestic Assistance*, the *Federal Register* is published in both print (available at twice the cost of the typical annual newspaper subscription) and electronic (available free) formats. Exhibit 7 shows the *Federal Register* home page at www.gpoaccess.gov/fr/index.html.

Clicking on the "Advanced Search" link allows you to select specific volumes and sections of the *Federal Register* as well as search by keyword and date. To illustrate, Exhibit 8 indicates how a keyword search for the terms "grant" and "housing" between January 1, 2007 and December 31, 2007 would be framed.

The single terms "housing" and "grant" have been linked with the Boolean operator AND.

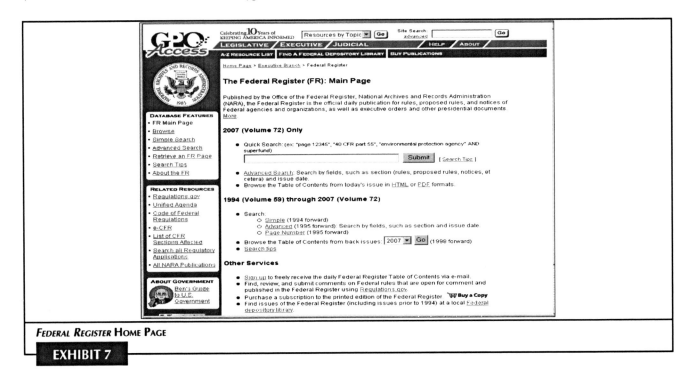

FEDERAL REGISTER HOME PAGE

EXHIBIT 7

KEYWORD SEARCH FOR HOUSING GRANTS DURING 2007

EXHIBIT 8

Federal Register Search Tips. Successful grantseekers have found the following tips useful to save time and improve search efficiency.

1. Monitor the *Federal Register* (FR) regularly, at least twice per month. Bookmark this address: www .gpoaccess.gov/fr/index.html.
2. Once you click on the current FR issue, open it up in the HTML format. Then use your computer's "find" command (See Chapter 15) and enter the word "grant" to locate all grant-related entries in the table of contents. This will save you considerable search time.
3. Use "wild cards," the asterisk symbol (*) or percent sign (%), for root words. For instance, *child** or *child%* will include searching such words as *child, child's, children, childhood,* and *childproof.*

Grants.gov, the *Catalog of Federal Domestic Assistance,* and the *Federal Register* all provide information about federal *grants* and *cooperative agreements.* In addition, there are also opportunities for *contract* dollars.

FedBizOpps

FedBizOpps (www.fedbizopps.gov) is the single source for federal government procurement opportunities that exceed $25,000. It is maintained by the U.S. General Services Administration. All federal agencies must use FedBizOpps to tell the public about these contract opportunities.

On a typical federal workday, the government publishes Uncle Sam's official shopping list of 500–1,000 procurement notices. More precisely, federal agencies use FedBizOpps to post any and all relevant procurement information on the Internet, including procurement notices, solicitations, drawings, and amendments. Grantseekers can sign up to automatically receive procurement information, by solicitation number, selected organizations, and product service classifications. A visit to the FedBizOpps home page reveals the screen as seen in Exhibit 9.

To get started, just insert your keywords into the "Quick Search" box in the upper left-hand corner of the home page. To review the current list of open contract opportunities, click on FedBizOpp Vendors, found on the home page.

As you review a contract solicitation, you may wonder whether it is truly open for competition; that is, does someone else already have the "inside track"? It's possible they do. One way to tell is to look at the length of the announcement. The longer the announcement, the greater the likelihood it is "wired." If it refers to prior work conducted by another organization, that group may have an advantage on the bidding.

If you are interested in a solicitation, begin your preproposal contacts (as described in Chapter 4). Tell your program officer about you, your organization, and the kind of projects that you are interested in. Through preproposal contacts, you will be able to judge whether you want to do business with this agency. One caution: contract support is relatively complex and certainly not for the uninitiated.

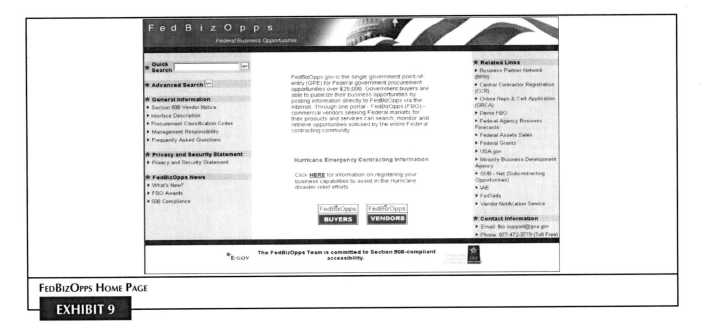

FedBizOpps Home Page

GOVERNMENT-SPONSORED FEDERAL AGENCY WEB SITES

Nearly all federal agencies maintain their own individual Web sites in addition to posting funding opportunities on Grants.gov and FedBizOpps. For convenience, the common federal Web sites are listed on the inside back cover of this book. As you would expect, these Web addresses are quick and easy reference tools for identifying grant opportunities and deadlines. However, these Web sites contain many other types of information as well, as the 20 examples in column two, Exhibit 10, exemplify.

Obviously, not all federal agencies provide all of the column two information. However, with the rapid changes occurring in Web-based information dissemination, the trend is to expand. As a result, the future will see more agencies providing more detailed information.

PRIVATE-SPONSORED FEDERAL AGENCY GRANT INFORMATION

Beyond the print and electronic newsletters and bulletins published **free** by federal agencies, a few private companies also provide grant information for a fee. To remain competitive, all are expanding the services they provide. Brief descriptions follow of five commercial vendors, along with Web addresses to seek additional information.

The Grant Advisor Plus. The Grant Advisor Plus publishes electronic information about grant and fellowship opportunities, especially targeted for faculty in U.S. institutions of higher education. An online newsletter covers grant opportunities from federal agencies (except the National Institutes of Health) as well as many independent organizations and foundations. Published monthly (except July), each issue contains 20–25 program reviews with descriptions, eligibility requirements, special criteria, funding amounts, and contact information (including phone and fax numbers, e-mail and Web addresses). The remainder of the newsletter is comprised of the Deadline Memo with more than 300 listings of grant and fellowship programs for the coming four months, organized into eight academic divisions: fine arts, humanities, sciences, social sciences, education, international, health related, and unrestricted/other. For more details, visit www.grantadvisor.com.

Illinois Research Information System (IRIS). IRIS is a unit of the University of Illinois Library at Urbana-Champaign. The IRIS Database of funding opportunities contains records on 9,000 federal and private funding opportunities in the sciences, social sciences, arts, and humanities. The IRIS Database is updated regularly and is available on the Web to subscribers. In addition to the IRIS Database, the IRIS office also maintains the IRIS Alert Service and the IRIS Expertise Service. The alert service allows users at subscribing institutions to create personal IRIS search profiles and receive funding alerts automatically. The expertise service enables faculty members to create detailed electronic CVs ("biosketches") and post them on the Web for viewing by colleagues at other institutions, program officers at federal and private funding agencies, and private companies. For details, visit www.library.uiuc.edu/iris.

Agency Name	Type of Information	Web Address*
Administration on Aging	Latest Agency Press Releases	www.aoa.dhhs.gov
Center for Medicare and Medicaid Services	How to Write a Final Report	www.cms.hhs.gov/ResearchDemoGrantsOpt/ 05_Authors_Guidelines_for_Grants_and_ Contracts.asp
National Endowment for the Arts	List of Recent Grant Awards	www.nea.gov/grants/recent/index.html
National Endowment for Democracy	Home Pages of Grantees	www.ned.org/grants/grants.html
National Endowment for the Humanities	Grant Deadlines	www.neh.gov/grants/grants.html
National Endowment for the Humanities	List of Recent Grant Awards	www.neh.gov/news/recentawards.html
National Historical Publications and Records Commission	What We Do/Don't Fund	www.archives.gov/nhprc/apply/eligibility.html
National Institutes of Health	Names of Current Reviewers	www.csr.nih.gov/Committees/rosterindex.asp
National Institutes of Health	Abstracts of Awards	crisp.cit.nih.gov
National Institutes of Health	Sample Funded Proposal	www.niaid.nih.gov/ncn/grants/app/default.htm
National Science Foundation	Video of NSF Mission Statement & Overview	www.nsf.gov/about
National Science Foundation	Staff Directory	www.nsf.gov/staff
National Science Foundation	Merit Review Process	www.nsf.gov/bfa/dias/policy/meritreview
Office of Management and Budget	Earmarks	earmarks.omb.gov
U.S. Department of Education	Prior Grant Awards	www.ed.gov/fund/data/award/edpicks.jhtml
U.S. Department of Health and Human Services	Organizational Chart	www.hhs.gov/about/orgchart.html
U.S. Department of Justice	Downloadable Application Kits	www.ojp.usdoj.gov/funding/solicitations.htm
U.S. Department of Transportation	Grant Management Regulations	www.dot.gov/ost/m60/grant/regs.htm
U.S. General Services Administration	Searchable Database of Federal Spending	www.federalspending.gov
White House	Faith Based and Community Initiatives	www.whitehouse.gov/government/fbci

*These Web addresses go directly to the type of information cited, which may or may not be on the home page of the agency.

TYPES OF WEB-BASED GOVERNMENT GRANT INFORMATION

EXHIBIT 10

Federal and Foundation Assistance Monitor. The Federal and Foundation Assistance Monitor features a comprehensive review of federal funding announcements, private grants, and legislative actions affecting community programs, including education, economic development, housing, children and youth services, substance abuse, and health care. Each grant notice is categorized by subject matter. For foundations, it indicates areas of interest and projected grant awards, as well as funding priorities for both national and regional organizations. In addition, each issue contains proposal-writing tips to help grant coordinators and development professionals write more successful applications. Finally, it also offers advice from grant officials on exactly what funders are looking for, and details key points from fundraising workshops sponsored by the Foundation Center, the Support Center, and other public and private agencies. To view a sample online newsletter, visit www.cdpublications.com.

SPINPlus. SPINPlus is a Web-based subscription package that bundles SPIN (Sponsored Programs Information Network), a funding opportunities database, with GENIUS, a flexible CV/Biosketch database, and SMARTS, an automated alerts system that matches investigators with grant and contract announcements based on their user profiles. Further details exist at www.infoed.org.

Community of Science (COS). COS provides rapid access to information about the funding of science and other projects across all disciplines. It is a global registry designed to provide accurate, timely, easy-to-access information about what new funding opportunities exist, and who is working on what subject, and where. Their comprehensive database contains more than 22,000 grant records. Their Web address is www.cos.org.

"PUSH" VERSUS "PULL" FUNDING INFORMATION

All of the public grant sources discussed so far have one thing in common—you must proactively seek the funding information; that is, you have to "pull" the information to you. An alternative exists. You can let the information come to you; that is, you can let someone else "push" the information your way. More precisely, there are some reference sources that you can subscribe to (many are free), which will automatically send you grant information on a regular basis. Some of these reference sources allow you to select key words or topics in your interest area; others just send out thumbnail sketches from which you pick and choose.

The advantage of the "push" approach is that it may save you time; you don't have to spend valuable time searching for grant information. The disadvantage is that you may get too much irrelevant information, such that "e-mail" becomes "eeek mail." Decide for yourself as you subscribe/unsubscribe to the following "push" approaches to finding public grant funds.

- *Federal Register*: Sign up to freely receive the daily *Federal Register* table of contents via e-mail at www.gpoaccess.gov/fr/index.html.
- Grants.gov: Register to receive free notifications of new grant postings delivered right to your e-mail inbox via www.grants.gov/applicants/email _subscription.jsp.
- National Endowment for the Humanities: Subscribe to the free monthly newsletter, *NEH Connect!*, and receive information on the latest

projects, upcoming events, and grant deadlines. Visit www.neh.gov/news/nehconnect.html.
- National Institutes of Health: Join the free listserv to receive an e-mail with table of contents information for that week's issue of the *NIH Guide*, www.nih.gov/grants/guide/listserv.htm.
- National Science Foundation: Sign up for free e-mail alerts from MyNSF at www.nsf.gov.

STATE GOVERNMENT FUNDING

The discussion so far has focused primarily on federal grants, cooperative agreements, and contracts, although some state dollars can be identified by use of the Applicant Eligibility browser in the *Catalog of Federal Domestic Assistance*. These funds are essentially federal "pass-through" dollars targeted for state distribution. Unfortunately, no state-level equivalent of the CFDA exists. Generally, states are just beginning to come online with basic grant information, even though it is still sparse for many of them. As a result, specific state-level funding opportunities must be searched out through electronic sources and personal contacts, as opposed to print directories.

Electronic Information Sources for State Government Funding

As a starting point to find state grant information, visit the generic address www.state.gov, inserting the name of your state as one word. For instance, if you live in North Carolina, you would visit www.northcarolina.gov. It would take you to the state government home page for North Carolina, as Exhibit 11 reveals. Enter "grant" into the search engine to identify state-level grants or find reports of prior grants, which suggest agencies that you may wish to approach.

Some states have specific Web sites announcing state grants, as Exhibit 12 from Wisconsin illustrates.

Wisconsin grants (http://doa.wi.gov/dir/wcca.asp) can be searched either by keyword or by functional category, as noted by the dual arrow.

For a directory of official state, county, and local government Web sites, visit www.statelocalgov.net. This Internet directory provides convenient one-stop access to the Web sites of thousands of state agencies and city and county governments. Use the drop-down menus on the left to view directory pages for states, topics, and local boroughs, counties, and parishes with cities, towns, townships,

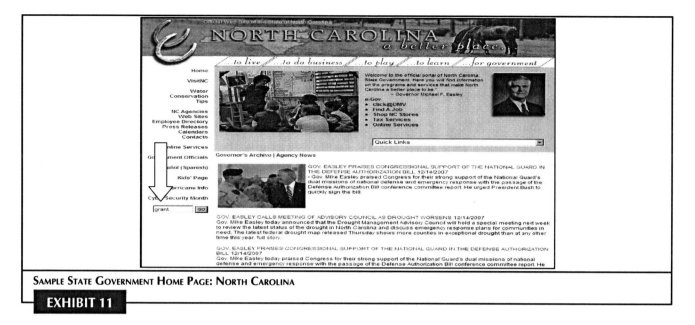

SAMPLE STATE GOVERNMENT HOME PAGE: NORTH CAROLINA

EXHIBIT 11

and villages. A sample Web page is indicated in Exhibit 13.

Human Information Sources for State Government Funding

Legislative Officials. Your state legislative officials can help identify pathways to grant programs, if you let them know your interests. To identify your legislative officials at both the state and federal levels, visit www.congress.org. One main job of legislators, of course, is to provide constituency services. As one of their constituents, it is appropriate for you to request their assistance, especially since they have access to comprehensive information networks and a support staff to help "dig" for information.

Agency Mission Statements. Review the mission statements from those state agencies whose broad interests match your needs. The Department of Health and Social Services might be interested in your approach to adolescent pregnancy prevention. The Department of Transportation might be interested in your ideas on improving highway resurfacing. The Department of Public Instruction might welcome your ideas on teaching geometry to middle school students. A few persistent phone calls or a walk down

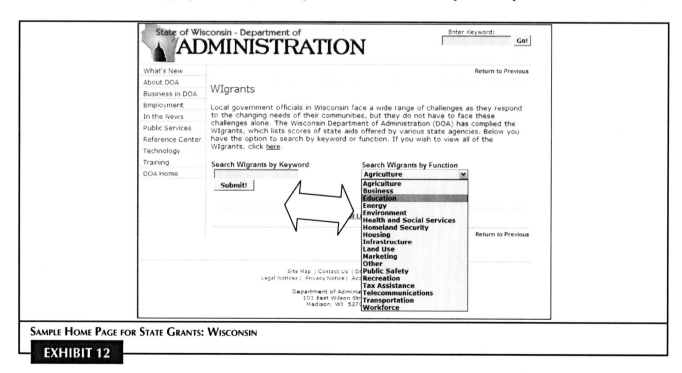

SAMPLE HOME PAGE FOR STATE GRANTS: WISCONSIN

EXHIBIT 12

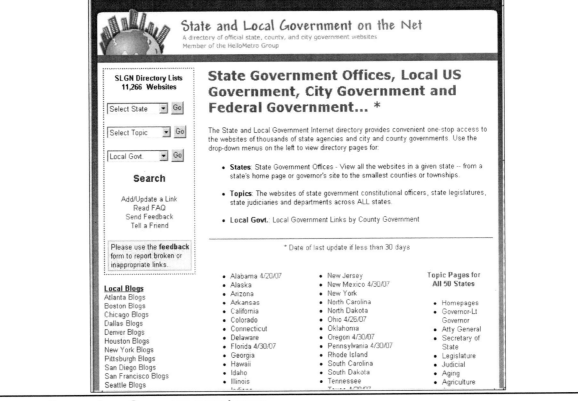

DIRECTORY OF STATE AND LOCAL GOVERNMENTS ON THE INTERNET

EXHIBIT 13

a few corridors in the state capitol building should identify existing grant opportunities in your area of interest, whether it is in education, health, social services, or technology development.

 ## Clip File Action Item # 6
Finding Public Funds

Build your Finding Public Funds clip file by including such information as the following:

- Copies of pertinent Grants.gov, *Catalog of Federal Domestic Assistance*, *Federal Register*, and FedBizOpps pages.
- Lists of past grant winners, found on Web sites or available from program officers.
- Model letters requesting application forms and guidelines.

- Web pages from federal and state grantmaking programs.
- Copies of successful public grant proposals, available under the Freedom of Information Act.
- Sign up to receive free electronic copies of the daily *Federal Register* table of contents and all new postings on Grants.gov. Follow instructions on each home page.

 ## Clip File Action Item # 7
Finding Public Funds

Set aside five minutes each day and explore the government Web sites listed on the inside back cover of this book. When you find sponsors who might fund your projects, copy that information and paste it in your Finding Public Funds clip file.

CHAPTER 3
Finding Private Funds

The impersonal hand of government can never replace the helping hand of a neighbor.

—Hubert H. Humphrey

OVERVIEW OF PRIVATE FUNDING

Vice President Humphrey recognized the importance of private philanthropy nearly 100 years ago: nongovernmental philanthropy is crucial. Private grant funding comes primarily from foundations and corporations. Although wealthy individuals also provide private funding, those dollars are seldom available for competitive grants because they are usually given at the sole discretion of the philanthropist. (Some information sources for seeking individual philanthropy are found in the Bibliography.) Accordingly, this chapter restricts itself to finding foundation and corporation grants. Specifically, in Chapter 3, you will learn the following:

- The different roles that foundations fulfill.
- Basic reference tools for finding private foundation grants.
- Basic reference tools for finding corporate grants.
- How to analyze foundation tax records.
- Five different types of foundations.
- Perspectives on corporate philanthropy.

The Web addresses in this chapter and on the back inside cover of this book will help you find private funding sources for your projects.

In comparison with public grants, private grants are usually shorter in length and less background information is available for prospect research. Private funds sometimes provide support in areas not extensively funded in the public sector, e.g., religion. Private proposals may take less time to prepare and, in many instances, offer a quicker funding decision. However, your choice is not necessarily between public or private funding; often, both can and should be solicited.

This chapter begins with a general discussion of foundations and their self-images, followed by sources of print and electronic information about finding funds. Next, it describes the five different foundation categories and their outlooks on giving: national foundations, community foundations, family foundations, special purpose foundations, and corporate foundations. While the corporate foundation is legally an independent tax-exempt organization, it conducts business more like a corporation than a foundation. The discussion of corporate foundations midway through this chapter serves as a segue into corporations: their cultures, funding options, and reference sources.

Basic Foundation Characteristics

A private foundation is a tax-exempt philanthropic organization concerned about injustices or inequities. In 2007, more than 90,000 private foundations were registered in the United States. Annually, they award more than $40 billion. While the figures vary slightly from year to year, the 10,000 largest foundations typically have 90 percent of the assets and make 80 percent of the awards. By federal law, foundations must give away 5 percent of their market value assets or interest income each year, whichever is greater. This law means, for example, that the Bill and Melinda Gates Foundation with $60+ billion in market assets must award at least $3 billion annually. Foundations are required to follow the 5 percent rule or risk losing their tax-exempt status.

Foundation Roles

Foundations see themselves in multiple roles; five are identified below, along with sample proposal language that reflects these differing values.

As *grantmakers*, foundations provide direct financial resources that target immediate or emerging concerns.

> *As a grantmaker, you perform an incalculable service by helping groups and individuals foster lasting improvement in the human condition.*

As *catalysts*, foundations help mobilize leaders and constituencies.

> *An extraordinary convergence of community need and immediate opportunity motivates us to seek your investment in triggering an overdue change—the primary reason for our special request. From a broader perspective, this proposal is a catalytic change agent to impact the lives of a vulnerable population through fierce dedication and warm compassion.*

As *community resources*, foundations provide services to donors, nonprofit organizations, and the community-at-large.

> *Our proposal concentrates on helping people build just and caring communities that nurture people, spur enterprise, bridge differences, foster fairness, and promote civility.*

As *resource developers*, foundations build a permanent unrestricted endowment.

> *This proposal develops crucial resources to build better futures that more effectively meet the needs of today's vulnerable children and families. The project outcomes will strengthen the support services, social networks, physical infrastructure, employment, self-determination, and economic vitality of our target community.*

As *stewards*, foundations receive and distribute community resources.

> *You and I share something in common—a profound stewardship responsibility to the local community. Accordingly, this proposal invites your shared partnership in making a difference.*

To help determine which roles your target foundation deems most important, read their "About Us" description on their Web site or mission statement in their annual report. Next, use your preproposal contacts (Chapter 4) to validate your first impressions and base your appeals on those roles, since they represent the psychological needs of foundations.

With these orienting perspectives on foundations, we now turn our attention to print and electronic information sources that explain funding priorities, application protocols, and often grant histories.

THE FOUNDATION CENTER

The Foundation Center is an independent national organization that provides information about philanthropic giving. National collections exist in their New York City headquarters and four field offices: Atlanta, Cleveland, San Francisco, and Washington, DC. Each location contains extensive reference materials about foundations and the broad spectrum of fundraising. Further, each state has one or more regional foundation collections to service people in its area—free. Each regional collection contains core Foundation Center publications plus supplementary information. To find the location of the collection nearest you, visit www.foundationcenter.org/about/locations.html or call the Foundation Center toll free at 1-800-424-9836.

The following sections discuss the Foundation Center print and electronic primary source materials. The print materials can either be purchased or read in your nearest regional foundation library. The electronic references are available on CD-ROM or through an online service, both at a fee. Details exist at the Foundation Center Web site. Our discussion of private foundation reference materials then turns to information sources from other grant publishers.

Foundation Directory

The *Foundation Directory* is the private foundation equivalent of the *Catalog of Federal Domestic Assistance*; that is, the *Foundation Directory* is a primary starting point to identify the larger foundations. For instance, the 2007 edition features key facts on the top 10,000 U.S. foundations by total giving—indexed by name, types of support, subject field, state, key officials. For ease of access, over 1,700 new entries to this edition are also indexed. Enhanced with more than 50,000 recently awarded foundation grants, the Directory provides valuable insight into foundation giving priorities.

While the 10,000 largest grantmaking foundations represent less than 15 percent of the total number of existing foundations, they control more than 90 percent of all foundation assets and award more than 80 percent of all foundation grants. The *Foundation Directory* has been a basic prospect research tool for many years. If you wish to locate information about smaller foundations, explore a companion publication: *The Foundation Directory: Part 2*. This research guide provides information on the next largest 10,000 grantmaking foundations. The information format is the same as the *Foundation Directory*, with obvious content differences. Collectively, both volumes present information on nearly 25 percent of all private foundations.

The *Foundation 1000*

Within the private foundation arena, substantial interest lies in the larger foundations because they, obviously, have the most money to distribute. The *Foundation 1000* provides detailed information about the 1000 largest U.S. foundations on the basis of total grants awarded; for instance, the 1000 foundations listed in the 2007 edition accounted for 65 percent of all foundation grants awarded, although they represented only 2 percent of all foundations. Each entry may be several pages long and includes contact information, purpose, limitations, key personnel, background information, analysis of giving patterns, types of support provided, types of recipients, partial listings of grants, application guidelines, and funding cycles. It is one of the most comprehensive directories available and is extremely valuable if it lists your foundation of interest. A hypothetical example from *Foundation 1000* follows in Exhibit 14.

Grant Guides

The Foundation Center *Grant Guides* provide you with descriptions of foundation grants of $10,000 or more awarded in twelve subject fields.

1. Grants for Arts, Culture & the Humanities
2. Grants for Children and Youth
3. Grants for Elementary and Secondary Education
4. Grants for Environmental Protection & Animal Welfare
5. Grants for Foreign & International Programs
6. Grants for Higher Education
7. Grants for Libraries & Information Services
8. Grants for Mental Health, Addictions, & Crisis Services
9. Grants for Minorities
10. Grants for People with Disabilities
11. Grants for Religion, Religious Welfare, & Religious Education
12. Grants for Women & Girls

You can search the Grant Guides by key words in the subject index to locate funders for your specific project. With the geographic index, you can discover the active grantmakers in your region. The recipient index enables you to track grants awarded to similar organizations in your field.

Foundation Center—Electronic Resources

The Foundation Center makes some grant information available free on the Internet, and, for a fee, on a CD-ROM. Each is described briefly.

Access to Free Foundation Center Information. Foundations have lagged behind the federal government but are beginning to come online. As of 2007, less than 10 percent of the private foundations had Web sites. Rather than go searching for each foundation at its own Web site, some foundations are accessible through the Foundation Center Web site at www.foundationcenter.org. At present, navigation is somewhat cludgy relative to finding grantmakers who might support your project. In addition to reviewing a list of the top funders in your state, you can search by the foundation name and by the subject area of interest.

Access to Fee-Based Foundation Center Information. Beyond the free Internet information, the Foundation Center also publishes several CD-ROMs and online services that are periodically updated. *FC Search* gives you access to the Foundation Center's comprehensive data of funders in either CD-ROM or online formats. It allows you to develop targeted prospect lists, quickly mark records, and save your customized search strategies. The *Foundation Directory*, mentioned above, exists in a CD-ROM as well as print format. Details are available at www.foundationcenter.org/findfunders/fundingsources/printcd.html. Organizations on a limited budget are advised to visit the nearest regional foundation center library, explore the free use of electronic information sources, download search findings into your flash drive and do further editing at home.

OTHER GRANTS PUBLICATIONS

State Foundation Directories

Most states publish a directory of their private foundations. These directories customarily present the basic identifying information for all statewide foundations, small and large. This document is particularly useful when you are seeking support for local or statewide

RAMSEY CHARLES FOUNDATION

Address: 505 Madison Avenue   Telephone: 212-506-9867
           New York, NY 10222   Contact: Sharon Belanger, VP

Purpose: Principal source of philanthropy for Ramsey Charles Corporation and its subsidiaries; scope is national, emphasizing support for institutions and projects in the areas of health care, social welfare, minority education and the arts. Aid to local communities provided primarily through the United Way.

Limitations: Giving primarily in areas of company operations. No grants to individuals or for religious organizations for sectarian purposes; local chapters of national organizations, elementary schools, medical or nursing schools; disease-related health associations, or for operating expenses. No support for operating budgets or endowments. Does not purchase advertisements or donate equipment.

Officers: Financial Data: (FY 06)
Ronald Lewis, President   Assets $68,647,921
Jane Griff, Vice President   Gifts Received $1,947,837
Arne Johnson, Vice President   Expenditures $17,221,933
Sharon Belanger, Vice President   Grants Paid $16,032,149
Michael Fredricks, Secretary   Number of Grants 943
June Smythe, Treasurer   High Grant $500,000
                                       Low Grant $100
                                       General Range $9,000–50,000

Trustees:
Randall Block, Chairman
Debra Jones
Ray Lazarus
Frank Abramoff
Susan Burch
Thaddeus Porter
Roy Clayton

Number of Staff: Eight full-time and three part-time professional, four full-time support.
Sponsoring Company: Ramsey Charles Company
Business: Oil
Employees: 24,500
Sales: $37.81 billion
Fortune 500 Ranking: 2006—3rd in sales, 6th in assets, and 10th in net income.

Corporate Locations: New York City (headquarters); Houston, New Orleans, Galveston, Tampa
Background: The Ramsey Charles Foundation was established in 1968 in New York with some of the proceeds from the sale of substantial quantities of oil. Their philanthropic giving has reduced during periods of oil shortages. Historically they have provided substantial support for worthy institutions and causes.

Ronald Lewis, president of the foundation, was formerly vice president for corporate communications at the Ramsey Charles Company. He has also served on the Community Services Agency of New York. In the academic world, he has served as an adjunct assistant professor in Lehman College's Department of Political Science.

Grants Analysis: In 2005, the foundation contributed $16,032,149 in grants. The largest portion (37 percent) was distributed to United Ways through the country. Educational organizations accounted for 33 percent of the allocations, including $100,000 or more to the University of Texas at Austin, Florida Atlantic University, and the Massachusetts

SAMPLE ENTRY FROM FOUNDATION 1000

EXHIBIT 14

Institute of Technology. The remaining 30 percent was dispersed throughout a wide range of social welfare and arts organizations; each received approximately $10,000.

Type	No. of Grants	Amount	Percent	Range
Health Care	168	1,603,215	10	5,000–50,000
Social Welfare	79	1,282,571	8	1,000–20,000
Education	212	5,290,609	33	1,000–500,000
Arts	32	1,923,859	12	100–100,000
United Way	452	5,931,895	37	100–300,000
Total	943	$16,032,149	100%	

Corporate Contributions Program: Through other corporate programs, Ramsey Charles gave further grants of $7,322,945 to nonprofit organizations. Most of it went to areas of company operations. A few selected universities received computer surplus equipment that was not open to applications.

SAMPLE ENTRY FROM FOUNDATION 1000

EXHIBIT 14 (Continued from page 26)

projects because many of the small- to mid-sized foundations concentrate their support on projects that serve their locale. The Foundation Center can identify where to obtain the directory for any given state. For example, *Foundations in Wisconsin: A Directory* is available through the Marquette University Funding Information Center (www.marquette.edu/fic); the *Directory of Illinois Foundations* is available through the Donors Forum of Chicago (www.donorsforum.org); and the *Michigan Foundation Directory* is available through the Council of Michigan Foundations (www.cmif.org).

Foundation Reporter

Currently in its 39th edition (2007), the *Foundation Reporter* profiles the top 1,000 leading private foundations in the United States that have at least $10 million in assets or whose annual giving totals $500,000 or more. Entries include foundation type, giving levels, assets, contact points, types of grants, officers and directors, application procedures, grants analyses, areas of interest, and sample grants. It presents more detailed information than is found in the *Foundation Directory* but less information than contained in the *Foundation 1000*.

The *Foundation Reporter* includes background information about major foundation officers, e.g., year and college of graduation, major corporate and noncorporate affiliations—mini "who's who" information that can be very useful when trying to adapt a proposal idea to a particular audience. Seven indexes—by state, grant recipient location, types of grants, field of interest, donor, list of foundations, and application deadlines—arrange foundations by the nature and distribution of their grant support and application deadlines. For more details, visit www.infotoday.com or call 609-654-6266.

Annual Register of Grant Support

Some reference sources include information on all types of grantmakers: foundations, government agencies, and corporations. For instance, a reference book containing information from different types of sponsors is the *Annual Register of Grant Support* (visit www.infotoday.com or call 609-654-6266). The 41st edition (2008) details more than 3,500 grant program from public and private sources. Because it lists so many different types of sponsors, it is a good starting point for prospect research using print reference sources. Entries are arranged by field of interest and cross-indexed. Entries include valuable information on how the grants are made, the ratio of applications to grants awarded, and application procedures and deadlines.

The Grants Register

The *Grants Register* is another prospect research tool that contains information about private and public funding sources. It differs from other reference works in that it contains information on international grant programs as well as those in the United States. More precisely, it provides information about (1) scholarships, fellowships, and research grants; (2) exchange opportunities and travel grants; (3) grants-in-aid; (4) grants for all kinds of artistic or scientific projects; (5) competitions, prizes, and honoraria; (6) professional and vocational awards; and (7) special awards. The 2008 edition contains information on 3,825 grantmakers from 58 different countries. Published by Palgrave Macmillan, additional information is available at www.palgrave.com.

Chronicle of Philanthropy

In addition to the books and newsletters that provide grant-related information, one biweekly newspaper publishes information about a wide range of philanthropic activities. The *Chronicle of Philanthropy* contains information about governmental, foundation, and corporation grants as well as individual gifts. It describes new grant trends and changes in personnel within the philanthropic community. Because it publishes information so frequently, it is an effective way to monitor subtle changes in the philanthropic scene or to obtain early access to information about new grant opportunities. Electronic updates are posted regularly at www.philanthropy.com, which is available free to regular print subscribers.

Private Foundation Web sites

At present, a small but growing number of the private foundations have Web sites available to disseminate grant-related information. At least three Web sites monitor private foundation activity and establish links to those Web sites once they are created.

- Foundation Center: www.foundationcenter.org
- Council on Foundations: www.cof.org
- Grant Advisor Plus: www.grantadvisor.com

Although the lists do overlap, most sites are clearly organized and easy to navigate. For instance, study the home page for the Bill and Melinda Gates Foundation (Exhibit 15). To locate grant information, you would click on "For Grantseekers" to learn more about *the* largest foundation in the world.

List of Cumulative Organizations

Finally, after exploring available reference directories and reviewing Web results from search engines such as Google (www.google.com), Web Crawler (www.webcrawler.com), and Yahoo! (www.yahoo.com), you may discover that you are unable to find information about a potential sponsor, although you have reason to believe it does provide some type of financial support. When all else fails, consult the Internal Revenue Service, U.S. Department of Treasury Web site (www.irs.gov) and conduct a keyword search for "Cumulative List of Organizations." This downloadable reference tool contains the names, cities, and states of all charitable organizations, including private foundations, religious organizations, nonprofit trusts, and so forth. You might open up this file and search for the name of a foundation to confirm that it does

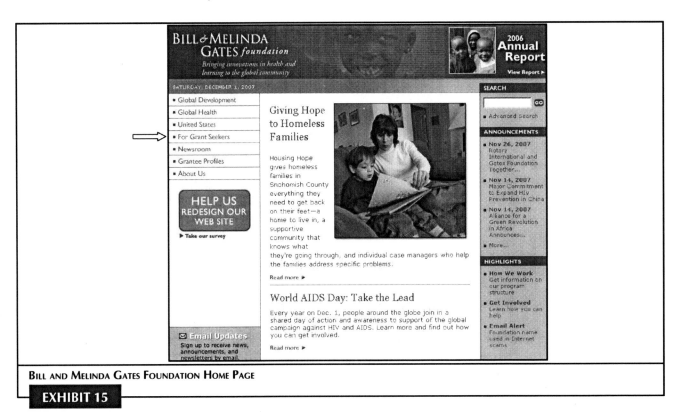

BILL AND MELINDA GATES FOUNDATION HOME PAGE

EXHIBIT 15

exist and that it has a legal nonprofit status; not all organizations with the word "Foundation" in their name are grantmaking foundations. Further, you might use your computer's "find" command (Chapter 15) to identify all charitable organizations in a particular city or state.

ANALYZING TAX RETURNS

From the reference sources listed so far, you will identify several potential sponsors that might be interested in supporting your organization. An important next step is to determine precisely where these organizations have spent their money in the past. Some publish annual reports or list recent grant winners on their Web site; that information is very valuable in analyzing giving patterns. In some instances, however, lists of grant recipients are simply not published by your target foundation. To gain additional financial and funding information about all foundations, large or small, you can review their tax records.

By law, foundations are required to submit IRS 990-AR (Annual Reports) or 990-PF (Private Foundation) returns. The 990s are the private foundation equivalents of your individual 1040 income tax records; the 990s are inching their way onto the Internet, thus inviting a new era of public scrutiny. Here are some Internet sites worth exploring.

- www.guidestar.org. A charity group working with the IRS to post tax records and comprehensive data on more than 1.7 million nonprofit organizations.
- www.foundationcenter.org/findfunders/990finder. You'll be able to locate and download (via PDF: Portable Document Format files) the tax records of more than 90,000 private foundations—and the number is growing regularly.

By looking at sections on the tax records that list giving patterns, award amounts, and board members, you can determine whether a foundation is a good match with your needs.

As you review these tax records, pay particular attention to three important pieces of information.

1. One section will identify the net assets of the foundation. If you multiply this value by 5 percent, you will know the minimum amount of money the foundation disbursed during the reporting year.
2. A second section will list the names of key foundation personnel. Circulate that list within your organization to identify possible linkages or networks.

3. A third section will list the recipients of the grants for the reporting year. Study the list and see whether you can identify organizations similar to yours that received foundation dollars.

Finally, remember that the vast majority of all foundations do not have any paid staff. Even among larger foundations—those giving away more than $100,000 annually or with assets of at least $1 million—approximately 15 percent have any paid employees. As a result, the 990 serves as the *only* source of information on activities of most smaller foundations.

APPEALING TO FOUNDATIONS

Foundations award grants to organizations that can help foundations reach their long-term goals. Your proposal appeals can assume several different forms. Some foundations make their money available for *specific purposes*, e.g., building funds, operating support, equipment, or seed capital. Other foundations target their funds for *specific populations*, e.g., frail elderly, minorities, or homeless. Still other foundations concentrate their dollars on *specific types of organizations*, e.g., hospitals, universities, or youth organizations. As another alternative, some foundations make their money available to *specific geographic areas*, e.g., a city, a county, a state, or a region. Finally, certain foundations have their own *specific priorities and interests* that determine the types of programs they support. With these considerations in mind, you will want to cast your project in a way that appeals to their self-defined mission.

TYPES OF FOUNDATIONS

Foundations vary considerably in market assets, staff size, funding priorities, review protocols, geographic giving patterns, and preferred approach. Some are eager to share information about themselves; others take a very constrained approach to information dissemination. As you search for private foundation funding sources, it is essential to understand the five different types of foundations. Note in particular the differences in types of projects funded by each type of foundation, as evidenced by actual funding examples.

National Foundations

National foundations are the largest and most familiar funding sources because they control a significant percentage of the philanthropic assets and make over 50 percent of all foundation awards. Ten of the larger national foundations (in terms of assets and giving) are listed below.

1. Bill and Melinda Gates Foundation: www.gatesfoundation.org
2. The David and Lucile Packard Foundation: www.packard.org
3. The Ford Foundation: www.fordfound.org
4. Lilly Endowment Inc.: www.lillyendowment.org
5. J. Paul Getty Trust: www.getty.edu/grant
6. The Rockefeller Foundation: www.rockfound.org
7. The Pew Charitable Trusts: www.pewtrusts.com
8. W.K. Kellogg Foundation: www.wkkf.org
9. John D. and Catherine T. MacArthur Foundation: www.macfdn.org
10. The Andrew W. Mellon Foundation: www.mellon.org

Because they are national in scope, such foundations prefer impact programs with high visibility. They are not good sources of requests for operating income or grants to extend old projects into new areas. "New ideas with national impact" are the watchwords for attracting national foundation dollars. Fortunately, information about national foundations is generally quite accessible. For example, a visit to the Ford Foundation Web site will list examples of recently funded projects. Three examples are shown in Exhibit 16.

National foundations are looking for projects that address national needs, or at least very widespread issues. Methodologically, they are interested in unique, cost-effective approaches. Decisions are usually made by an independent board of directors.

Community Foundations

Community foundations are the best places to go for strictly local support. They are very responsive to programs serving local or community needs. They seek creative solutions to community problems. Their focus is on long-term community betterment. They are generally available to all nonprofit organizations regardless of their programmatic area. They are quite willing to disseminate information about their programs and priorities. Examples of community foundations include the following:

1. The New York Community Trust: www.nyct-cfi.org
2. Houston Endowment Inc.: www.houstonendowment.org
3. The Cleveland Foundation: www.clevelandfoundation.org
4. The Marin Community Foundation: www.marincf.org
5. The Chicago Community Trust and Affiliates: www.cct.org
6. The San Francisco Foundation: www.sff.org
7. The Columbus Foundation: www.columbusfoundation.org
8. The Saint Paul Foundation, Inc.: www.saintpaulfoundation.org
9. California Community Foundation: www.calfund.org
10. The Greater Milwaukee Foundation: www.greatermilwaukeefoundation.org

As an example, the California Community Foundation, established in 1915, was Los Angeles's first grantmaking institution and is the country's second-oldest community foundation. The Foundation makes grants to organizations serving the greater Los Angeles region in the following areas: human services, children and youth, community development, civic affairs, community health, community education, arts and culture, the environment, and animal welfare.

Visitors to the California Community Foundation's Web site will find a range of useful information, including grant guidelines, a downloadable version

---

$175,000 to Arkansas State University for a tourism development program for minority and distressed communities

$1,250,000 to Center for Puppetry Arts Inc. (Atlanta) to advance exemplary artistic initiatives by increasing permanent capital, expanding the individual donor base, and enhancing board leadership

$75,000 to Los Angeles Alliance for a New Economy to increase government and corporate accountability regarding job subsidies and tax incentive programs

SAMPLE FORD FOUNDATION GRANTS: A NATIONAL FOUNDATION

EXHIBIT 16

of the Foundation's grant application form, a list of recent grants, brief bios of selected donors, a list of Foundation-sponsored publications, and a calendar of upcoming Foundation-related events. Exhibit 17 lists examples of three grants among many made by the California Community Foundation.

Contacts with the community foundations are essential. If you can demonstrate credibility and project need, you can overcome the lack of prior grant experience. A board of directors representing the diversity of the community typically makes decisions.

Family Foundations

Family foundations are generally small and controlled by the donor or the donor's family. The special family interests determine their granting priorities. Often geographic limitations are apparent in their giving patterns. Networking through preproposal contacts (Chapter 4) discloses top funding priorities. Fewer family foundations have Web sites than any other type of foundation; examples of family foundations with a Web presence include the following.

1. William and Flora Hewlett Foundation: www.hewlett.org
2. Hall Family Foundation: www.hallfamilyfoundation.org
3. The Henry J. Kaiser Family Foundation: www.kff.org
4. The Ford Family Foundation: www.tfff.org
5. Walton Family Foundation: www.waltonfamilyfoundation.org
6. Orfalea Family Foundation: www.orfaleafamilyfoundation.org
7. The Perrin Family Foundation: www.perrinfamilyfoundation.org
8. The Jay and Rose Phillips Family Foundation: www.phillipsfnd.org

9. Carol and Eloise Polhad Family Foundation: www.pohladfamilygiving.org
10. Helen Bader Foundation: www.hbf.org

One example of a family foundation is the William and Flora Hewlett Foundation. The Palo Alto industrialist William R. Hewlett; his wife, Flora Lamson Hewlett; and their eldest son, Walter B. Hewlett, incorporated it as a private foundation in the State of California in 1966. The Foundation concentrates its resources on activities in education, performing arts, environment, population, global development, and philanthropy. In its grantmaking decisions as well as in its interests and activities, the Hewlett Foundation is wholly independent of the Hewlett-Packard Company and the Hewlett-Packard Company Foundation. Three sample grants recently made by the William and Flora Hewlett Foundation follow in Exhibit 18.

Special Purpose Foundations

Special purpose foundations serve very precise purposes. For instance, the Wallace H. Coulter Foundation restricts its support to biomedical research. The Research Corporation supports projects primarily in the physical and life sciences. Many special purpose foundations are health related and concentrate on a specific medical conditions, e.g., cancer, heart, or lung problems. Others are more academically focused and support faculty in particular disciplines, e.g., chemistry or philosophy. Examples of special purpose foundations follow.

1. Robert Wood Johnson Foundation: www.rwjf.org
2. Wallace H. Coulter Foundation: www.whcf.org
3. Research Corporation: www.rescorp.org
4. American Philosophical Society: www.amphilsoc.org
5. American Chemical Society: www.acs.org

$120,000 to Asian Pacific Health Care Venture, Inc., Los Angeles, CA to expand prenatal care services for pregnant, Asian Pacific Islander women in Los Angeles

$140,860 to Centinela Valley Juvenile Diversion Project, Hawthorne, CA to support mental health services and medical referrals for at-risk youth residing in Hawthorne, Inglewood and selected areas of South Los Angeles

$100,000 to Children's Dental Center, Inglewood, CA to continue preventive and basic dental care treatment for low-income children residing in Hawthorne, Inglewood, and selected areas of South Los Angeles

SAMPLE CALIFORNIA COMMUNITY FOUNDATION GRANTS: A COMMUNITY FOUNDATION

EXHIBIT 17

$200,000 over two years to Goodwill Industries of the Greater East Bay, Oakland, CA for the Family Based Skills project, a job training program for low-income working parents

$200,000 over two years to Mission Hiring Hall, San Francisco, CA for the Construction Administration Training and Employer Linkage Program

$200,000 over two years to Bay Area Industry Education Council, Fremont, CA for the Machine Technology Workforce Development Model project

SAMPLE WILLIAM AND FLORA HEWLETT GRANTS: A FAMILY FOUNDATION

EXHIBIT 18

6. American Heart Association: www.americanheart.org
7. American Diabetes Association: www.diabetes.org
8. American Council for Learned Societies: www.acls.org
9. American Psychological Association: www.apa.org
10. Ronald McDonald House Charities: www.rmhc.org

Perhaps the best known special purpose foundation is the Robert Wood Johnson Foundation, www.rwjf.org, which specializes in funding health care. Seventy-five percent of their funds are set aside for Foundation priorities and 25 percent is reserved for unsolicited proposals. The Robert Wood Johnson Foundation supports research, training, and service demonstrations. They like to field test promising ideas and evaluate the results; take proven ideas and approaches to scale; give heightened visibility to an issue, idea, or intervention; cause coalitions of like-minded or disparate individuals and groups to form and act around a problem or issue; and reach and engage organizations and institutions that would not otherwise seek philanthropic support. Three examples of recently funded projects appear in Exhibit 19.

Your needs statement should be documented in terms of their priorities. Your methodology should be viewed as unique in this area. Networking with people who are experts is especially important. Their board of directors usually makes funding decisions after receiving input from technical specialists.

Corporate Foundation Funding

Corporate foundations represent the philanthropic arm of their corporate parents. Generally, corporate foundations are especially interested in funding programs in communities where their companies have plant operations. As a result, they are particularly responsive to the needs of their workers in those communities. To attract corporation foundation dollars, specify what you have to offer that will affect their workers, products, or corporate concerns. Networking through your contacts can help reveal funding priorities. Examples of major corporate foundations follow.

1. 3M Foundation: www.3Mgiving.com
2. Alcoa Foundation: www.alcoa.com/global/en/community/foundation.asp
3. Bank of America Foundation, Inc.: www.bankofamerica.com/foundation
4. Coca-Cola Foundation: www.thecoca-colacompany.com/citizenship/index.html

$1,993,698 over three years to State of North Carolina Department of Health and Human Services, Raleigh, NC for statewide youth-led program to prevent tobacco use by young people

$74,708 to Oregon Pacific Research Institute, Eugene, OR for surveying changes in spit tobacco use among Major and Minor League Baseball players

$994,697 over four years to Child Welfare League of America, Inc. Washington, DC for technical assistance to promote health and social services in distressed public housing

SAMPLE ROBERT WOOD JOHNSON GRANTS: A SPECIAL PURPOSE FOUNDATION

EXHIBIT 19

5. GE Foundation: www.ge.com/foundation/index.html
6. Starbucks Foundation: www.starbucks.com/aboutus/foundation.asp
7. Target Foundation: www.targetfoundation.org
8. Toyota USA Foundation: www.toyota.com/foundation
9. Verizon Foundation: foundation.verizon.com
10. Wal-Mart Foundation: www.walmartfoundation.org

An example of a corporate foundation is the Toyota USA Foundation. One of its major priorities is to build bridges that lead to improvements in mathematics and science education, as Exhibit 20 indicates.

Prior grant experience is important when seeking corporate funds. Corporate foundations give money to those organizations they trust. A board of directors, who are usually corporate officials as well, makes funding decisions. Study the corporate culture to understand how to approach the corporate foundation.

Corporate foundation funding represents one of three different sources of corporate-related money. The remainder of this chapter shifts its focus from the nonprofit world of foundations to the for-profit world of corporations and offers concrete tips on securing their dollars.

PERSPECTIVES ON CORPORATE PHILANTHROPY

Overview

In larger corporations—those with net annual sales in excess of $10 million and more than 200 employees—grantseekers can usually find three different "pots of money."

1. **Corporate Foundation Funding.** Some corporations establish separate foundations for social and legal purposes. Technically, these funds are independent of the parent corporation and are legally classified as a foundation. In reality, they behave like corporations and they are best approached from the corporate perspective. Suggestions for securing corporate foundation funding were cited above.

2. **Corporate General Philanthropy Funding.** Some corporations establish a pool of pretax corporate earnings to distribute for general philanthropic purposes. Depending on the health of the economy, those philanthropic dollars represent 1–3 percent of pretax profits. Usually, the grants are made to those projects for which the corporation can also benefit.

3. **Corporate Research and Development (R&D) Funding.** Some corporations rely on outside organizations like universities and research institutes to develop new products or services, especially in those instances when corporations lack the in-house expertise or equipment to conduct the needed R&D. Usually, strong collaborations need to be established before funding is secured.

This chapter concludes by offering practical tips on the basic approaches to both general and R&D corporate funding, including pertinent examples, and electronic and print corporate information sources.

Corporate General Philanthropy Funding

Approach to Corporate General Philanthropy Funding. Because corporations award shareholder profits as they make grants, corporate officials are particularly selective in identifying their recipients. When corporations award grants, they follow a concept of

---

$185,000 over two years to Santa Fe, New Mexico public schools to develop a Rainforest Exploration curriculum for fourth and fifth graders. The curriculum and teachers' guide will include inquiry-based activities and experiments related to the rainforest ecosystem

$400,000 over three years to the University of Southern California's Integrated Media Systems Center to study, evaluate, and develop interactive visualization content materials and tools for high school biology. These interactive modules will utilize manipulative 3-D representations of biological objects and processes

$390,000 over two years to WNET New York to assist schools in integrating environmental education in their science programs. Entitled "What's Up in the Environment," this multimedia program will enable educators and students to make connections with the natural and social sciences, as well as mathematics, arts, and humanities

SAMPLE TOYOTA USA GRANTS: A CORPORATE FOUNDATION

EXHIBIT 20

"profitable philanthropy"; that is, they often fund those projects that will bring them better products, happier or healthier employees, lower costs, better brand awareness, or good public relations—all things from which they can benefit, the "What's in it for me" syndrome. As a corporate grantseeker, your challenge is to describe your project in terms that will benefit the corporation.

Example of Corporate General Philanthropy Funding. Organizations can attract corporate funding by making it a "win-win" situation for all. Recently, the Healthy Baby Agency was concerned generally about the high incidence of adolescent pregnancy in its inner city, and more specifically was alarmed at the low birth weight and poor nutrition received by the newborns. Visiting nurses reported that mothers were cutting off the end of the nipples on baby bottles so the infants could consume their nourishment faster; additionally, the nurses observed that the infant formula consisted of sugar water instead of healthy nutrients. The problem: these new mothers lacked information on the benefits of good infant nutrition. The Healthy Baby Agency went to a manufacturer of baby food formula and gained $25,000 to develop a video on infant nutrition that would be played for mothers of newborns while they were in the hospital, postdelivery. What was in it for the corporation? Two things: their products were prominently displayed during the filming of the video (but not commercially plugged) and the corporation was generously acknowledged during the credits at the end of the video. This project was so successful, in fact, that the corporation later sponsored additional videos in languages other than English.

The Healthy Baby Agency found that crucial point of "connect" with the corporation: an innovative project that underscored the importance of their corporate mission, namely, developing healthy babies. The corporation was able to secure substantial publicity from this project, letting others know what a good corporate citizen they were. What is your point of "connect" with a corporation? These organizations found "hot buttons" with corporations and were successful in obtaining philanthropic support.

- A university approached a corporation that hires many of its engineering graduates and obtained funding for minority student scholarships.
- A museum first loaned paintings to help decorate a new corporate office and then later received funding for an art restoration project.

- A hospital received corporate support for a diabetes research project from a corporation whose CEO had a family history of diabetes.

How do you find your corporate "hot button?" Through prospect research.

Corporate Research and Development (R&D) Funding

Approach to Corporate R&D Funding. Corporations are "for-profit" firms. This descriptor pretty well sums up the major purpose of any corporation—to make money for its owners, who range from the sole owner/entrepreneur of a small company simply looking to support his family, to a large publicly traded company holding millions of shares of stock. Corporate R&D funding represents the pinnacle of profitable philanthropy. Corporations fund those projects for which they believe a long-term—but often "more immediate"—gain will be received.

Example of Corporate R&D Funding. Profitable philanthropy worked for both parties in a recent case where a university laboratory was conducting cutting-edge research on sensors and their use in liquid environments. The laboratory director approached an automobile manufacturer and explained how the sensors could detect when it was time to change the oil in an automobile; that is, instead of changing the oil automatically every 3,000 miles as most people do, the research professor gave details how his sensors could determine when the oil became dirty enough to change regardless of miles driven, thereby more efficiently reducing engine wear. The corporation supported the R&D project and now includes the sensors in all automobiles it manufactures. The research laboratory received funding for their R&D project as well as a nice revenue stream from royalty sales and patents. It was a win-win situation for both parties.

Corporate Internet References

Foundation Center. At present, few direct sources of corporate funding information reside on the Internet. The Foundation Center maintains an online database of corporate giving. This subscription-based service profiles 3,700 companies, 2,700 company-sponsored foundations, 1,400 direct corporate giving programs, and records of 97,000 recently awarded grants. Further details regarding *Corporate Giving Online* are available at www.foundationcenter.org/findfunders/funding sources/cgo.html. The online subscription databases for SPIN, IRIS, and Community of Science, discussed in Chapter 2, also contain corporate sponsorship information.

Thomas Register. Thomas Register, a 100-year-old company, has established an online presence for its well-known directory; registration is free. The directory lists 700,000 U.S. and Canadian companies that provide industrial products and services in 65,000 different categories. It also includes links to online catalogs and corporate Web sites. Search engines permit use of keywords and Boolean terms: AND, OR, NOT. Visit www.thomasnet.com.

How can you use Thomas Register to bolster your corporate grantseeking? First, determine what type of business might be interested in supporting your project; then use Thomas Register to find those corporations with similar commercial interests. For instance, if your project deals with infant nutrition, Thomas Register could identify for you those firms that manufacture baby food and infant formula. If you have a health or wellness project, consider insurance companies or HMO providers. At your next office staff meeting, identify five different types of corporations that might support your organization, and then seek them out in Thomas Register.

Corporate Web sites. Beyond the Foundation Center and Thomas Register sites, you can explore corporate commercial sites, most of which follow the standard address: www.organizationname.com. Often, you will encounter corporate descriptions, not specific grant-related information, although there are some exceptions, as the IBM address www.ibm.com/IBM/IBMGives (Exhibit 21) reveals.

SEC Information. If you are contemplating a corporate solicitation, study the Securities and Exchange Commission Web site. It'll provide very useful information about the prospect's values and financial history. Go to www.sec.gov and click on the EDGAR database to search for actual company filings with the SEC. A friendly tutorial is available to help you interpret the SEC forms.

U.S. Patent and Trademark Office. The U.S. Patent and Trademark Office maintains an excellent Web site at www.uspto.gov of all patents and trademarks ever issued in this country. This database is very current, with patents typically listed in their entirety within a week of being issued. Patent applications and provisional patent applications are not yet listed, but some may become available in the future under the American Inventors Protection Act.

Patent information often gives another useful insight on a company's product development interests and needs. This database obviously is a good place to begin a search of a company's patent portfolio, to identify patents that the company might be asked to donate or otherwise make available at no cost to your organization. One caveat, however, is that it takes two to three years for a patent to issue after its original application. In some cases, by the time a patent issues, the company may have moved away from that technology. In such cases, a company might be willing to donate nonessential patents to your organization.

CORPORATE GRANTMAKER HOME PAGE: IBM

EXHIBIT 21

State Corporate Records Files. Most states require corporations—and in many cases, other business entities such as LLCs (limited liability companies)—to file brief annual reports that list the company's registered agent and registered address at a minimum, plus other information that varies from state to state. Such information may include names of officers, names of board members, and previous names and addresses the company has used. Most often, such records are kept by a state's Secretary of State office, but sometimes the records are more difficult to locate. Some states such as Wisconsin, California, and Georgia provide this information at no cost over the Internet to residents and nonresidents alike. To find state corporate records, go to the state home page, www.xx.gov (where xx is the name of your state with no spaces) and then look under the Secretary of State's entry.

Corporate Grant Print References

Information on government grants is quite accessible and is even backed legally by the Freedom of Information Act. Information about private foundation grants is somewhat less accessible than in the government arena, although many foundations go to considerable effort and expense to publish information about their interests. Additionally, the public accessibility of foundation tax records keeps philanthropic information flowing. Access to information becomes quite restricted in the case of corporations. As private, independent organizations, they have no obligation to disseminate information about their philanthropic activities. Corporations are responsible to their stockholders, not the general public. The stockholders have access to company finances, including philanthropic activities.

You can start gathering your corporate background information by requesting a copy of an annual report (for publicly held companies only) from the public relations office of your target corporation. It will provide you with a view of the world as seen through corporate eyes. It may or may not indicate the total dollar volume contributed for philanthropic purposes. Even if such information is disclosed, you may not find the level of detail you may wish, namely, the names of grant recipients, their grant titles, and their grant amounts.

If you are having trouble getting corporate information through the usual channels, try getting the information from a stockholder—or buy one share of stock and become a stockholder yourself. As a stockholder, you will have privileged access to information about charitable corporate contributions.

If your organization doesn't have a history of attracting corporate donations, start small and request larger grants as you establish credibility. For your first approach, you may wish to request nonmonetary support, e.g., donation of a used computer or "borrow" an executive. Corporations are very cost conscious; therefore, challenge grants have special appeal because corporations feel they are getting the most for their dollar. While there are nearly 2.5 million corporations, only about one-third of them make general contributions to nonprofit organizations.

Corporate Giving Directory. Unlike government and foundation grants, few reference books list corporate giving preferences. One basic reference document is the Information Today publication, *Corporate Giving Directory.* The 29th edition (2007) provides detailed profiles of the 1,000 top corporate charitable giving programs in the United States. Collectively, these corporations awarded more than $5 billion in grants. Each listing includes biographical data on corporate officers and trustees, types of grants given, giving priorities and budgets, typical recipients, contact person, application procedures, and relevant data on sponsoring company. Its multiple indexes cross-reference sponsors by headquarters state, operating location, type of grant, nonmonetary support, recipient type, application deadlines, and names and background information on key personnel.

National Directory of Corporate Giving. *The National Directory of Corporate Giving*, 13th edition (2007), published by the Foundation Center, gives you reliable, fact-filled, and up-to-date entries on approximately 3,687 corporations awarding grants to nonprofit organizations. Each entry features such essential information as application procedures, names of key personnel, types of support generally awarded, giving limitations, financial data, and purpose and activities statements. Many entries include descriptions of recently awarded grants, an excellent indication of funding priorities. Many of the large corporate entries include program analyses to further illustrate their grantmaker's interests. In addition to details on corporate grantmaking activities, all entries include the company's name and address, a review of the types of business, financial data, plant and subsidiary locations, and Fortune 1000 ranking. Seven indexes help you target the best funding prospects for your program.

Corporate General Business References

Beyond the prospect research tools that provide direct information about corporate grant information sources, several large business directories might be useful for grantseeking purposes. None contain specific grant information. However, they contain contact and financial information that could point you along the right path. The following corporate business references are available in the business section of most public libraries. As you peruse these references, look for linkages, connections, and networks that can help establish a contact between your organization and the corporation.

1. **Fortune 500 Directory.** It lists the 500 largest industrial corporations and pertinent information about sales, profits, assets, market value, earnings per share, and total return to investors. Visit http://money.cnn.com to see the complete list.

2. **Fortune Magazine.** The late May or early June issues list the top 500 industrial and top 500 service corporations. Read the online version at http://money.cnn.com.

3. **Forbes Market 500.** Forbes ranks both industrial and nonindustrial corporations and includes information on market value, sales volume, assets, and profits.

4. **Dun and Bradstreet's Million Dollar Directory.** This reference tool lists information on corporations with a net worth of over $1 million. Electronic information is available at www .dnbmdd.com/mddi.

5. **Standard and Poor's Register of Corporations, Executives, and Industries.** A good beginning point in your search for corporate grants, the entries include corporate name, address, phone; a list of major corporate officers; sales volume; number of employees; primary bank; and description of products, including corporate trademarks.

6. **State Manufacturing Directories.** To research corporations within your state, locate your state manufacturing association directory in your public library. Most states have one that lists names of key personnel, company size and dollar volume, products manufactured, and locations of company plants. Check with the nearest Business Reference Librarian for specifics.

7. **Business Journals.** The larger metropolitan areas publish a regular business journal, a business newspaper that reports regional business information. It is a valuable source of detail about the financial and philanthropic health of business firms in your areas. To read online versions of business journals, visit www.newspapers.com and click on "Business Publications."

Not all of the references cited above have online Web sites; some online references are free, while other do charge an access fee. After reviewing these basic business materials, start networking with your corporate contacts following the suggestions in Chapter 4, Preproposal Contacts.

Clip File Action Item # 8
Finding Private Funds

As you expand your Finding Private Funds clip file, consider including items such as the following:

- Copies of grant opportunities from the print and electronic reference sources cited above.
- Names of past grant winners.
- Model letters requesting application forms and guidelines.
- Tax records from private foundations.
- Annual reports from foundations and corporations.
- Copies of successful proposals.

CHAPTER 4
Preproposal Contacts

Personal relationships are the fertile soil from which all advancement, all success, all achievement in real life grows.

—Ben Stein

OVERVIEW

You now have several ideas for seeking grants (Chapter 1). You've looked at public and private funding sources (Chapters 2 and 3) for your ideas. Next, you wonder which "suspects," among many, offer the best chance of getting funded; that is, which "suspects" are really the best "prospects?" It's now time to heed Ben Stein's advice and launch some new personal relationships.

This chapter details the many things you can do to increase your chances of getting funded by using preproposal contacts. Specifically, in Chapter 4, you will learn the following:

- How to pick the sponsors that have the highest probability of funding your projects.
- Questions you should ask program officers.
- Questions you should ask past grant winners.
- Questions you should ask past grant reviewers.

At the moment, your list of "suspects" falls into a "maybe" category: "maybe" they will fund you, "maybe" they won't. You can move those "suspects" from the "maybe" category to either a "yes" or "no" category by following the four-step process described below. The outcome will identify your real "prospects," those sponsors with a higher probability of funding your proposals.

RATIONALE

Preproposal contact is a process that helps you see the grant world from the sponsor's perspective. You already know your viewpoint. Preproposal contact lets you judge how well your needs match those of the sponsor. In essence, you are evaluating them first, before they evaluate your proposal. Ask yourself questions like these:

- "Are these the kind of people I can and want to do business with?"
- "Can my services solve their problems?"
- "Should I send them a proposal?"
- "If so, what are they looking for?"

In order to produce a win-win situation, both you and the sponsor must be satisfied with each other.

You can make successful preproposal contacts by following these four steps that will validate the information obtained from your initial funding search to identify potential public and private grantseekers.

1. Write to the program officer requesting basic application information
2. Call a past grant winner to learn success secrets
3. Call a past grant reviewer to learn proposal evaluation policies and procedures
4. Call the program officer to validate prospect information

After making these contacts, detailed below, you can easily decide whether you should submit a proposal to any given sponsor on your "suspect" list. If the answer is "yes," you substantially increase your likelihood of getting funded. If the answer is "no," then you have not wasted your time in writing a proposal for this sponsor; instead, move on to another one that is a better match for your situation.

This chapter explains precisely how to conduct your preproposal contacts by specifying to whom you should talk, what questions you should ask, and how you can interpret their answers.

The initial tendency of beginning grantseekers is to just write, mail, and hope for the best. Frankly, we know of no better way to get turned down. In contrast, experienced grantseekers know the value of preproposal contact and typically report three benefits:

1. It is crucial in selecting a sponsor who is highly likely to fund your proposal.
2. It pinpoints what is required to put together a winning proposal.
3. It prepares for possible site visits, if you end up on the "short-short" list for funding.

Beginning grantseekers, on the other hand, are sometimes reluctant to contact people who can provide valuable grant information; they develop a bad case of the "jitters."

Overcoming Preproposal Contact Jitters

Making preproposal contacts, whether through calls, visits, letters, or e-mails with grant officers, is a key first step in grant writing. If you are stalled at this point, you may be suffering from PCJ (Preproposal Contact Jitters), a common malady that strikes all grantseekers.

The typical symptoms of PCJ include fear of failure, anxiety, vacillating between making the contact and postponing it, helplessness, and lack of focus. The basic cause of PCJ is lack of preparation.

Imagine that at four o'clock this afternoon you get a letter saying you have been funded. Ask yourself: "What's the first thing I will do in the morning?" You can't really answer this question unless you've first answered questions like these:

- "What do I specifically want to accomplish in this project?"
- "What have I done, up to now, to get the project started?"
- "How's it working out?"
- "What else could I do?"
- "What will happen to the project if it doesn't get funded?
- "Exactly what are my resources (people, equipment, experience, money) for this project?"
- "Precisely what do I want from the grantor?"
- "Have I talked with everyone involved and clearly planned the project?"

- "Specifically, when, where, and how will I make the preproposal contact?"

You will think of more questions that you must answer before you make your preproposal contact, and we will list many that you'll find helpful. Most grant officers welcome contacts from well-prepared potential applicants. Knowing that you are a likely fit saves both of you time and effort.

Another manifestation of PCJ arises when beginning grantseekers wonder, "Why would the program officer want to talk to me?" The answer: program officers would much rather formally review a strong as opposed to a weak proposal. The preproposal communication affords the program officer with opportunities to strengthen the quality of proposals officially received. Since not all worthy proposals can be funded, program officers sometimes use the high quality of rejected proposals as a basis for seeking increased funding for the next fiscal year.

When asked about the importance of preproposal contact before submitting an application, a federal program officer recently said it best: "It's THE most important thing to do." Moreover, it sometimes yields unexpected dividends. For example, experienced grantseekers have, because of preproposal contacts, done the following:

- Learned about new grant opportunities not yet announced
- Critiqued draft proposal application forms and guidelines
- Been asked to serve as beta test sites on new computerized grantseeking ventures

All of these outcomes provide you early access to valuable grant information.

Beginning grantseekers sometimes feel that while preproposal contacts have value, the program officers are much like sales people for their agencies, only looking out for their interests and not yours. In other words, agency staff members benefit when the number of proposals in their interest area increases. Encouragement from program officers to submit a proposal needs to be weighed carefully; their optimism and hope can sometimes mask very real barriers to funding, such as budget constraints, geographic award criteria, or changing funding priorities. Successful grantseekers gather information from multiple sources (program officers, past grant winners, prior grant reviewers) before deciding whether to submit a proposal. Triangulating your information and resources will maximize your likelihood of getting funded.

STEP ONE: INITIAL CONTACT WITH PROGRAM OFFICER

Why Do Step One?

Making initial contact with the program officer satisfies two objectives. First, you obtain the application forms and guidelines to follow should you decide to submit a proposal. When these materials arrive, study them to determine whether you have the interest and capacity to respond. Second, it is an important beginning step in relationship building with the program officer.

Who to Contact—and How

Contact the program officer who was identified from your initial prospect research. If you have no prior relationship with the program officer, send a letter, since it will help build the name recognition of your organization, in addition to securing basic grant-seeking information. If you have dealt with this program officer in the past, a phone call or e-mail will suffice.

A federal program officer recently offered this advice to grantseekers: "Consolidate your questions; too many e-mails can be annoying." E-mail has become too user friendly. It's too easy to fire off a question whenever you think of one. Moreover, because e-mail is so easy, we also expect realistic and immediate responses. This program officer added, "I e-mail back and forth twice, then I pick up the phone and call." Her rationale: phone calls allow for verbal clues, e.g., pauses that alert her to and allow her to clear up potential misunderstandings.

What to Request—and Why

Contact the program officer when you are ready to evaluate your funding prospects. You are seeking three pieces of information.

1. A copy of the current application forms and guidelines.
2. The names of several past grant winners.
3. The names of several past grant reviewers.

You do not need to explain your project in any detail. On the contrary, you want to know what the sponsor considers important in order to determine how you might cast your proposal. At this point, any detailed description of your proposal to the program officer is premature and should await the finding from your preproposal contacts.

Contacting the past grant reviewers will give you valuable insights into the review process. To submit a successful proposal, you need to know how your proposal will be reviewed, especially time frames and points awarded for proposal sections. Learning from the experiences of past grant reviewers and knowing what they were instructed to look for in their reviews will help you decide whether to submit your proposal.

Sample Letter to Program Officer

Your letter to a program officer should do the following:

1. Introduce yourself and your organization.
2. State a benefit that appeals to them, based on your initial prospect research.
3. Explain that to deliver your potential benefits, you need more information.

The following sample letter in Exhibit 22 was used by a social service agency to seek basic information from a local private foundation. It could easily be modified to other types of sponsors. Be sure to use your organization's letterhead; you want the sponsor to begin to recognize your agency's name and logo.

As you review this sample letter, note first that the administrative assistant opening the letter reads the phrase "Letter Requesting Grant Application Information." This heading phrase helps the reader determine the purpose of the letter without having to read it in detail; that is, the heading provides a quick basis for referral or response. Second, the heading also signals that this letter is *not* a grant application and should not be treated as such. Finally, notice the enclosures. Some sponsors have response packets already assembled in sealed envelopes. If that is the case, they appreciate your thoughtfulness in providing a gummed address label. On the other hand, if they don't have information packets preassembled, they can gather pertinent materials and put them in your large manila, self-addressed envelope bearing plenty of postage in case they have large information packets. Either way, this courtesy makes it easier for them to respond, you'll get your information much sooner, and you'll be taking an important first step in establishing your organizational efficiency.

In sum, Step One represents a reconnaissance, information-gathering stage. You must gather information before deciding whether you should submit, and these three individuals—program officers, past winners, and past reviewers—can furnish crucial information. Step One happens quickly: a generic letter, once

Today's Date

Ms. Program Officer Name
Agency Title
Agency Name
Mailing Address

Dear Ms. Program Officer:

Teen Pregnancy Services specializes in working with inner city teenage mothers in Atlanta, helping them ensure their infants receive good nutrition, while, at the same time, reducing developmental health problems. Recently, the Governor of Georgia cited our work as a "role model for social service agencies throughout the state."

We have some ideas that may be of value to you and the Healthy Baby Foundation. Accordingly, we request three specific items:

_____1. A copy of your current application forms and guidelines.
_____2. A list of your recent grant winners.
_____3. Names of three past grant reviewers.

These three items will help us understand better your current priorities to see whether our ideas would be worthwhile for you to look at in a formal proposal.

Sincerely,

Your Name
Title

Enclosure
    Address Label
    Self-addressed, Stamped Envelope

LETTER REQUESTING GRANT APPLICATION INFORMATION

EXHIBIT 22

on your word processor, can easily be adapted in less than two minutes—well worth the time investment!

STEP TWO: CONTACT A PAST GRANT WINNER

Why Do Step Two?

You want to contact past grant winners to learn their secrets of success. Obviously, they did something right, because they were funded. Their success tips and experiences in dealing with the sponsor will help you decide whether to submit your proposal. You will not be asking their feedback on your proposal idea; rather, you will be idea mining for those good information nuggets that might be useful as you develop your proposal. Experience is a wonderful teacher and you can profit from their experience.

Who to Contact—and How

From the information you received in Step One, you want to contact a project director who received a grant from your target sponsor, preferably an organization that is similar to yours or working on a project like yours, although this is not always possible.

Government organizations are very open about identifying their grant recipients; it is one means of encouraging other grant applicants. Besides, the names of government grant winners are in the public domain and available under the Freedom of Information Act, a federal law (5 U.S.C. §552) that ensures government records are available for public inspection.

The situation is a little different with private sponsors. Some private foundations volunteer the names of their grant recipients, for they like to be known for doing charitable good. About 15 percent of the private foundations publish annual reports that often include lists of recipient names. For those foundations that neither publish grant winner names nor include them in your Step One request, your fallback position is to examine the sponsor's tax records (Form 990, see Chapter 3) to learn the names of recipients; that information is public.

Corporate grant award information is less available than private foundations. If your potential corporate sponsor does not include names of past grant winners in response to your Step One letter, then a shareholder or stockbroker may be able to secure this information for you. If not, your fallback position is to ask the corporate sponsor directly for a profile of a typical grant winner: type of organization, size, and geographic location. If your profile is substantially different from their typical grant winner, then you should discuss this fact with the sponsor to determine whether you should apply.

In sum, you should be able to identify the names of all past public grant winners and many (but not all) private grant winners. The preferred method of contact is by telephone: it's easier, cheaper, quicker, and most important, the informants will often say things verbally they would be reluctant to put in writing. Your telephone approach has two key parts: the opening statement and some follow-up questions. Both parts are described below.

The Opening Statement to Past Grant Winners

You want to use an attention-getting opening statement that will pique their curiosity and elicit further communications. Within the first few seconds, you'll either create interest or resistance. TV advertisers, for example, have known this for years: if you don't get viewers' attention immediately, they will go channel surfing or head for the refrigerator.

Here's a three-step formula for opening success on the telephone. Briefly, explain the following.

1. **Who** are you? Introduce yourself and organization.
2. **Why** are you calling? State an interest-stimulating, curiosity-creating benefit that appeals to their desire to gain, or avoid loss.

3. **What's** in it for them? Involve them in the conversation; you want to do more listening than talking. Tell them that in order to deliver potential benefits, you need to get information.

Beginning grantseekers often wonder, "Why should a past grant winner talk to me? Won't they see me as competition? Why should they share their success secrets with me?"

These are good questions that deserve solid answers! People who worry that past grant winners won't talk freely can counter those concerns by offering something of value: information exchanges, collaboration possibilities, proposals swaps. Consider these opening statements to winners of government, private foundation, and corporate grants.

Call from a university history professor to winner of a federal humanities grant:

> Dr. Maki, Fred Johnson from the National Endowment for the Humanities suggested I give you a call [Why]. I'm Bob Iacopino with the Children's History Institute at Midwest University [Who]. Like you, we're investigating the role of children in the Civil War. Fred thought since our efforts seem to overlap, it might make sense to consider some type of mutually beneficial collaboration [What]. If I've caught you at a good time, I'd like to learn more about your project, tell you what we're doing, and ask you some questions about your experiences with NEH. (95 words)

Call from a youth agency to winner of a national foundation grant:

> Hi, Mr. Rockefeller. I'm Shandel Lear with the Why Care Agency [Who]. I understand you recently got a grant from the Ford Foundation to teach geometry to middle school children. Congratulations. We are also doing something similar in this area. I'm calling today because depending on your situation, there's a possibility we might be able to informally collaborate in some fashion [What]. If I've caught you at a good time, I'd like to exchange project information and discuss your experiences with Ford [Why]. (81 words)

Call from a nonprofit dental clinic to winner of a corporate grant:

> Hello, Mr. Metal. I'm Dr. Mona Molar with Midwest Dental Associates [Who]. I understand you were recently selected as a winner of a Sullivan Community Oral Health Grant.

The reason I'm call is this: depending on your priorities, there's a good chance our ideas might dovetail with your project [What]. If I've caught you at a good time, I'd like to get a brief update on your project, explore possible linkages, and learn more about your experiences with Sullivan Dental Products Company [Why]. (81 words)

These opening statements are designed to get consent to move on to the next phase, the investigating, questioning stage. These three examples can be uttered in 30–40 seconds. Write out your opening statement, verbatim, 45 seconds—max! (The average adult speaks approximately 160 words per minute.)

Follow-up Questions to Past Grant Winners

Questioning is the foundation of preproposal contacts, getting essential background information to decide (1) whether you should submit a proposal, and (2) if you submit, how best to frame the proposal so it matches the "values glasses" of the sponsor. The list of questions that one could pose to a past grant winner is theoretically endless. Nevertheless, if you want to write a successful grant, you must PREP first, where PREP is an acronym to distinguish between four basic types of questions.

1. **Position:** what are the baseline situations, present circumstances, and basic facts?
2. **Rationale:** what are the problems, needs, and injustices that exist today?
3. **Expectation:** what are the implications for addressing these problems?
4. **Priority:** what approaches are most likely to lead to an improved situation now?

Collectively, PREP questions span a continuum of time from past actions to future intentions. Beginning grantseekers often ask too many **Position** questions and too few **Rationale-Expectation-Priority** questions. Here are some "starter questions" in each category, to which you will undoubtedly add your own.

Position Questions: The Baseline Situation. Position questions explore baseline information and relationships with the sponsor from the perspective of past grant winners, and lay the foundation for more probing types of questions.

- "Did you call or go see the sponsor before writing the proposal?"

Preproposal Contact. This question will reveal the extent to which the grantee engaged in preproposal contact.
- "What materials did you find most helpful in developing your proposals?"
Proposal Development Materials. This answer will suggest those reference materials and tools that the grantee found valuable in writing the proposal, e.g., Web sites, government reports, primary and secondary text references.
- "Who did you find most helpful on the funding source staff?"
Internal Advocate. This query will help identify an "in-house hero," an agency staff person who may be the best source of inside information for you.
- "Did you use any special advocates on your behalf?"
Special Advocates. This question will indicate what role, if any, people outside of their organization (board officials, lobbyists, politicians) played in securing the grant.
- "Did the funding source review a preproposal or a proposal draft prior to final submission?"
Review Drafts. This query identifies their receptivity to preproposal contact. Most agencies welcome this contact, given sufficient lead time. One federal program officer recently commented, "Less than 1 percent of our proposals are funded 'cold' without any preproposal contact."
- "How close was your initial budget to the awarded amount?"
Budgets. The answer to this question identifies the extent to which budget negotiations took place. What was cut or increased? What level of documentation was required to justify budget items?
- "Did you have a site visit?"
Site Visit. If one occurred, ask what took place; that is, who attended, how long did it last, were you able to supplement your proposal with additional materials, to whom did they speak, and so forth.

Rationale Questions: Problems Existing Today. Rationale questions go to the heart of sponsor-giving from the perspective of past grant winners: the problems, needs, and injustices that exist today. Problems may be either (1) in your topic area if it's the same as past grant winners, or (2) in an area different than yours, in which case your interest is in learning about sponsor motivations in funding past grant winners' projects.

- "You got funded because the sponsor was convinced you could solve some big problems they

were concerned about. What were those big problems?"
Big Picture Problems. Look for big picture problems that really trouble the sponsor.

- "What are some of the biggest dissatisfactions with the current approaches to this problem?"
Current Failures. Listen for sore spots and raw nerves.

- "Generally speaking, what are the disadvantages of the way these problems are being handled now?"
Status Quo Shortcomings. Pay attention to what's wrong today and will become worse tomorrow.

- "Are there problems or difficulties in this area that are particularly challenging now?"
Major Hurdles. Take note of priorities among complex problems: what are the top issues?

- "What kinds of problems are the biggest at the moment? Personnel problems? Financial problems? Management problems? Training problems? Reliability problems? Quality problems? Other?"
Problem Categories. Help your informant focus on different dimensions of the problem.

Obviously, the questions are not discrete. The overlap is intentional; good interviewers know the importance of asking a question more than one way to get at the heart of an issue.

Expectation Questions: Basic Implications for Addressing Problems.

Expectation questions look at the "so what?" implications of the rationale questions from the vantage point of past grant winners. These questions also identify the sponsor's outlook for changing the problem situation.

- "Was there a hidden agenda to the program's guidelines?"
Hidden Agenda. Priorities change and what was top priority at the time the grantee's proposal was funded may have changed again as you plan to submit now.

- "Given the problems you identified, what are the implications of those difficulties?"
Implications. Get the informant talking about the consequences of existing problems.

- "What's the desired impact on these problems, balancing project breadth, depth, and financial resources available?"
Project Balance. Proposals can be too broad or too narrow. The answer to this question helps you find a proper balance within budgetary constraints.

- "What are some other implications?"
More Implications. One of the most revealing questions in interviewing: "What else?"

- "Among the many consequences of these problems, which ones are most significant? Reduced self-esteem, workplace bottlenecks, lost hopes, limited aspirations, impaired health status, financial drains, personnel turnover, high training costs, lost productivity, dependency on others, higher costs, slowed down expansion, reduced output, other?"
Implication Priorities. One final pass at "What else?"

- "What would you do differently next time?"
Things to Change. Invariably, people learn from the positive experience of getting a grant and have concrete suggestions about things they would change to strengthen their next grant proposal.

Priority Questions: Approaches for an Improved Situation.

Priority questions concentrate on identifying the top activities that will effectively and efficiently improve the conditions surrounding the identified problems, needs, and injustices that exist today, as seen by past grant winners.

- "Why did the sponsor think it important to solve the problem you identified?"
Significance. Look for the sponsor's motivation in solving the problem.

- "How does your project really help?"
Solution Impact. What are the key features of your proposed solution?

- "What are the benefits you see of your approach?"
General Benefits. Look for reasons why the sponsor found this solution so useful.

- "Would this approach be useful for cost reasons or something else?"
Economic Benefits. Narrow the general benefits to that major motivator: money.

- "Will your approach reduce the frequency or severity of the problem?"
Programmatic Benefits. Look for the things that will change, e.g., the incidence or magnitude of the problem.

- "Could you clarify how this would help?"
Additional Benefits. One last call for "What else?"

Do you need to ask all of these questions? Absolutely not! Choose those from each category that you will find most helpful, recognizing that other questions will arise in the natural course of the conversation. In the course of a 10-minute phone conversation, you will have a much better idea how your needs mesh with those of the sponsor.

STEP THREE: CALL TO PAST GRANT REVIEWERS

Why Do Step Three?

Past grant reviewers had firsthand experience in evaluating proposals like yours. They actually measured the psychological impact of the proposals they read. Your goal in contacting past grant reviewers is to learn about the specific process to be followed when your proposal is reviewed. For example, if a reviewer has only three minutes to review your proposal, you will write differently than if the reviewer has three hours to review it. As another benefit of talking with past grant reviewers, you will learn about the scoring system used to review proposals; some proposal sections may be more important than others.

Who to Contact—and How

Step One should have identified the names of some past grant reviewers. They may be specialists in the field or internal staff members. Sometimes, one can find the names of federal program reviewers on agency Web sites. Private sponsors may or may not provide the names of reviewers. If not, ask your program officer for information about a typical reviewer's profile, since your proposal should be written to the level of expertise of the reviewer. Just like your contact with past grant winners in Step Two, you need both an opening statement to pique interest and information-yielding follow-up questions.

The Opening Statement to Past Grant Reviewers

These opening statements follow the same model discussed for past grant winners, although the actual content is different, as the following examples illustrate.

Call from a researcher in a local environmental protection agency to a recent reviewer of a federal grant:

> Hi, Dr. Beach. I'm Gary Grant with the Sand-Crab Agency [Who]. I understand you recently served as a reviewer for the National Institute of Seashells. We are in the process of putting together a proposal to NIS [Why]. I'm calling today to request a friendly favor. If I've caught you at a good time, I'd like to discuss your experiences with NIS so we can see whether our proposal would be of value to them [What]. (74 words)

Call from a health agency administrator to a reviewer of health care foundation proposals:

> Hello, Ms. Lawson, I'm June Thompson with the Atlanta Lung Society [Who]. Dr. Barry Gimbel mentioned that you recently reviewed grant proposals for the National Breathright Association. We are completing a proposal to the NBA and I'm calling today wondering if we can exchange professional favors? [Why]. If I've caught you at a good time, I'd like to discuss your experiences with NBA so we can be sure that what we propose would be of value to them. In turn, I'd like to send you a copy of our proposal, if that would be of interest [What]. We've done this successfully in the past and actually ended up collaborating with our new-found friends. May I send you a proposal copy? (118 words)

Call from a fire chief to a reviewer of corporate proposals:

> Hello, This is Chief John Hunkel from the Detroit Fire Department calling [Who]. The folks at Mitsubishi Communications said you recently served as a reviewer for their Emergency Communications Program. We're targeting a proposal to them for their next deadline. As you know, you won't be reviewing our proposal since they regularly rotate reviewers in each competition cycle. So I'm wondering if you can extend to us a professional courtesy [What]. If I've caught you at a good time, I'd like to get your perspectives on the proposals you reviewed [Why]. What were the typical shortcomings of the proposals you looked at? (99 words)

Follow-up Questions to Past Grant Reviewers

Again, many PREP questions could be asked; those that follow are suggestive, not prescriptive.

Position Questions: The Baseline Situation. Position questions explore baseline information and relationships with the sponsor, and lay the foundation for more probing types of questions from the viewpoint of past grant reviewers.

- "How did you get to be a reviewer?"
  Selection as Reviewer. Usually you just submit a resume and express an interest, showing how your background and expertise meshes with agency priorities. Consider being a reviewer yourself (see Chapter 16). It's an easy way to get "inside information" and improve your success rate.

- "Did you review the proposals at the sponsor's office or at home?"
  Review Environment. The difference here is between a mail and a panel review. Mail reviews are done under more relaxed conditions but often require greater documentation whereas a panel review is apt to be done quicker, placing a higher premium on proposal readability and scanability.
- "Did you review electronic or hard copies of the proposals?"
  Proposal Presentation. The trend, especially at the federal government level, is to review electronic copies of proposals. Some agencies have greater experience than others relative to handling electronic copies of proposals. You are especially interested in knowing whether formatting problems existed when reading electronic copies.
- "Did you follow a particular scoring system?"
  Proposal Scoring System. Invariably some portions of a proposal carry greater weight than other portions. This information will enable you to concentrate your efforts on the highest scoring portions.
- "How much time did you have to read the proposals?"
  Review Time. If the reviewers have essentially unlimited time to read a proposal (as in a mail review) then you write one way, but if they are under severe time constraints, then you write another way. One reviewer recently noted that in a panel review situation he could allow approximately 20 seconds per page to finish the review process on time. While that is not the norm for proposal review, it does suggest that one uses different proposal-writing strategies under such conditions, e.g., simple and short sentences, creative use of headings and subheadings, lots of white space, boldface for emphasis, and bulleted lists.

Rationale Questions: Problems Existing Today.

Rationale questions go to the heart of sponsor-giving from the vantage point of past grant reviewers: the problems, needs, and injustices that exist today. Whether the past grant reviewer evaluated proposals in your topic area or another area, your interest is in learning about what motivates sponsors to fund projects.

- "What were you told to look for?"
  Identification of Problems. Invariably the reviewers are told to look especially at the statement of the problem or need. Any special "red flags" raised by the reviewers should be addressed as you develop your proposal. Sometimes, reviewers are instructed to look for elements of proposals that are not requested in the application guidelines. Your proposal should respond to all items on the application guidelines and the reviewer's evaluation form.
- "How often did you notice this problem in proposals?"
  Frequency of Problems. This answer will help determine the more frequently occurring proposal problems. The problems may deal with proposal content or format. For instance, one reviewer lamented that proposals were written in ten point type. Although this was allowable according to the guidelines, the reviewer found it very tiring to read.
- "What were the disadvantages of the way this problem area was being approached in the proposals you read?"
  General Barriers. This answer highlights the reviewers' insights into problems not being addressed in the proposals they reviewed, problems that you may be able to incorporate into your proposals.
- "What are the biggest hurdles people face in reaching their grant objectives?"
  Specific Barriers. This answer prioritizes existing problems in meeting grant objectives.
- "What difficulties linger that still are not being addressed?"
  Unanswered Issues. This answer spotlights existing problems that are still being avoided.
- "How does the existing data support this problem?"
  Need Documentation. This answer indicates data sources for quantifying existing problems.

Expectation Questions: Basic Implications for Addressing Problems.

Expectation questions look at the "so what" implications of the rationale questions, as seen by past grant reviewers. They also identify the sponsor's outlook for changing the problem situation.

- "What were the most common mistakes you saw?"
  Avoiding Common Errors. The resulting answers should clearly list those errors that you want to be sure and avoid, errors like failing to number the pages or to list the resumes of project directors or consultants, or math mistakes on the budget.
- "What are the implications of those mistakes?"
  Implications of Mistakes. The answer indicates both the logical and psychological dimensions of proposal errors and suggests ways in which proposals could be improved.

- "What happens when those proposal problems occur?"
  Consequences. This answer implies a relationship between proposal problems and their impact on reviewers.
- "How does this problem relate to the bigger picture?"
  Impact on Bigger Picture. This response places the current problems in a larger context.
- "If there were no budget limits, what should have been proposed that wasn't?"
  Overcoming Financial Barriers. Playing "what if," this answer invites creative solutions that are not fiscally constrained.
- "Of the many probable causes, which one is most significant?"
  Causation. While most problems have multiple causes, this question probes for the most significant factors.
- "Could a higher scoring proposal get bumped out in favor of a lower scoring proposal that meets other special criteria?"
  Special Criteria. This question recognizes that awards are made sometimes on a basis other than merit, e.g., geographic location of the applicant, type of organization, extensive collaborative relationships, or prior relationships with sponsor.
- Was there a staff review following your peer review?"
  Staff versus Peer Review. This answer suggests what happens after the review process is over. You especially want to find out how much discretionary authority the program officers have over the peer review results.
- "How would you write a proposal differently now that you have been a reviewer?"
  Avoiding Reviewer Aggravation. People invariably learn from the positive experience of seeing the inside process of awarding grants and have a number of suggestions about things they would do if they were asked to write a proposal again—something that is called "learning."

Priority Questions: Approaches for an Improved Situation. Priority questions concentrate on identifying the top activities that will effectively and efficiently improve the conditions surrounding the identified problems, needs, and injustices that exist today from the perspective of past grant reviewers.

- "What's not happening in this area that should?"
  Intervention Failure. This answer highlights areas needing intervention.
- "How would that close the gap?"
  Needed Intervention. The response suggests how to intervene.
- "Which actions are most likely to solve the problem?"
  Intervention Options. This reply implies probable intervention options.
- "What would be the key features of an ideal solution?"
  Ideal Intervention. Among various options, this answer indicates the components of an ideal solution.
- "Why would this solution be useful?"
  Intervention Justification. This query probes why the ideal solution has value.
- "What might be the benefits from this approach?"
  Intervention Benefits. The response compiles the benefits list for the intervention strategy.
- "Are there other ways this might help?"
  Other Outcomes. This question explores for other anticipated outcomes.

Answers to questions like these, resulting from a 10-minute phone conversation, will help shape your proposal format and content.

STEP FOUR: FOLLOW-UP CONTACT WITH PROGRAM OFFICER

Why do Step Four?

The information you gain in Steps One through Three will leave you with some preliminary ideas about the final scope of your proposal, along with some unanswered questions. Your follow-up contact with the program officer enables you to draw the final parameters around your proposal: what to emphasize, include, and exclude. In completing Step Four, you synthesize grant information from multiple sources to develop a highly competitive proposal, should you decide to proceed with submission.

Who to Contact—and How

You are now going back to contact the same individual you wrote to in Step One, this time with a phone call or e-mail to thank the program officer for the information you recently received. Indicate while you have studied the information carefully, you still have additional questions that were not covered in the material you received.

Early in your relationship with program officers, ask them whether they prefer phone, fax, or e-mail communications. Before you pick up the phone or send off a quick e-mail, ask yourself:

- Do I need this answered immediately?
- What other questions will I need answered?
- Can I wait a day or two to see whether I come up with any additional questions?

Consolidate as many of your questions as possible into one concise message. Include your e-mail address and phone number at the end of your e-mail message. It may be easier for the program officer to answer your questions with a two-minute phone call than type a two-page e-mail response.

Once again, your phone call consists of two parts: an opening statement and follow-up questions.

The Opening Statement to a Program Officer

Note that each opening statement consists of 80–90 words and takes approximately 40 seconds to present.

Call from a university researcher to a federal government program officer regarding a biosensors program:

> Hello, Dr. Jones. I'm Libby Johnson with the Neuroscience Research Laboratory at Midwest Medical College [Who]. Thanks for sending the recent application materials. I'm calling today because depending on your current interests in biosensors, there's a possibility we might be able to help cut down on the time biomedical researchers spend preparing liquid phase sensors, while also increasing their accuracy and speed [What]. If I've caught you at a good time, I'd like to discuss your situation to see if our approach is something you'd like more information on [Why]. (89 words)

Call from a school administrator to a private foundation youth violence program officer:

> Hello, Mr. Bancroft. I'm Charlie Jones, principal of the West Division High School in Cleveland [Who]. Thanks for sending the recent application materials. I'm calling about your "Cops in Schools" program that was just announced [Why]. Depending on your main interests, there's a possibility our past experiences and existing networks might be of value. If your calendar permits, I'd like to ask some questions that were not addressed in the recent materials you sent me to see whether our

proposal ideas might be of value to you [What]. (85 words)

Call from a hospital administrator to a regional corporation:

> Hi, Mr. Goodwrench. I'm Evie Richards with the Midwest Hospital [Who]. Thanks for sending the recent application materials. I'm calling today because depending on your current commitment to serving disabled adults, there's a possibility we might be able to reduce your difficulty in hiring physically challenged individuals while at the same time increasing your staff diversity [Why]. If I've caught you at a good time, I'd like to ask a few questions that were not addressed in your materials to see if this is something you'd like more information on [What]. (88 words)

Follow-up Questions to a Program Officer

When talking with program officers, explain you analyzed their guidelines carefully, but still have some unanswered questions that you'd like to raise to ensure that your proposal would be of value to their agency. Briefly describe your project, stressing objectives and outcomes. Then ask the following types of PREP questions.

Position Questions: The Baseline Situation. Position questions explore baseline information and relationships with the sponsor, and lay the foundation for more probing types of questions from the viewpoint of the program officer.

- "What is your current budget?"
  Program Budget Amount. This answer will tell you how much money is allocated for your grant program, a starting point for the next more crucial question.
- "How much of that money will be available for new awards as opposed to noncompeting continuation awards?"
  Program Budget New Money. This answer will tell you how much money is actually available for new projects like the one you propose.
- "What is the anticipated application/award ratio?"
  Application Competitiveness. The funding odds will tell you your mathematical chances for success. Just remember that the grants business offers no guarantees. Funding odds are highly variable among grant programs and range from 5 to 50 percent.
- "Does the program provide one-time-only support, or will it permit other funding opportunities?"

Continuation Funding. This answer will let you know if you can go back with future funding requests or if you are likely to receive only one award.

- "Would you review our preproposal (two- to three-page concept paper)?"
  Preproposal Review. If they will (and many do), then you will have an important opportunity to better match your proposal with their priorities.

- "Would you review our draft proposal if we got it to you early?"
  Draft Proposal Review. Again, a favorable response will help you better cast your proposal to their expectations. Do give them enough response time; don't expect them to do this three weeks before the program deadline.

- "Who officially reviews our final proposal?"
  Reviewer Expertise. Since proposals should be written to the expertise level of the reviewers, this answer will help determine the amount of technical detail you write.

- "How do you review proposals? Who does it? Outside experts? Board members? Staff?"
  Review Procedures. This information will help you analyze your reviewer audience and the conditions under which they read proposals. To illustrate, three individuals were assigned recently to review some federal grant proposals. Because of traffic delays, one reviewer was stuck at an airport and a backup reviewer was called in and given one hour to read a 30-page proposal and write up 10 pages of evaluation. At best, this reviewer could skim-read a proposal, not read for elaborate details.

- "How are the proposals being evaluated? Against what yardstick are the proposals being measured?"
  Evaluation Criteria. The response suggests in general terms how your proposal will be evaluated. Are they scored independently against the guidelines? Are they ranked against each other? Are they prioritized within sponsor funding categories? Are proposals evaluated on a first-come, first-funded basis?

- "Do you plan to offer a workshop, teleconference, or preproposal conference to explain how to prepare an application?"
  Presubmission Training. Some sponsors conduct training sessions to help applicants prepare a proposal, either through group meetings or conference calls. These sessions help you not only better understand how to prepare a competitive proposal but also provide insights into people who will be guiding your proposal review process.

Rationale Questions: Problems Existing Today.
Rationale questions go to the heart of sponsor-giving from the vantage point of the program officer: the problems, needs, and injustices that exist today. Rationale questions explore sponsor motivations in funding projects.

- "Why does this problem persist?"
  Duration of Problem. This answer implies major barriers to problem resolution.

- "What are the major variables in this larger problem?"
  Dimensions of Problem. This answer suggests the different facets of the problem you seek to address.

- "What are the biggest hurdles in this area now?"
  Problematic Barriers. The response points out the biggest challenges people in the field now face.

- "Is the problem getting worse or better?"
  Changes Over Time. The reply draws a verbal trend line for the severity of the problem.

- "What are the biggest sources of dissatisfaction with current approaches?"
  Current Failures. This query probes to discover what hasn't worked to date.

- "Which dimensions of this problem need to be addressed next?"
  Problem Priorities. This answer points to the "big impact" needs.

- "Why have you targeted your program dollars to this problem?"
  Financial Priorities. This answer explains why money will solve the problem.

Expectation Questions: Basic Implications for Addressing Problems. Expectation questions look at the "so what" implications of the rationale questions from the perspective of the program officer. Expectation questions also identify the sponsor's outlook for changing the problem situation.

- "Does my project fall within your current priorities?"
  Matching Your Project with Sponsor Priorities. If it does, begin writing. If it doesn't, explore different objectives that might yield a better fit or ask for suggestions of other grant programs that might be interested in your project.

- "Since your average award last year was $xx,xxx dollars, do you expect that to change?"
  Budget Request. This answer will help you determine the budget size you should request.

- "Will awards be made on the basis of any special criteria, e.g., geography or type or organization?"
  Special Award Criteria. This answer will help reveal

legal or administrative considerations in the decision-making process. For instance, they may be especially interested in receiving proposals from small organizations in the Midwest or private hospitals in the Southeast.

- "Are there any unannounced programs or unsolicited funds in my area to support my project?"
  "Hip Pocket" Dollars. Sometimes you will discover unobligated or uncommitted funds in the "hip pocket" of the program officer by asking this question.
- "What are the most common mistakes in proposals you receive?"
  Typical Proposal Errors. Pay particular attention to the answer, for they are things you want to avoid.
- "What would you like to see addressed in a proposal that other applicants may have overlooked?"
  Pet Ideas. Many program officers like to feel a partner relationship in the proposal development process. This question provides them with an opportunity to articulate their pet ideas.
- "Would you recommend a previously funded proposal for us to read for format and style?"
  Getting Sample Proposals. Sometimes a model proposal is helpful to review. Either they will provide you with a copy or refer you to a source where you can get it, e.g., project director.
- "Should the proposal be written for reviewers with nontechnical backgrounds?"
  Proposal Technical Writing Style. The level of technicality in your proposal should be geared to the background of your reviewers.
- "What percentage of your awards is made in response to unsolicited proposals?"
  Competitiveness of Unsolicited Proposals. If they fund few unsolicited proposals, you may be wasting your time. Responses vary among program officers. One mission-oriented agency may award less than 5 percent of its funds in response to unsolicited proposals while another may award 95 percent.
- "Can you provide me with a copy of the reviewer's evaluation form?"
  Reviewer's Evaluation Form. Use this form to organize your proposal, using the same headings and subheadings, even if they differ from those in the application guidelines. Sometimes discrepancies exist between the application guidelines and reviewer's evaluation form, an agency oversight that often occurs when two different people are responsible for developing the documents. One person prepares the guidelines while another

develops the evaluation criteria. In cases of conflict, follow the reviewer's evaluation criteria.

Priority Questions: Approaches for an Improved Situation. Priority questions concentrate on identifying the top activities that will effectively and efficiently improve the conditions surrounding the identified problems, needs, and injustices that exist today in the opinion of the program officer.

- "What's essential that isn't happening now?"
  Clarification of Need. The answer focuses on the key dimensions of today's problem.
- "Why solve this problem?"
  Magnitude of Need. This answer tells how big your problem is; the bigger, the better.
- "What's needed to close the gap?"
  Bridging the Gap. Another question that tells how to narrow the discrepancy between "what is" and "what should be."
- "Would this approach produce what is needed?"
  Solution Feasibility. This answer provides a "trial balloon" response to your proposed action plan.
- "How do you think this would work?"
  Implementation Strategies. This answer helps map out a successful action plan to solve the problem.
- "How would this really help?"
  Distinctive Benefits. This answer points out the distinctive benefits or payoff of your solution.
- "What are the long-term benefits of this solution?
  Long-Range Payoffs. This answer describes the long-range implications of your solution.
- "What outcomes do you expect from grantees?"
  Program Officer Expectations. This answer clarifies what the program officer will expect from you.

Again, a 10-minute phone call will give you a substantial competitive edge. This four-step process is one that successful grantseekers follow. After looking at the information gleaned from following it, you can see the disadvantage you would face if you **didn't** follow it.

In sum, the purpose of conducting preproposal contact is to narrow down your list of "suspects" and identify those sponsors who appear to be a good match with your organization's needs. You do not always need to go through all four steps. Sometimes the feedback you gain in Steps Two or Three will be sufficient for you to determine that the match is not a good one. In that case, scratch the potential sponsor's name off of your list and move on to the next one. Doing this homework before starting to write will pay dividends later on.

TRACKING PREPROPOSAL CONTACTS

Over time, successful grantseekers contact many individuals. Database programs, such as Access, allow you to create and maintain files of facts, figures, names, mailing lists, grant ideas, sponsor contact histories, and the like. With database programs, you can define new databases, specifying the type and length of information allowed into each field. It is an easy matter to add, delete, edit, and display information from your files. All such programs let you generate customized reports, complete with subtotals, totals, counts, and simple arithmetic operations on numeric fields. Usually you can search or sort for specific information within a record, regardless of upper and lower case letters. Further, you can search for certain records and replace any or all of the information contained in them. It is a simple matter to create new databases from existing ones, adding new fields within the record and discarding unneeded ones. As appropriate, you can export the information in databases to word processors, spreadsheets, or other database packages.

One of your first database applications should be to configure a file of preproposal contacts that includes information about program officers, past grant winners, and prior grant reviewers. Each of the following could be a separate element in your database: name, title, address, phone, fax, e-mail, Web address, sponsor type (public or private), contact type (program officer, past grant winner, prior grant reviewer), program name, deadline, last contact date, eligibility requirements, restrictions on funding, special linkages, average grant size, initial contact preferred, special comments, and whatever else might suit your particular needs. You may wish to create a special form for this purpose using a "Wizard" that accompanies most software programs, a self-instructional pathway to easily creating your own customized application.

Clip File Action Item # 9
Preproposal Contacts

Develop your Preproposal Contacts clip file by taking the following actions:

- Write out sample opening statements that you could use on the telephone to past grant winners, prior reviewers, and program officers; adapt the models in this chapter to your situation.
- Generate an electronic list of the four question categories that can be used with past grant winners, prior reviewers, and program officers. Have the list on your computer screen when you make the calls; type in answers during the telephone conversations. Use a headset to talk so your hands are free to type in answers.
- Create a database to track your preproposal contacts, including contact information, who you talked to, date, information learned, and impressions.

PART II
Writing Private Foundation and Corporation Proposals

OVERVIEW OF PART II

Part I focused on the process of proposal planning. It identified the major print and electronic sources needed to find sponsors who might fund your proposals. Once an initial suspect pool was determined, pre-proposal contact is needed to narrow down the list of potential funders and settle on those that have the highest probably of granting you funds. A four-step model was presented to help you gain pertinent background information from program officers, past grant reviewers, and past grant winners.

In Part II and Part III, we turn our attention from proposal planning to proposal writing. Specifically, in Part II, we analyze the approach to writing grant proposals to private sources. In Part III, we follow-up with strategies for writing grant proposals to public funding sources.

Private grantmakers—foundations and corporations—often require short proposals, typically a few pages in length. The letter proposal format is perhaps the most commonly written type of private grant. It is ideally suited for those situations where the private grantmaker has no specific form to follow; they just want you to submit a brief synopsis of your project. Accordingly, Chapter 5 presents a seven-step template to develop your own letter proposal. Those proposal elements are as follows:

- Part One: *Summary*—a one-sentence proposal overview
- Part Two: *Appeal*—rationale for approaching the sponsor
- Part Three: *Problem*—description of need or gap
- Part Four: *Solution*—method for solving a problem
- Part Five: *Capabilities*—your credentials to solve the problem
- Part Six: *Budget*—your specific request for funds
- Part Seven: *Closing*—a check-writing nudge to the sponsor

For each proposal element, we provide you with examples and questions to help you start writing. In essence, the letter proposal is a versatile tool that can be adapted to many different circumstances.

In Chapter 6, we take the basic seven-step template presented in Chapter 5 and modify it for use in other grant situations. Specifically, we present seven different examples of complete letter proposals using this model. Further, we show how it can be tailored for use with government agencies or in those situations where private grantmakers have an actual form to use in preparing your proposal.

CHAPTER 5
Letter Proposal Template

More than kisses, letters mingle souls.

—*John Donne*

OVERVIEW

A letter proposal is a short grant proposal, usually two to five pages long. As the name implies, it is written in letter form and used in those instances when a foundation or corporation has no specific submission guidelines to follow, hopefully for some soul mingling, as poet John Donne suggests.

In Chapter 5, you will learn the following:

- The difference between letter proposals, letters of intent, and letters of inquiry.
- The seven essential ingredients of a letter proposal.
- Tips for writing each part of a letter proposal.

Often private sponsors will decide whether to fund you on the basis of your brief letter proposal, regardless if you are asking for $100 or $1 million. A few private sponsors use the letter proposal as a screening device and request an expanded proposal if your idea captures their interest. In either case, final draft or screening device, you face the challenge of writing a short, clear, concise, and persuasive document.

The grants community is not consistent in its use of three terms: letter proposals, letters of intent, and letters of inquiry. What one sponsor may mean by the term "letter of intent," another may mean "letter of inquiry." Still others may use the two terms interchangeably. This chapter begins with a brief discussion of all three terms as they are used in the majority of instances in various grant documents. As you respond to these calls for information about your grant ideas, be certain you understand exactly what the sponsors mean by the terms they are using.

LETTER PROPOSALS, LETTERS OF INTENT, AND LETTERS OF INQUIRY

All three—letter proposals, letters of intent, and letters of inquiry—share similar characteristics: they are short and communicate to potential grantmakers information they seek. They are different in the information they transmit.

- A **Letter Proposal** is a short grant proposal written in a letter format. It contains an abridged version of the basic proposal elements: summary, need, objectives, methods, applicant credentials, and budget.
- A **Letter of Intent** alerts the sponsor of your plan to submit a formal proposal. It may contain your name and a tentative working title, but little else.
- A **Letter of Inquiry** is similar to a Letter Proposal except it is not written in a letter format. It does include the same essential grant proposal elements, but they are presented in a more formal layout that usually includes a cover page and appropriate headings and subheadings.

Consider, for example Exhibit 23, the Carnegie Corporation of New York's instructions for preparing a **Letter of Inquiry,** which is their first step in applying for a grant.

In essence, Carnegie is seeking a five-page synopsis of your project. In responding to their guidelines, your cover page (not counted in the five-page limit) would include project title, collaborators (if any), and appropriate contact information. In the five-page narrative, you would restate the major headings and subheadings implicit in their eight bulleted points. Put differently, your proposal outline for Carnegie might be as indicated in Exhibit 24.

A letter of inquiry clearly and concisely describes the project, its aims, its significance, its duration, and the amount of funds required. The document should not exceed five pages. Please address the following points in a letter of inquiry.

- What problem does your project address? Why is this issue significant? What is the relationship of the problem/issue to the Corporation's current program interests as noted in its Information Pamphlet and Web site?
- What strengths and skills does your organization and personnel bring to this project? What makes your organization the right one to conduct this project?
- Who will lead the project? Identify key personnel and attach resumes.
- What do you intend to demonstrate or prove? What means will you use? If the project is already under way, what have you accomplished so far?
- If you are requesting funding from Carnegie Corporation for a component(s) of a larger project, specify which activities you are requesting the Corporation to fund and how they relate to the larger project.
- What outcomes do you expect, both immediate and long term?
- If you have requested funds from other sources (or plan to), please list those sources and note the status of your request.
- What plans do you have to disseminate information to the public about your project?

LETTER OF INQUIRY GUIDELINES FOR THE CARNEGIE CORPORATION OF NEW YORK

EXHIBIT 23

The end product in Exhibit 24 is a brief document the sponsor can evaluate and determine whether you should receive an invitation to submit a full proposal. It also prevents grantmakers from spending unnecessary time assembling application materials for projects that are a fundamental mismatch with sponsor priorities and thus would ultimately be unsuccessful.

A **Letter of Intent** is requested by sponsors in those instances when they want to get an approximate idea of how many applications to anticipate. Armed with this estimate of anticipated proposals, they can more efficiently organize the review process, e.g., determine size of staff needed to administer the reviews and respond to applicant postsubmission inquiries.

To illustrate, a request for a letter of intent was published in the *Federal Register* by the Centers for Disease Control and Prevention. It read as follows:

> A one-page non-binding letter of intent (LOI) is requested to enable CDC to determine the level of interest in this announcement. The LOI should provide a brief description of the proposed project and identify the principal investigator, organizations actively involved in the proposed project, and the address and telephone number for key contacts.

This CDC request is typical of most issued by private foundations and government agencies. Corporations seldom request an LOI. Letters of intent are issued in response to a specific request for proposals; in contrast, letter proposals may be submitted in response to both solicited and unsolicited proposals. In essence, an LOI simply notifies the sponsor of your plan to submit a proposal, as Exhibit 25 indicates.

ELEMENTS OF A LETTER PROPOSAL

In certain respects, a short **Letter Proposal** is more challenging to write than a longer full proposal because each sentence must carry a heavy information load. Accordingly, it is helpful to segment the writing process into seven different components.

Part One: *Summary*—a one-sentence proposal overview
Part Two: *Appeal*—rationale for approaching the sponsor
Part Three: *Problem*—description of need or gap
Part Four: *Solution*—method for solving a problem
Part Five: *Capabilities*—your credentials to solve the problem
Part Six: *Budget*—your specific request for funds
Part Seven: *Closing*—a check-writing nudge to the sponsor

In seven brief sections, you anticipate and answer the major questions that private sponsors will be asking as they read your letter proposal. These seven proposal parts are suggestive, not prescriptive. Deviate without guilt from the letter proposal format when it makes sense to do so. In the illustrations that follow, each part identifies what you are trying to accomplish as you write that section and provides some sample paragraphs to help you start writing.

PART ONE: SUMMARY

Objective: To summarize the entire proposal in one or two sentences.

I. Statement of Problem

   A. Significance
   B. Relevance to Carnegie Priorities

II. Organizational Capacity

   A. Strengths
   B. Personnel and Skills
   C. Uniqueness to Conduct Project

III. Key Project Personnel

   A. Project Director
   B. Other Key Project Personnel

IV. Project Goals and Objectives

   A. Methods for Achieving Goals and Objectives
   B. Project Timelines
   C. Current Project Status

V. Carnegie Funding Request

   A. From Carnegie
   B. Relationship to Larger Project

VI. Project Outcomes

   A. Immediate
   B. Long-Term

VII. Funding from Other Sources

   A. Sources and Amounts
   B. Status of Requests

VIII. Dissemination

   A. Target Audiences
   B. Dissemination Messages
   C. Dissemination Methods

OUTLINE OF LETTER OF INQUIRY TO CARNEGIE CORPORATION OF NEW YORK

EXHIBIT 24

Preparing to Write

Study the critical elements of the model sentence, including

- *Self-Identification:* State your organizational name.
- *Organizational Uniqueness:* Cite a brief "claim to fame" from a mission statement that explains your reason for being.
- *Sponsor Expectation:* Explain what you want them to do.
- *Budget Request:* Identify how much money you are requesting.
- *Project Benefit:* Describe the major project outcome for the sponsor, not you.

The model summary sentence takes on the following structure:

> [Identification], [uniqueness], [expectation] in a [request] that [benefits].

Examples

As you study the following five examples, note how they all include the five critical summary elements. These examples represent a range of funding requests and can be adapted easily to your situation. An example of a complete letter proposal can be found at the end of this chapter. In Chapter 6, you will find seven additional examples of complete letter proposals.

Today's Date

Ms. Jerri Kurri, President
Finnish Athletic Foundation
123 Maki Drive
Helsinki, California 90120

RE: Letter of Intent
Your Proposal Title
Your Organizational Name

Dear Ms. Kurri:

This letter conveys our intent to submit a formal proposal in response to your recent initiative on dental implant research with toothless hockey players. Our 10-year history of implant research enables us to bring unique value to your programmatic goals. The collaborators for this project include the California Sports Authority, three California dental schools, and the California Dental Association. You will receive the required original and six proposal copies in advance of your October 3rd deadline. In the meantime, feel free to contact me for further information.

Sincerely,

Your Name
Your Title

LETTER OF INTENT

EXHIBIT 25

One final complete letter proposal is included in Chapter 15.

1. The basic summary sentence for a university research project:

> Midwest University [identification], as Wisconsin's largest independent educational institution [uniqueness], invites the investment of the Big Gene Corporation [expectation] in a $250,000 research project [request] that builds the long-term infrastructure for scientific advancements in biomedical research [benefit]. (32 words; one sentence)

2. A welfare agency seeking foundation support for an HIV/AIDS prevention project:

> The Family Welfare Agency, the largest welfare agency in Horton County, seeks $20,000 from the Happy Family Foundation to teach HIV/AIDS prevention to urban teens. (26 words; one sentence)

3. A public school seeking foundation funding for a cultural diversity project:

> Quinkleberry High School, recently described by the Governor of Wisconsin as "a benchmark of public school excellence that others should strive to follow," invites your participation in a $200,000 special project to increase the multicultural learning experiences of its students. (42 words; one sentence)

4. A multispecialty medical clinic seeking corporate support to increase its service delivery:

> Advanced Healthcare Medical Clinic, the most comprehensive healthcare facility within the eastern region of the state, invites your investment in a $500,000 service project that would increase access to and improve the delivery of rural healthcare services. (37 words; one sentence)

5. A faith-based organization seeking foundation funding for a food pantry program:

> Houston Unity Church, the most centrally located church in the inner city, invites you to share in a $15,000 service project to coordinate disjointed food programs for the poor. (30 words; one sentence)

As you now write your summary statement for your proposal, avoid the trap that beginning grant writers often encounter: expressing the benefit to themselves instead of to the sponsors. Contrast these pairs of examples as tabled below.

Self-Oriented Benefits	Sponsor-Oriented Benefits
Lincolnwood Fire Department, exclusively responsible for the fire safety of 85,000 residences and 12,000 businesses, invites your investment in a $750,000 grant to buy a new fire truck.	Lincolnwood Fire Department, exclusively responsible for the fire safety of 137,000 individuals and $42 million in property, invites your investment in a $750,000 grant to ensure continued community welfare during a period of increased vulnerability.
The Family Welfare Agency, Atlanta's only urban family crisis intervention agency, respectfully requests a grant of $75,000 to meet its operating expenses.	The Family Welfare Agency, Atlanta's only urban family crisis intervention agency, respectfully requests a grant of $75,000 to sustain the delivery of crucial welfare services to victims of violence and abuse.
Fairview middle school, recently recognized by the Governor as a "Center for Educational Excellence," requests a $5,000 grant to pay for a guest speaker who will talk about teen bullying.	Fairview middle school, recently recognized by the Governor as a "Center for Educational Excellence," requests a $5,000 grant to help decrease bullying behavior among teens.

In these pairs of examples, the message is clear and simple: sponsors usually give money to organizations that help other people; sponsors seldom give money to organizations that only help themselves. After you write your summary sentence, reread it and see whether it presents a self- or sponsor-oriented benefit.

PART TWO: APPEAL

Objective: To explain why you are appealing to the sponsor for funding.

Preparing to Write

These tips will help explain why you "knock on their door."

- Conduct prospect research on the sponsor as described in Chapter 4.
- From your prospect research, identify values that the sponsor seems to cherish, e.g., high-risk projects not normally funded by the government, cutting-edge research, demonstration projects with a national impact, or low-cost/high-benefit projects.
- Summarize key funding patterns that attract you to the sponsor, e.g., "80 percent of your award dollars in the last two years have gone to support projects like this," or "Last year, you awarded $2.5 million to private universities in support of projects on technology transfer." When you analyze a sponsor's giving history, you can usually find a pattern of giving that attracts you to them.

Examples

Six examples follow: three targeting foundations and three targeting corporations. As you write your

sponsor appeal paragraph in your next letter proposal, you may wish to "cherry pick" the sentences that best fit your situation. Each sample paragraph ends with a word count; while there is no "ideal" number of words, many paragraphs will range from 80 to 150 words.

1. An Alzheimer's research center seeking foundation support for a neuroscience project:

> We are encouraged that the R.U. Rich Foundation supports new frontiers in the neuroscience of memory; over 75 percent of your grant dollars during the last three years have been invested in cutting-edge genetics technology research. The Foundation has been an inspiration because you have supported biomedical projects over the years with absolute consistency. Clearly, your support fills a valuable niche in light of the more conservative and traditional funding offered by the federal government. This strong commitment to innovative research is shared by researchers in our Biomedical Research Institute. (90 words; four sentences)

2. An interfaith council seeking foundation support for an international missionary project:

> The best ideas are ones that help people. For decades, you have directed your resources to promoting the religious and educational well-being of millions. Since 1969, you have systematically examined the increasing impact of missionary work on almost every aspect of our lives. For instance, your current list of grant awards shows over $400,000 in project support targeted for missionary service. Because of your unprecedented concern for the needs of the financially and spiritually impoverished in third-world countries as well as your position of leadership in the philanthropic community,

we turn to the Big Bucks Foundation for its support of a $90,000 international missionary project. (109 words; five sentences)

3. A private university seeking foundation support for student scholarships:

> We are encouraged that the George and Martha Washington Foundation has given $681,389, or 53 percent of all its awards in the last two years to private colleges and universities. This type of recognition is essential for independent universities that are tuition-dependent and lack state financial support. Midwest University wants to attract the brightest students into our ranks: people with fresh perspectives on current issues who we can encourage to become tomorrow's top leaders. Midwest has a national reputation for providing a values-based, liberal arts education; this reputation, in turn, attracts many top-caliber applicants. Unfortunately, the number of academically talented students in all areas of study who deserve our help strains our limited scholarship funds. Your contribution will be especially important in providing vital student assistance to our nation's future leaders. (133 words; six sentences)

4. A child welfare agency seeking corporate support for a social services project:

> In our shared commitment to making our community a better place to live and work, we look forward to finding avenues of mutual support. Such a partnership is particularly timely since public funding for human services and civic needs continues to decline at a dramatic rate. Because of your demonstrated concern for children as well as your position of leadership in our city, we turn to the Big Bucks Corporation for its support in expanding community outreach services to at-risk youth. (82 words; three sentences)

5. A health agency seeking corporate support for a community health program:

> We recognize your commitment to being an outstanding corporate citizen, and we appreciate the fact that you are as concerned about the health of our community as you are with the health of your business. Indeed, it is sometimes difficult to determine where business interests end and community interests begin. Since you provide important work for the good of others, your investment in this project would contribute significantly to maintaining a community health program of the highest quality and national distinction, based here in San Antonio. Moreover, it would also serve as a standard of committed civic responsibility, inspiring others to support this important fund-raising effort. As a result, your philanthropic generosity could be leveraged to attract additional support from the business community. (124 words; five sentences)

6. A local police department seeking corporate matching funds for a juvenile justice project:

> Like many communities, the Evergreen Police Department (EPD) must cope with the consequences of escalating juvenile crimes. The rising crime rate comes at a time when local government budgets are retrenching due to our dwindling tax base. Accordingly, EPD must rely on support from external sources if it is to remain financially healthy and meet community service obligations. We have been fortunate in attracting partial funding from the Department of Justice through their Community Oriented Policing program. Their matching grant will provide three-year funding to hire one juvenile justice officer, provided the community will fund a second officer. In response, the City Council has committed one-half salary for a second officer, wishing that the budget allowed full matching funds. Since your support over the years has played a catalytic role in local efforts to help nurture and challenge ideas that are locally developed, we now seek your generous support to secure this co-funding opportunity—and secure the future of our troubled youth. We hope you are able to take advantage of this opportunity to leverage your support dollars in continued partnership with the City. (185 words; eight sentences)

PART THREE: PROBLEM

Objective: To briefly summarize the current problem and its long-term implications.

Preparing to Write

Focus the problem or need statement from the sponsor's perspective, not yours. Funding your project is not their end goal. You must show how funding your project can be a means for them to reach their end goal, namely, their mission.

A "need" is really a gap between "what is" and "what ought to be." Document that gap with statistics, quotations, reasoning, or surveys and express it in human terms. Limit your documentation to brief but clear statements. Beware of the excessive use of statistics, which may only confuse the reader.

Examples

Four examples follow, two each seeking foundation and corporate support. Because the need section is a crucial proposal section, it is longer and contains more detail than other proposal elements.

1. A research institute seeking foundation equipment funding:

> As you know, interdisciplinary research combined with genetic technology fuels the rapid advancements in the modern life sciences. To remain at the cutting edge of these discoveries, Institute researchers must consolidate and expand the analytical methods they now use to study the expression of gene regulation. Currently, our researchers lack the capability for genomic analysis at levels of detail now possible with new technology. This lack of powerful and productive equipment inhibits our ability to use state-of-the-art methodology, to perform critical experiments, and to develop more efficient, definitive, and versatile research programs.
>
> There are two major consequences from this lack of modern equipment. First, it presents insurmountable barriers to scientific progress in understanding the mechanisms underlying such diseases as Alzheimer's and cancer. Neuroscience questions on the mechanisms that alter gene functions often require equipment support that extends beyond the financial boundaries of individual research projects. Maintaining state-of-the-art equipment has become prohibitive. Second, the Institute has a serious responsibility to train scientists who will contribute to an ever-changing technological society in the future. To meet this challenge, our laboratories must be equipped with modern, sophisticated instrumentation. (186 words; 10 sentences)

2. A community mental health proposal to a community foundation:

> The purpose of this proposal is to initiate a psychological support service for inner-city families with teenage parents. The results of a recent Community Life Survey revealed 68 percent of the households in the 53206 zip code region have single mothers with an average of 2.3 children. These families—mothers, grandmothers, and great grandmothers alike—experience a growing strain in trying to balance family and work responsibilities. As a result, there is a significant and spiraling gap between the stress levels in urban and suburban households in our community.
>
> The problem is further exacerbated by the collision between service providers in the two communities. Suburban households have more financial resources and coping mechanisms to deal with stressors than what exists in corresponding urban environments. Bottom line: very few service providers have the cultural expertise or multicultural staff to be seen as credible and affordable helping agencies. Clearly, this lag in inner-city family support services is a problem that needs to be creatively addressed. (163 words; eight sentences)

3. A medical school curriculum development proposal to a pharmaceutical corporation:

> Genetics is one of the most rapidly developing areas of neuroscience.
>
> While physicians must understand genes and their function in health and disease, today's medical students receive little training in human genetics: its basic science concepts or clinical applications.
>
> A recent survey of American medical schools revealed medical students receive an average of only 18 hours of genetics instruction. Now that the human genomic code has been cracked, demands for genetic testing are coming with growing demands from patients and insurance companies alike. Additionally, new issues in confidentiality, patient counseling, informed consent, and societal perceptions have added new dimensions of complexity for medical students.
>
> To close the gap between rapid advances in medical science and the training received by future physicians, there is a need to develop a model course in medical genetics that could be integrated into medical school curricula nationwide. By reason of its multiplier effect, education is one of the most constructive longer-term approaches to ameliorating troubling genetics questions. (162 words; seven sentences)

4. An elder care agency seeking corporate support for consolidation of services:

The rationale for this project is driven by the demographics of aging. The elderly population is increasing in size.

- By 2020, 40% of our population will be over age 65.
- One-half of the elderly will be 75-plus years old.
- Elderly women will outnumber elderly men three to two.
- At age 85, there will be 4 men for every 10 women.

As a result of these demographics, there will be a marked increase in consumer demands for specialized health care services. Presently, local health services for the elderly are fragmented. Geographically, they exist in many different locations. Their disparate locations result in reduced purchasing power, ineffective case management, and duplication of records. (116 words; nine sentences)

PART FOUR: SOLUTION

Objective: To describe your approach to the problem.

Preparing to Write

Remember to justify your selection of methodology. While most problems can be solved using multiple approaches, explain why you chose your preferred one. Summarize the outcomes that your approach will generate. Convey confidence that you can solve the problem. Use a one-page attached time and task chart (see Chapter 9) to detail your methodology.

Examples

Four examples follow, including approaches to both foundations and a corporation.

1. A day care center proposal seeking foundation support to train parents of preschool children:

This proposal addresses a crucial service to our community: counseling and support for parents of preschool children. In recent months, we have witnessed a tragic series of cases of children who have been neglected and abused. The plight of these youngsters is dramatic evidence of the need for young parents to learn proper care and development of their children —one of the most important responsibilities of their lives. The Parenting Center was established to meet these needs. Its centerpiece is a

theory-driven training program called STAR: Stop, Think, Assess, Respond. This four-step response to childlike behaviors is preferable to the more customary use of corporal punishment for our target population. STAR has an established track record across various culture groups and is ready for implementation here. (128 words; seven sentences)

2. A hospital seeking corporate funding for a teen smoking prevention project:

Our intervention strategy directly addresses the number-one teen health hazard: smoking. The project approach will close the health hazard gap by getting at the root causes that lead to addiction. We will avoid the two primary unsuccessful techniques used in the past: (1) Fear of death: too remote of a concern during the teen years; and (2) Health impairment: permanent lung damage has little stimulus value to change behavior. Instead, we will initiate a five-pronged approach that is targeted at the average age of the first-time smoker: 13 years old. Our campaign, called Butt Out Now, will

- Develop in-house program to fight tobacco use in middle schools
- Create Web sites to discourage youth smoking
- Empower teen smokers to quit successfully
- Enact peer teaching programs to defend youth against advertising and peer pressure
- Remind physicians to take a proactive role

Our accompanying Time and Task Chart describes in detail how campaign phases interrelate. (158 words; 11 sentences)

3. A battered women's shelter organization seeking foundation funding for research on families at-risk for domestic violence:

Our approach uses both qualitative and quantitative methods. We will use interviews and questionnaires to determine responses to aggression and its impact on the family. Two key questionnaires are the Ryder Aggression Scale and the Intent to Institutionalize Scale. Both instruments will be given to a random selection of the clients at the Family Wellness Center over the next two years. To interpret the resulting scale values, focus group interviews will be conducted with the clients to better understand their perceptions of core family values. The outcome of this research has implications for the training of social welfare personnel and will be submitted for publication to the

Journal of Domestic Tranquility. (111 words; six sentences)

4. A collaborative university/community agency proposal seeking foundation funding for adult literacy training:

> The attached Time and Task Chart summarizes the project methodology, including major milestones, responsible personnel, and duration. The innovative aspects of the project include close supervision of tutors, emphasis on family approaches to literacy training for adults, and the inclusion of graduate students earning academic credit. Since methods of teaching reading to children are not directly transferable to adults, the method of choice is the Randolph Reading Review, which presents adult level stimulus material in a combined phonetic and sight vocabulary approach. A 2006 study by Chenitz documented the effectiveness of this technique with a similar population, when compared with other common intervention strategies. (105 words; four sentences)

PART FIVE: CAPABILITIES

Objective: To establish your credentials to carry out the project.

Preparing to Write

As you write this section, your task is to establish three types of credibility: (1) your organization, showing you work in an environment capable of supporting the project; (2) your project idea, indicating that you have identified a unique problem that you are capable of solving; and (3) your key project staff, demonstrating that you have experienced and credentialed personnel to ensure project success.

Examples

Two corporate and two foundation examples follow.

1. A pediatric hospital seeking foundation funding to work with emotionally disturbed preschoolers:

> The State Pediatric Hospital has been meeting the needs of emotionally disturbed preschoolers for 13 years. The trained staff represents over 300 years of experience in this specialized area. The hospital's geographic location is less than a two-hour drive for 80% of the state's population. The hospital is in a unique position to conduct this project for two reasons. First,

veteran pediatricians and child psychiatrists with extensive national networks will conduct this project. Second, as a private institution not dependent upon public funding, it can provide a detached perspective without the constraints that publicly funded hospitals might experience. (99 words; six sentences)

2. A university biology department seeking corporate funding for genetics research:

> Here are some things you should know about us. Our biology department is uniquely suited to conduct this crucial genetics research. Stemming from the department's solid past of 30 years of doctoral studies in biological science, its faculty includes Drs. Smith, Johnson, and O'Connor. This distinguished academic core cumulatively represents 224 years of productive research experience at our university. With special focus on the molecular basis of oncogenesis, our current research uses unique systems to analyze the genetic and hormonal factors responsible for gene regulation. While these systems are not widely studied in established programs of cell biology, they are most suitable for answering the cutting-edge questions of gene expression and regulation—and our department is endowed with the intellectual talent to succeed. (124 words; seven sentences)

3. A county department of aging institute seeking foundation funding to coordinate services for the elderly:

> The Grant County Department of Aging is uniquely positioned to develop an integrated system of geriatric medical and nonhealth services. Since 1980, the Department has provided quality health, education, and research services. As a result, it serves a full range of seniors' needs. The Department has a 20 plus year history of positive networking with the business community. Accordingly, this project represents a systematic continuation of prior geriatric efforts in the area where we've transformed vision into success. It organically grows out of our past activities in the area of integration of essential services. We are solidly endowed with the intellectual resources, a skilled population, and healthy attitude to successfully implement our action plan. (114 words; seven sentences)

4. An environmentally conscious agency seeking corporate funding to train volunteers:

The Greenspace Society is similar to many other organizations that are dedicated, as our mission statement says, to environmental protection and preservation. During the past two years, we have successfully trained volunteers as evidenced by the fact that annual volunteer hours now exceed 18,000 (up 46%) and donations total $25,000 (up 12%). As a result, we now request funding to systematically develop a formal training model, complete with a curriculum and instructional materials; since we are like other environmentally conscious volunteer organizations, a training model developed here can be replicated in many other equivalent institutions. (96 words; four sentences)

PART SIX: BUDGET

Objective: To request a specific dollar amount in the proposal.

Preparing to Write

Be certain to ask for a precise amount. Base your request on your preproposal contact information. Express your request in meaningful units, e.g., hours of instruction, numbers of students, or healthy patients; if the per unit costs are too high, spread the figures out over several years. Advise the sponsor if you plan to submit this or a similar proposal to other sponsors as well.

Examples

Two corporate and two foundation examples follow.

1. An elementary school requesting corporate support for new computers:

> To meet our obligation of training computer-literate children, it is essential that they have access to today's technology; otherwise, we would be guilty of educating technological orphans. The cost of maintaining state-of-the-art computer technologies is quickly becoming prohibitive. Quite frankly, this project extends beyond the financial boundaries of our school. Accordingly, we must now reach out for assistance in what surely is a vital service to our entire community. Although we are expanding our budget allocations for technology upgrades as rapidly as possible, we intend to build an endowment that will provide ongoing support for suitable technology and staff without relying

on annual operating dollars—but that takes time. With the interest that you've shown in this area, we are requesting a grant in the amount of $150,000. This represents an investment of $1.25 in every student that will use these computers in the next five years, or a cost of $0.018 per hour of instruction. (157 words; seven sentences)

2. A social service agency seeking corporate funding for a conference on rural poverty:

> It is in the spirit of this beneficial synergism between business and the community it serves that I respectfully request the John Doe Tractor Corporation grant $10,000 to provide funds for a conference on rural poverty. This project would not only flow logically from your great corporate interest in supporting communities in which your employees live and work, but it would also yield fresh perspectives on the plight faced by many of your rural customers. In making such a contribution, the John Doe Tractor Corporation will join the Rural Social Service Agency and the state Bureau of Agriculture in this effort to serve our community by finding contemporary solutions to nagging problems. Corporate marketing professionals, government policy makers, and social service agencies can use the conference findings to strength the vitality of rural communities throughout the nation. (138 words; four sentences)

3. A local library seeking foundation funding to digitize its holdings:

> With the commitment shown by the Brush Foundation to promote literary and educational efforts, we are seeking a $25,000 grant to digitize our entire library holding of more than 100,000 volumes. Over a 10-year period, your support will touch the lives of 50,000 library patrons. Such a gift will assure not only that timely and quality services are provided, but also extend its outreach to turn every community household into a "virtual library." Clearly, this project will enrich the lives of all whom it reaches. The average library checkout entails four books; this project has the attractive investment of five cents (5¢) per person. (105 words; five sentences)

4. A small college seeking private foundation funding support for curricular development:

> With the demonstrated concern that you have shown for preparing a professional workforce

to successfully address issues of aging, we request a grant of $6,000. Funds will support: curriculum development ($3,000); development of the experiential learning component ($1,000); library resources ($500); honoraria for guest speakers ($500) and for consultation and evaluation ($1,000). Once the course is designed, the College will assume the expense of offering it in the future, including teaching and attendant costs. Over a three-year period, this course will help transform the lives of nearly 100 college students. (90 words; four sentences)

PART SEVEN: CLOSING

Objective: To nudge the sponsor to a favorable funding decision.

Preparing to Write

Avoid the hackneyed "We'd be happy to talk with you further about this. Please call if you want more information." Identify a contact person that could provide more details, if requested. Have a "heavyweight" sign the letter.

Examples

Three foundation and one corporate examples follow.

1. A private school seeking student financial aid from a foundation:

We hope the Marcy Foundation will be able to support these Marcy scholars as they continue their tradition of the pursuit of knowledge. In making such a contribution, Marcy—and indeed, society—will benefit by investing in the ideas of the future. Quite simply, your investment will perpetuate excellent educational opportunities for future leaders throughout the nation. Dr. Robert Wheeler, Director of Student Financial Aid, can provide additional information or answer questions via telephone (414-234-5678) or e-mail (robert.wheeler@midwest.edu). (80 words; four sentences)

2. A biofeedback clinic seeking corporate support for a pain management project:

Your support really does make a difference. The impact of your contribution will last for years to come as a key player in the management of pain

in patients with advanced disease. Your support will contribute to the only business worth pursuing, as Albert Schweitzer noted, "The business of doing purposeful good." Although this proposal follows the businesslike brevity your guidelines request, Dr. Griffin Boyes can be reached at 210-123-4567 to answer questions or give further information. (77 words; four sentences)

3. A family resource center seeking foundation support for a family values project:

Strengthening family ties is clearly a priority in our country. This is evidenced by collaborations between myriad local agencies to achieve these goals and the increased demand for family support services in cases where family values are absent. With your investment we will be able to foster healthy relationships between parents and their children. Please contact Sarah Spencer directly to answer questions or provide additional information by phone (202) 123-4567 or e-mail: Sarah.Spencer@frc.org. (73 words; four sentences)

4. A college seeking private foundation support for a capital building project:

Winston Churchill once observed, "At first we shape our buildings. Thereafter, our buildings shape us." Nowhere is this more evident than in a library. As the accompanying drawings highlight, this new Library will secure its place as the academic heart and information hub of the campus. This modern Library will serve as a place that houses great books and physical collections as well as an electronic portal to information from all over the world. It will, as Churchill noted, shape the lives of generations of College students.

This new facility will build on a rich tradition of success and be an important part of our unwavering commitment to academic excellence. The generosity of your support will help attract more students of the highest caliber to campus. The Library will exemplify the core values of a College education, which seeks to develop students' full potential in understanding and serving their world. I look forward to hearing from you soon. You can reach me directly by phone: (608) 987-6543 or e-mail: Kelly.Ball@college.edu. (170 words; 10 sentences)

COMPLETE LETTER PROPOSAL

Orienting Observations

An example of a complete 648-word letter proposal to a private foundation that seeks support for a project to improve police-community relations follows in Exhibit 26. It contains all seven sections described above and makes good use of headings. Further, notice that the proposal is left margin justified instead of having both left and right margins justified. The reasons: double justification forces proportional spacing, causing little white "rivers" down the page. Also, the eye sweep from the end of one line to the beginning of the next line is more difficult with double margin justification. Finally, the two most common attachments for a letter proposal are (1) a copy of your IRS letter certifying that you are a nonprofit organization, and (2) a time and task chart.

Today's Date

Mr. Hubert Williams, President
Law Enforcement Foundation
1001 23rd Street, N.W., Suite 200
Washington, DC 20037

Dear Mr. Williams:

The Center for Urban Problems (CUP), as Washington's largest organization dealing with police-community relations, invites your investment in a $66,240 special project to improve community relations among minorities.

We are encouraged that the Law Enforcement Foundation supports innovative projects that improve the delivery of police services. Over 85 percent of your grant dollars during that past three years have been invested at the local community level. Clearly, your support fills a valuable niche in light of the more conservative funding offered by the federal government. The researchers and evaluation specialists at CUP share your strong commitment to unique community-based projects.

The Problem: Spiraling Tensions. Despite proactive community relations programs, an unchecked tension exists between municipal police and minority community members. Relationships between law enforcement officers and minorities—Hispanics and African-Americans—are at a critical stage. One out of every three arrests in Washington, DC currently involves a member of a minority community; the incidence is even higher in such cities as San Antonio, Kansas City, and Los Angeles.

Many factors contribute to the growing minority community-police tensions: unemployment, inadequate housing, and the increasing complexity of urban life. Although the police did not create these nationwide social problems, they must cope with the consequences of these problems. This vast social dislocation spawns minority attitudes of prejudice and contempt. To counterbalance these problems, many police communities have adopted public relations programs to "sell" their departments to the minority communities without the concomitant need to work with them. As a result, there is an ever-widening split between present and potential minority community acceptance of police behavior. Long term, this spiraling gap further alienates citizens, limits cooperation, and erects barriers to community development.

The Solution: Evaluating Police/Community Relations Bureaus. The most effective approach to successful community-based mediation lies in forming citizen/government collaborations (often called "bureaus"), according to the latest community action research. However, success claims regarding the effectiveness of police/community relations bureaus remain undocumented. Police departments often adopt a new fad without understanding the key components of a police/community relations program. Some features of the bureau approach appear to work; others don't. This project has two specific objectives: By July, 2008, we will (1) identify the successful features of existing bureaus, and (2) disseminate those "best practices" to 350 police departments serving substantial numbers of minority citizens. The CUP research staff will follow standard social science research techniques as detailed in our Project Planner, Attachment A.

SAMPLE LETTER PROPOSAL

EXHIBIT 26

CUP Credentials: National Experience and Networks. CUP is uniquely suited to conduct this evaluation project on police/community relations bureaus. As a nonpolice-linked organization we can objectively and independently assess current practices. This project represents a systematic continuation of prior CUP efforts in this area with state and municipal organizations and private police-related associations. Our staff has a cumulative 127 years of experience in evaluating the outcomes of police-related projects. Finally, location and national networking with 28 regional offices makes CUP well postured to effectively conduct this assessment.

Budget Request: $66,240. With the demonstrated concern that you've shown in the delivery of police services to minorities, we are requesting a grant of $66,240. Quite frankly, this project extends beyond the financial boundaries of CUP. Accordingly, we must now reach out to the community for assistance in what surely is a vital service to the police community. The outcome of this project will touch the operations of over 6,000 law enforcement groups nationwide, resulting in a $13 investment in each existing municipal and state police organization, or a cost of seven cents (7¢) per police official.

In making this investment, the Law Enforcement Foundation will be supporting a cost-effective approach to the delivery of police services for the minority communities where major problems exist. Ms. Neva Shelby, National Program Director for CUP, can be reached at (202) 123-4567 or Neva.Shelby@cup.org to answer questions or give further information.

Sincerely,

Colleen McDonald
Executive Director

P.S. Come visit us and see for yourself how this project helps people in need.

Enclosure: Attachment A: Project Planner
            Attachment B: IRS Nonprofit Certification

SAMPLE LETTER PROPOSAL

EXHIBIT 26 (Continued from page 66)

Specific Comments

The Project Planner, Attachment A, referenced in the Enclosure, is a combination of a Time and Task Chart (Chapter 9) and a Budget (Chapter 12). For the complete copy of Attachment A, cited above, see Exhibit 43 for specifics. Note further that the proposal uses single spacing within paragraphs and double spacing between paragraphs.

Chapter 5 provided a detailed discussion of the seven elements in letter proposals along with 31 examples. Obviously, the examples can be adapted to multiple grant writing situations. To facilitate the adaptation process, this chapter concludes with a crosswalk among the examples (Exhibit 27). The first column in the crosswalk table indicates the general topic area of the example. The second column

identifies the type of applicant who might be writing the example. The third column specifies the type of sponsor (foundation or corporation) to which the example is targeted. The fourth column cites the page number where the example is found.

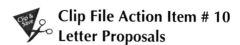

Clip File Action Item # 10
Letter Proposals

Start your Letter Proposals clip file by doing the following:

- Add an electronic copy of a letter proposal used as a transmittal letter (Exhibit 34).
- Choose sample electronic paragraphs for all seven sections of a letter proposal that can be edited and adapted as you write your next one.

Topic	Applicant	Sponsor	Page
Adult Literacy	University/Community Collaboration	Foundation	63
Biomedical Research	University	Corporation	58
Capital Building Project	College	Foundation	65
Community Health	Health Agency	Corporation	60
Computer Equipment	Elementary School	Corporation	64
Conference Support	Social Service Agency	Corporation	64
Counseling	Community Mental Health Agency	Foundation	61
Cultural Diversity	Public School	Foundation	58
Curriculum Development	College	Foundation	64
Curriculum Development	Medical School	Corporation	61
Digitize Holdings	Community Library	Foundation	64
Domestic Violence	Battered Women's Shelter	Foundation	62
Emotionally Disturbed	Pediatric Hospital	Foundation	63
Equipment	Research Institute	Foundation	61
Family Values	Family Resource Center	Foundation	65
Food Pantry	Faith-Based Organization	Foundation	58
Genetics	University	Corporation	63
HIV/AIDS Prevention	Welfare Agency	Foundation	58
Juvenile Justice	Police Department	Corporation	60
Missionary	Inter-Faith Council	Foundation	59
Neuroscience	Alzheimer's Research Center	Foundation	59
One-Stop Shopping	Elder Care Agency	Corporation	61
Pain Management	Biofeedback Clinic	Corporation	65
Parent Training	Day Care Center	Foundation	62
Scholarships	University	Foundation	60
Service Coordination	County Department of Aging	Foundation	63
Service Delivery	Medical Clinic	Corporation	58
Social Services	Child Welfare Agency	Corporation	60
Student Financial Aid	Private School	Foundation	65
Teen Smoking Prevention	Hospital	Corporation	62
Volunteer Training	Environmental Agency	Corporation	63

CROSS-WALK TO LETTER PROPOSAL EXAMPLES

EXHIBIT 27

CHAPTER 6
Letter Proposal Examples

Letters are expectations packaged in an envelope.
—Shana Alexander

OVERVIEW

The previous chapter provided you with a seven-step template for writing a persuasive letter proposal. From a broad perspective, your letter proposals communicate the expectation, as Shana Alexander notes, that you have identified a significant problem which you propose to solve. Exhibit 26 identified the problem of spiraling tensions between the police and members of the minority community and proposed to reduce those tensions by researching best practices that would be disseminated nationwide. That is just one example among many how a letter proposal can be crafted to solve a crucial problem.

In Chapter 6, we provide seven additional examples showing how the letter proposal template can be applied to various grant writing situations. For each example, we provide some orienting observations about the type of grant and some specific comments about the particular request. More concretely, in this chapter, you will learn how a letter proposal can be applied to the following:

- A health education center request for operating support.
- A performing arts request for physical facilities renovation.
- A minority youth request for capital campaign support.
- A developmentally disabled request for vocational training support.
- A senior citizen request for coordination of service delivery.
- A transmittal letter that accompanies sponsor application forms.
- A concept paper for federal government grants.

In sum, these seven examples show how a letter proposal can be used with private foundations and corporations who have no specific application guidelines, as is the case with many sponsors. Additionally, the examples illustrate how the letter proposal template can be adapted for use with private foundations and corporations who do have specific application guidelines but are deemed to be constraining. Finally, the last example demonstrates how the letter proposal template can be modified for use with federal grant guidelines through initial submission of a concept paper, a preproposal designed to ensure your idea matches with sponsor priorities. The letter proposal template is a versatile grant writing approach that has generated millions of dollars for beginning and seasoned grantseekers.

HEALTH EDUCATION CENTER REQUEST FOR OPERATING SUPPORT

Orienting Observations

As we conduct grant workshops around the county, one of the most common questions we hear is "How do you write a grant to get operating support?" Since most grantmakers provide project support, not operating support, we respond by saying that the challenge is to cast your proposal so that it de facto becomes a request for project support. The grantmakers that do provide operating support are most likely to be local community or family foundations. The letter proposal in Exhibit 28 to the Dominic Michael Family Foundation is an example of how a request for operating support can be written.

Today's Date

Mr. Lee K. Wallet, President
The Dominic Michael Foundation
802 Josephine Way
Hartford, CT 02207-1799

Dear Mr. Wallet:

The Patrick Ignatius Center for Health Education, Connecticut's largest independent provider of health education for young people, invites your contribution of $10,000 to help provide high-quality outreach programs that teach children in grades 6-12 how to make better life choices.

We are encouraged that The Dominic Michael Foundation provides funding to support the operations of innovative programs that improve the health and quality of life for children. Over the past three decades, your foundation has made important investments at critical moments to ensure that community-based educational programs are responsive to local needs. This gift request is a systematic continuation of our mutual interest in serving the greater Hartford area.

The Problem: Health Risks and Chronic Illnesses

Four priority health risks and chronic illnesses have a considerable negative impact on students' development and academic performance. These behaviors, often established during childhood and early adolescence, include: (1) alcohol, tobacco, and other drug use; (2) pediatric asthma; (3) poor diets and limited physical activity; and (4) risky sexual behaviors. Left unchecked, these behaviors contribute to the leading causes of death, disability, and social problems in the U.S.

Alcohol, Tobacco, and Other Drug Abuse. The most recent Youth Risk Behavior Survey reveals alarming data about the percentage of students in Connecticut who, in the past month, have: drank alcohol = 47%; episodic heavy drinking = 28%; drank alcohol on school property = 7%; smoked cigarettes = 35%; smoked cigarettes on $\geq$ 20 days = 18%; smoked cigarettes on school property = 19%; used marijuana = 22%; used marijuana on school property = 8%.

Asthma. Asthma is the most common chronic illnesses of childhood, affecting an estimated 100,000 of the state's children under age 18. As a result, asthma is the leading cause of health-related school absenteeism. Nationwide, children with asthma miss an average 7.2 school days per year compared to 3.4 days per year for children without asthma. More locally, research from clinics and schools suggests that asthma affects 15% of Hartford's urban school-age children.

Obesity. Childhood obesity is a public health problem that has reached epidemic proportions. Obesity rates in the United States for children have doubled since 1990. In Connecticut, 1 in 5 children is obese or overweight; girls are at a greater risk than boys. Research indicates that obesity increases the risk of cardiovascular disease and diabetes, and may contribute to asthma. Due to state budget cuts, many schools are eliminating physical fitness and health education programs.

Sexual Behaviors. Despite recent improvements, too many high school students in Connecticut are still engaging in risky sexual behaviors. The Youth Risk Behavior Survey reveals that 44% of high school students have had sexual intercourse and 33% have had sexual intercourse in the past three months. Nearly half (45%) did not use a condom during their last sexual intercourse and almost three-fourths (72%) did not use birth control pills during their last sexual intercourse.

REQUEST FOR OPERATING SUPPORT

EXHIBIT 28

The Solution: Quality Health Education Programs

The Patrick Ignatius Center is dedicated exclusively to ensuring access to timely health education for young people. Our mission is to motivate students to recognize that their values, reflected in their attitudes and choices, determine the course and quality of their individual lives. During the last year, the Center reached 175,000 students from 150 schools across the state. Since opening in 1973, nearly five million students have benefited from Center programs.

Aided by highly sophisticated and visually stimulating exhibits, Center programs utilize resources which no single school or school system can duplicate. Each of the basic programs at the Center has its own rationale, instructional objectives, and balance of cognitive and affective components. Nevertheless all programs share a common underlying philosophy that is centered on preventive education. Research shows that the best way to address childhood health problems is through prevention. That's why instructional programming is always focused on helping students internalize targeted messages of personal responsibility and respect for the human body.

Outreach programs allow us to take health education messages into the community and deliver customized programs to students at their schools. Our innovative programs include:

1. **"What Takes Your Breath Away?"**—educates children, parents, and teachers about controlling asthma through trigger avoidance, taking medications, and frequent monitoring.
2. **"No Weigh!"**—employs a research-based design to promote healthy lifestyles among students by encouraging participation in lifetime fitness activities and nutrition habits.
3. **"High on Friends"**—uses trained peer leaders to educate other students about the dangers of alcohol and drug abuse, and offers constructive alternatives to these unhealthy behaviors.
4. **"The Birds, The Bees and Teens"**—is designed to help parents and teens be more open, honest, and comfortable when talking to each other about sex.

Center Capabilities: Measured Success

The Patrick Ignatius Center for Health Education specializes in presenting high-quality programs that are powerful, inspirational, and motivational. The Center employs 18 staff who have a cumulative 200 years of experience in teaching general health, family living/sex education, and alcohol and drug abuse prevention. Outreach programs are regularly evaluated by Center staff (administrators and instructors) and participants (students, parents, and teachers) to ensure that the information provided is accurate, timely, and in the best format possible.

- Students complete pre- and post-tests during the program, and follow-up questionnaires 6 months later, which measure changes in knowledge, attitudes, and behaviors.
- Teachers and parents complete a written evaluation at the conclusion of the program rating the quality of the information presented, the instructors, the exhibits and handouts.
- Instructors are evaluated quarterly on their teaching methods and ability to relate to students.
- Center administrators and instructors review programs on an annual basis to ensure that content is up-to-date, developmentally appropriate, culturally sensitive, timely and engaging.

Based upon these criteria, The Patrick Ignatius Center for Health Education is viewed as "very effective" by the public and private school teachers who use the outreach service, with over 75% of program requests coming from repeat customers. In addition, Midwest University recently conducted an independent evaluation of the "What Takes Your Breath Away?" program. Their final report gives the Center high marks for significantly increasing student knowledge and for an instructional approach that helps them retain this information long afterward.

Budget Request: $10,000

With the demonstrated concern that The Dominic Michael Foundation has shown for improving the health and quality of life of children, we respectfully request a contribution of $10,000 to support general program needs. Your funds

REQUEST FOR OPERATING SUPPORT

EXHIBIT 28 (Continued from page 70)

will help the Center to offer a variety of outreach programs to children, parents, and teachers, and to acquire new teaching resources and exhibits.

Although the Center charges schools a modest $3.50 per child for providing health education programs, this fee does not cover the full cost of the outreach programs. The true cost per child is $6.35. However, the current state fiscal crisis has taken away the ability to pass on increased operating costs to the schools, teachers, and parents. This price sensitivity forces us to rely heavily on the generosity of donors. Thanks to the gifts of charitable contributors, the Center is able to provide programs to school districts across the state in spite of rising program costs.

The total operating budget for the Center this current year is $1,109,800. Revenue from program fees is projected to cover 35%, endowment income 23%, and charitable donations 42%. Because the Center is frugally managed and expenditures are carefully planned, general operating support gifts, in reality, are scholarships for students to participate in health education programs. They are also a means to ensure the Center's value to area schools, teachers, parents and children.

In making this $10,000 investment, The Dominic Michael Foundation will be supporting a cost-effective approach to the delivery of quality outreach health education programs, and at the same time, enable the Center to make maximum progress toward fulfilling its mission. The outcome of this project will touch the lives of more than 175,000 students from 150 schools across the state, resulting in a five cent (5¢) investment in each child, or a cost of one cent (1¢) per hour of instruction. Please contact Mr. Jonathan Christopher, Outreach Director, to answer questions or provide additional information—phone: (860) 123-4567; e-mail: JChristopher@piche.org.

Sincerely,

Jessica Kwasny
President

P.S. Please come visit us and see this important project for yourself!

Enclosures
    IRS Nonprofit Certification
    Current Officers and Board Members
    Audited Financial Statement

REQUEST FOR OPERATING SUPPORT
EXHIBIT 28 (Continued from page 71)

Specific Comments

Content. This 1,384 word letter proposal from a health education center was really seeking general operating support. They recognized that few sponsors provide such funding. Their persuasive writing approach equated grant support to student scholarship support. On a per capita basis, student admission fees represented slightly more than one-half of total instructional costs. The full costs included, of course, such operating costs as instructor salaries and fringe benefits, facility costs, and so forth. The foundation "scholarship support" closed the gap between full operating costs and off-setting student admission fees.

Format. From a writing perspective, note the use of indented paragraphs as opposed to block paragraphing;

the extra white space provides the reader with a visual clue that a new thought is being advanced.

PERFORMING ARTS REQUEST FOR PHYSICAL FACILITIES RENOVATION

Orienting Observations

Of the many different types of grants available, Exhibit 29 is a letter proposal submitted to a private foundation seeking challenge grant funds for a performing arts project. The college has already received partial funding for the project and is now attempting to use that money as a magnet to attract additional support.

Today's Date

Mr. Brychan William, Director
Philanthropic Program: Cultural Heritage
American Arts Foundation
1 Rockefeller Center
New York, NY 10285-4804

Dear Mr. William:

Norman College, Vermont's only college to receive national recognition for character development in students, invites your investment of $50,000 in a special project to enrich performing arts experiences for the Northeastern Vermont community.

The American Arts Foundation has been an inspiration because of your long-standing commitment to art and culture. Indeed, in *Arts & Economic Prosperity*, Mary Beth Salerno, Foundation President, said it best: "the arts are central to the economic growth and vitality of communities around the world. . . .investing in the arts is good policy and good business." This request is a systematic extension of our mutual interest toward enriching the wider community.

Organization Information.   Norman College
                                  100 Grant Street
                                  Witt, VT 05005

Contact Person.   Aidan Tyler, Director of Theatre Facilities
                                  Phone: 802-403-3124—Fax: 802-403-4081
                                  E-mail: Aidan.Tyler@nc.edu

Funds Requested. $50,000

Geographic Area Served. Norman College is a private liberal arts school that provides a superior education that is personally, intellectually, and spiritually challenging. Located in Witt, Vermont, 125 miles north of Boston, we enroll over 2,000 undergraduates in 33 majors and 100 graduate students in three masters programs. Over 70% of students are from Vermont. Also of note, for 2007, we are ranked #4 among the top 10 best comprehensive colleges in the Northeast in *U.S. News & World Report's* guide to "America's Best Colleges."

The College's Madison Theatre and Monroe Theatre host over 680 musicals, plays, concerts, practices, speeches, and rehearsals a year for the campus and Witt community. Last year, more than 32,200 individuals attended ticketed events in these theatres. Nearly 45% of these patrons attended performances put on in collaboration with community partners such as the National Arts Program, Evergreen Productions, and the Dance Company. Compared to 10 major communities across the state, Witt ranks #2 in total nonprofit arts industry spending at $45.5 million in 2006. Only arts organizations and audiences in Dover spent more.

Project Description. The arts are an essential and integral part of every day life. They help us to better understand and interpret the world around us. They offer us the opportunity to communicate our most profound thoughts and deepest feelings. Or in the words of Robert L. Lynch, President and CEO, Americans for the Arts, the fundamental value of the arts is that "they foster beauty, creativity, originality, and vitality. The arts inspire us, sooth us, provoke us, involve us, and connect us. . .but they also create jobs and contribute to the economy."

   Goals and Objectives. The **goal** of this project is to enhance performing arts experiences for the greater Witt community. Specific project objectives are:

REQUEST FOR PHYSICAL FACILITIES RENOVATION

EXHIBIT 29

Objective #1: To create a theatre environment that captivates community arts patrons.

Objective #2: To provide budding student performers and theatre technicians with quality training experiences using the latest tools and technology of their trade.

Beneficiaries. Direct beneficiaries include over 32,000 theatre patrons annually from Northeastern Vermont who attend performances in the Monroe and Madison Theatres. Indirect beneficiaries include the local businesses such as hotels, restaurants, and retail stores who profit from event-related spending by arts audiences. The *Arts & Economic Prosperity* report (2006) indicates that nationally arts attendees spend an average of $22.87 above the cost of admission.

Our Theatre Department is an important source for promoting the performing arts profession. Dozens of students are intimately involved in all aspects of producing shows: the acting, technical production, and community relations. Further, budding theatre technicians studying at the College learn their trade through experience with the latest tools and technology. These students work on scenery, props, lighting and sound for the various productions, as well as work lights and sound for touring companies, nationally known speakers, and other events that occur in the two theatres. This lighting project will give students first-hand practice with the latest theatre technologies, and teach them the skills necessary to visually enhance theatre experiences.

Implementation Plan. To achieve the project goal and objectives, we will replace 180 antiquated 1,000 watt lighting fixtures with state-of-the-art 575 watt fixtures. Some of the existing fixtures are as old as the building—46 years. New fixtures are designed to be more effective and energy efficient, saving an estimated 176,342 kilowatts a year. Lighting systems will be installed in time for the Summer 2008 productions in the College's Madison and Monroe Theatres. These fixtures will provide the maximum viewing pleasure for spectators and superior light setting experiences for student performers and theatre technicians.

Expected Outcomes. Evaluation is essential for achieving project success. Aidan Tyler, Director of Theatre Facilities, will monitor project activity and submit a progress report to the American Arts Foundation following its completion. For this project, we anticipate two key outcomes: (1) an increase in the total numbers of community patrons who attend theatre performances, and (2) an increase in student satisfaction with theatre training experiences.

Timeline. Project funding is necessary by June 1, 2008. Fixtures will be ordered from the Lighthouse, a Boston theatrical and stage lighting equipment wholesaler. Mr. Tyler will ensure that light fixtures will be installed within ten days of delivery. The College anticipates the implementation of the project for its June 2008 musical comedy production of "I do! I do!" by Tom Jones and Harvey Schmidt and its July 2008 production of "Children of Eden" by score composer Stephen Schwartz. Your gift will enhance the visual appreciation of performing arts productions for more than 32,000 theatre goers per year.

Project Budget. With the demonstrated concern your company has shown for enriching community arts experiences, we request a grant of $50,000. Funds will be used to purchase energy efficient light fixtures that will enhance theatre productions. This project represents a portion of a larger challenge grant from the Vermont Focus on Energy, which has already pledged $40,000 toward the total project cost of $150,000. To make up the remaining difference, we have targeted specific requests to other sponsors who support arts and culture projects. The specific budget request is as follows:

1. ETS Source 4 Ellispoidal Reflector Spotlights (152 @ $296 each) = $45,4000
2. ETC Source 4 Panels (16 @ $178 each)   = $ 2,900
3. ETC Source 4 PARS (12 @ $178 each)   = $ 2,100

    Total Requested   **$50,000**

Evaluating Results. Norman College has established systems to track and measure project results. For example, from 2000 to 2005, the number of tickets sold for community-sponsored events increased from 9,900 to 14,500. At the conclusion of theatre courses, students complete a standardized survey that evaluates the instructor, course content, and the learning experience. In addition, the "Norman College Graduating Student Follow-Up Survey" was recently enhanced to collect information about the value of internship experiences in preparing students for their first job out of school. Mr. Tyler will use information from these and other sources when reporting project progress and results to the American Arts Foundation.

Thank you for your consideration of our proposal. Your support for this one-time project will help to enhance performing arts experiences for hundreds of theatre performers and student technicians, and thousands of community patrons in the greater Witt area. Please contact Adian Tyler to answer questions or provide additional information.

Sincerely,

Mikael M. Victoria, Ph.D.
President

P.S. Please come visit us and see—firsthand—how your support will make a difference!

REQUEST FOR PHYSICAL FACILITIES RENOVATION

EXHIBIT 29 (Continued from page 74)

While this letter proposal follows the general template presented in Chapter 5, it was modified to meet the few specific proposal submission requirements requested by the sponsor. The seven-step template is a guide, not a straight jacket.

Specific Comments

Content. This 1,198 word letter proposal from Norman College wants to upgrade the physical facilities in the theatre. Notice the persuasive writing approach that they took. They stressed the value of the performing arts—fostering beauty, creativity, and originality—and emphasized that theatre patrons benefit from attractive performing environments. Norman College recognized a fundamental principle of grantseeking: people fund people, they don't fund things. Norman College wisely stressed the people benefits of their proposal and downplayed the benefits of improved physical facilities, which were only a means to the end of improved performances that patrons will appreciate. The fact that partial funding has already been secured also serves to enhance the credibility of the project.

Format. Finally, from a writing perspective, note the use of a serif font for the narrative (e.g., Times Roman, Garamond, Courier) and a sans serif typeface for headings (e.g., Arial, Gothic, Universal). Serif fonts are more readable than sans serif fonts. The use of a different font style for headings provides the reviewers with another visual signal that they will be entering a new proposal section.

MINORITY YOUTH REQUEST FOR CAPITAL CAMPAIGN SUPPORT

Orienting Observations

Grant funding for operating support is difficult—but not impossible—to obtain. The same is true of capital campaign support. Usually capital campaigns for "bricks and mortar" are approached through such fundraising mechanisms as major gifts or planned giving. Nevertheless, occasions do arise where grants can help support the construction of new buildings, especially in those instances where a strong relationship exists between the sponsor and the applicant. Exhibit 30 contains an example of how one letter proposal was crafted to seek support for a new building that would provide services to inner-city minority youth and their families.

Specific Comments

Content. Obviously, this 1,536 letter proposal targets a corporation as opposed to a private foundation. The same seven-step template works for either type of private sponsor. With corporations, you must appeal to features that are profitable for them. This particular corporation placed great emphasis on "corporate social responsibility," a phrase that was repeated throughout their Web site. Corporations subscribe to the concept

Today's Date

Mr. John Calder, President
The Berger Corporation
P. O. Box 13390
Los Angeles, CA 92255-3390

Dear Mr. Calder:

Since 1996, Central City Mission (CCM) has provided educational activities and human services to the San Bernardino inner city. Over 55,000 children, youth and adults of Latino, African American, Hispanic and Caucasian cultures are the recipients of these services. Because of our shared values, CCM invites your investment in a $100,000 capital campaign project, the Empowerment Through Education (ETE) Center, that will reduce cultural barriers and increase cooperation, thereby empowering neighbors to become self-sustaining and melding into a community of hope.

We are encouraged that The Berger Corporation supports unique challenges in education, health and culture. Your past support of teens (Haven House), Big Brothers and Sisters, pediatric AIDS and Women's Work illustrate your concern for a broad spectrum of people and their needs. Equally important, your support sets a high standard of corporate social responsibility for the Greater Los Angeles area that we both serve. Our project presents a unique opportunity to corporations such as yours who have the vision and creativity to see the social benefits and value of building cultural diversity into a productive and contributing community. Education and training are the keys to the success of this project as CCM has already demonstrated. Wouldn't it be rewarding to know that The Berger Corporation has played a key role in this long-term effort to close a spiraling gap between need and resources?

The elements of the challenges and goals for this project follow.

The Problem: Mounting Educational Needs vs. Dwindling Resources

Education is the key to community empowerment. Our inner-city educational baseline falls significantly short of minimum acceptable standards. To illustrate,

- 90% of children are from families on some form of public assistance
- 70% of students suspended or expelled from San Bernardino schools live in this area
- 67% of students entering ninth grade fail to graduate from high school
- 73% of the high school graduates don't meet California university admission standards
- 36% of youth in CCM programs have been homeless at least once
- 24% of students are learning English for the first time but rely primarily on their native language

Clearly, the children and families in the CCM catchment area are the poorest, hardest to serve and most underserved in San Bernardino, the eighth largest city in California. Few minority children, regardless of academic standing, are encouraged to apply for college admission by school counselors; most are pushed toward jobs and trade schools.

There are two major consequences resulting from this lack of an empowered education community. First, it presents insurmountable barriers to attracting the resources essential for community development, especially service providers with a multicultural staff. Second, the community does not and cannot meet its serious responsibility to train individuals who will contribute to this ever-changing multicultural society. Bottom line: this lag in inner city educational support services is a critical and increasing problem that needs to be addressed creatively and immediately.

The Solution: Empowerment Through Education

Education is the most constructive long-term approach to changing the course of marginalization and its destructive impact while empowering youth and their families to take control of their community. Education means positive growth that multiplies geometrically over time. The end result is family and community stability.

REQUEST FOR CAPITAL CAMPAIGN SUPPORT

EXHIBIT 30

Precisely, CCM is creating an Empowerment Through Education (ETE) Center that will promote literacy at all levels—child, youth, and adult—and provide life-changing opportunities through the following programs that are currently operational from early morning to mid-evening.

After School Program: Working with the San Bernardino Unified School District, neighborhood children and youth study and play on weekdays after school. Heavy emphasis is placed on tutoring, homework assistance, cultural interaction and enrichment activities. As a result, tracking data show that 90% of children in this program advance in grade in the regular schools. Much individual attention is given, especially to our youth with special learning needs related to witnessing violence at an early age. Post traumatic stress syndrome is increasingly evident. Addressing these problems head-on is resulting in improved educational performance. At present, 100 children are enrolled.

- **Project Objective:** To increase enrollment by 100% in the next five years
- **Project Outcome:** Significantly more children will experience school success, overcome the stresses of poverty and violence, and achieve at higher academic levels

Power Teen Program: Teenagers from 13 to 15 years of age "learn and earn" by working with mentors while receiving a modest stipend. They support the Mission staff and Peer Educators in After School, Adolescent Health Care and other programs. From experience, it is known that "peer learning" is often more effective than adult-based learning. This program targets neighborhood youth because they are most susceptible to enrollment in gangs. Our program provides significant time during alternative hours when schools are closed and parents are working. At present 27 Power Teens are actively involved in programs or are in training.

- **Project Objective:** To increase the number of teen participants by 100% in the next five years
- **Project Outcome:** The presence of Power Teens, as role models in the neighborhood, attracts other youth who are school delinquent or involved in gang activities. Additional Power Teens will expand this attraction effect and provide additional support to all programming

Peer Educators Program: Young adults aged 16–21 are trained to assume leadership positions and direct programs with assistance from Power Teens. They earn a modest stipend. This program develops job readiness skills, encourages school completion and provides role models for Power Teens. Active involvement in this program has shown that our youth have a lower interaction with the juvenile justice system, lower rates for STDs and teen pregnancy and a higher level of school retention. At present there are 54 Peer Educators.

- **Project Objective:** To increase the number of Peer Educators by 100% in the next five years
- **Project Outcome:** Peer Educators foster ambition and desire to grow among Power Teens as they work together in various programs. Additional Peer Educators will support the expanding education, health and inter-cultural programs that are currently in place and will develop in the ETE Center

English as a Second Language: Nonnative English speaking children, youth and adults learn to function in an English language environment. In an innovative initiative, the Mexican government is providing satellite-based instruction to approximately 58 adults, many of whom have low literacy skills in their Spanish native language while dealing with the challenges of mastering English as a second language. Our English as a Second Language (ESL) teaching techniques focus on survival skills necessary to negotiate the education, health care and work site systems.

- **Project Objective:** To expand the number of participants by 100% in the next five years
- **Project Outcome:** Children and youth with improved English language skills will perform better in school. Adults with functional English language literacy will be more productive in the workforce, improve their ability to communicate with other social groups, and expand their leadership potential

REQUEST FOR CAPITAL CAMPAIGN SUPPORT

EXHIBIT 30 (Continued from page 76)

Capabilities

CCM is uniquely postured to conduct and complete this project for two reasons. First, its trained staff represents over 150 years of cumulative experience in working with at-risk youth and families. Second, through its documented record of success, CCM has garnered the trust, respect, and confidence of community residents and local government officials. It has received national recognition from such philanthropic groups as the Robert Wood Johnson Foundation. Its Board of Trustees fully supports and actively participates in the projects in support of the Executive Director, his staff and the youth and adults who have dedicated themselves to the success of the Mission and the control of their personal and family life.

Budget Request: $100,000 Towards Building Construction Costs

The Berger Corporation has repeatedly recognized the importance of and has demonstrated its support for higher education. CCM's programs remind us that higher education is built on a foundation of accessible education at the pre-school, elementary and secondary levels. Significant numbers are deprived of these basic education opportunities because of social and environmental barriers they cannot control.

To close this gap, CCM is requesting $100,000 towards the construction of a 3,240 square foot building whose total cost is $500,000. The requested funds represent the cost of one 25 by 25 square foot room in the new Empowerment Through Education Center. Quite frankly, this budget extends well beyond the financial boundaries of CCM. Accordingly, we must reach out to the philanthropic community for what surely is a vital service: building a community of hope through education. While the requested funds will be pooled (but not comingled) with others being raised to construct the ETE Center, the physical facility is a means to the end of educationally empowering community residents.

This letter describes a set of needs and problems that have current and long-term solutions that contain the unanimous and unqualified endorsement of our Board of Directors. We are prepared to discuss further details, including the overall fundraising strategy, architectural drawings, and full documentation of the educational services to be provided. In making this investment, you will be supporting the ideas, dreams and hopes for the future to perpetuate educational opportunities where many think none could exist.

Sincerely,

Rev. Calvin Key
Pastor/Executive Director

P.S. Come visit us and see for yourself the needs of the people we serve.

REQUEST FOR CAPITAL CAMPAIGN SUPPORT

EXHIBIT 30 (Continued from page 77)

of "profitable philanthropy." What do you have to offer them in your next proposal? Happier employees? Healthier employees? An improved transportation or communication system? Better training for their future employees? A safer community? A boost in brand awareness? Your prospect research (Chapter 3) and preproposal contact information (Chapter 4) should indicate their business priorities, which you can reflect in your proposal.

Format. From a proposal writing perspective, set all of your margins (left, right, top, bottom) to one inch. The white space border helps frame your proposal much the way a mat border accentuates a framed oil painting.

DEVELOPMENTALLY DISABLED REQUEST FOR VOCATIONAL TRAINING SUPPORT

Orienting Observations

Many social service, welfare, and educational grant requests center on seeking support to provide training for target audiences. The following proposal (Exhibit 31) targets providing horticultural training for developmentally disabled adults in order to increase their employability. Since reviewers are apt to question whether this proposal will succeed, including a statement regarding a successful 12-month pilot project is particularly persuasive.

Today's Date

Mr. Cameron Nicholaus, President
Vocational Rehabilitation Foundation
123 Main Street
Denver, CO 80010

Dear Mr. Nicholaus:

Adult Rehabilitation Center (ARC), the only rehabilitation center for adults with developmental disabilities in Denver, invites your investment in a $10,000 vocational education project.

The Vocational Rehabilitation Foundation invests more than one-third of its contributions in social service projects for people with disabilities. Because of your unprecedented concern for the welfare of the developmentally disabled, we turn to Vocational Rehabilitation Foundation for its support to expand vocational training services for a special needs population.

The Problem: The Gap between Competence and Performance. One of people's great needs is the ability to achieve, and through achievement, experience psychological and financial growth. Developmentally disabled adults have limited aspirations and lost choices. Right now, only 15 percent of those capable of holding gainful employment have paying jobs. In specific terms, this means that the Greater Denver Area has over 1,200 unemployed developmentally disabled adults. The challenge for this special needs population is to identify important work environments where they can develop and nourish job skills.

People with disabilities can work independently in only a handful of job settings. As a result, they can seldom put their restricted talents to full use and rarely experience job satisfaction commensurate with their abilities. Since the number of developmentally disabled people is growing faster than the general population, the need for job training is escalating as more of them experience this competence-performance gap.

The Solution: Job Training in Plant Care. This project will close the competence-performance gap by training developmentally disabled adults in the care of plants and flowers. Two major factors justify this horticultural project. First, the results of our needs assessment documents that over 75 greenhouse owners are willing to hire such people if they can work reliably. Second, a 12-month pilot project with six developmentally disabled adults demonstrated that with proper training, these individuals can and do achieve functional independence.

ARC has a greenhouse and a three-person groundskeeper crew to maintain the appearance of our 20-acre facility. The botanical expertise already resides at the School where the staff has a collective 79 years of greenhouse experience in such things as soil analysis, seeds, germination conditions, watering, fertilization, planting and pruning.

Credential: Botany Expertise and Job Networks. This project naturally grows out of our philosophy of maximizing existing resources. The current greenhouse also represents a botanical learning laboratory, where special people can be trained in a nonthreatening environment. The staff has developed specific learning objectives for each botany area. Administrators have secured agreements for tentative job placement sites as Attachment One shows. Accordingly, this project represents a systematic approach of ARC's prior efforts in "mainstreaming," by which we have transformed vision into success since 1904.

Budget Request: $10,000. With the demonstrated concern that the Vocational Rehabilitation Foundation has shown in this area, we are requesting a grant of $10,000. This represents an investment of $0.04 per hour in the 350 developmentally disabled adults over the next five years who will graduate from our three month training program.

REQUEST FOR VOCATIONAL TRAINING SUPPORT

EXHIBIT 31

The funds will be used to expand our worksites from five to 20 stations where our staff can provide essential job readiness skills. In making this investment the Foundation will be supporting a cost-effective approach to the delivery of vocation training for the developmentally disabled. Such a grant will assure the quality and regularity of the botany training program; more important, it will enrich many lives and, indirectly, create taxpayers, not tax takers.

Your support will make a critical difference, one that will last for years as job training services expand. Most of all, you will be investing in the ideas that will help exceptional people for decades. Please contact Mrs. Abby Scott, Director of Development, at 915-555-1212 or Abby.Scott@arc.org to answer questions or provide additional information.

Sincerely,

Grace Hill
President

P.S. Come visit us and let Randy tell you about his flower garden.

Enclosures
    Attachment One: Tentative Job Placement Sites
    Attachment Two: Letters of Commitment from Potential Employers
    Attachment Three: IRS Tax Exempt Certification

REQUEST FOR VOCATIONAL TRAINING SUPPORT

EXHIBIT 31 (Continued from page 79)

Specific Comments

Content. These 660 words present a succinct but persuasive appeal for project support. Note the use of Attachments One and Two to strengthen proposal credibility by showing that the marketplace is ready to hire trained developmentally disabled adults.

Format. From a writing perspective, use 12 point type size; it is easily readable and increasingly sponsors stipulate 12 point text as a minimum requirement.

SENIOR CITIZEN REQUEST FOR COORDINATION OF SERVICE DELIVERY

Orienting Observations

While many proposals seek support to provide education or training, as noted in Exhibit 32, a number of proposals concentrate on service delivery. These service delivery proposals may entail providing new services for existing markets, offering new services for new markets, entering new markets with existing services, increasing current market penetration, providing excess capacity to others, entering coalitions, using personnel more efficiently, or coordinating the delivery of multiple services, which is the topic of the following letter proposal.

Specific Comments

Content. This 922 word letter proposal is organized, contains essential information and is highly readable. Note the judicious use of statistics in the problem statement to document the need for this project.

Format. Note in particular the use of headings and the bolded sentences at the end of key paragraphs. The use of bolding for text emphasis is more readable than other comparable techniques such as the use of underlining, italics, or all capital letters. These persuasive writing techniques facilitate skim reading on the part of the reviewers. From a writing perspective, don't try to write perfect copy initially. Remember the grant writing maxim: the first draft is for getting down, not getting good. You get the proposal "good" through subsequent editing: Chapter 15.

LETTER PROPOSAL USE WITH EXISTING SPONSOR GUIDELINES

So far, this chapter has focused on how to write a letter proposal to private foundations and corporations who **do not** have particular guidelines to follow. And that is the case for most—but not all—of them. This chapter now concludes with strategies for writing

Today's Date

Mr. Gray American, President
Senior Foundation
123 Any Street
Memphis, TN 40239

Dear Mr. American:

The Roxbury Elder Institute, the largest hospital-based senior service system in Memphis, invites your investment in a $250,000 special project to centralize 50 elderly services.

We are encouraged that the Senior Foundation supports innovative projects that improve the delivery of elderly services. Over 69% of your grant dollars in the past three years have been invested at the local community level. Clearly, your support fills a valuable niche in light of the more conservative and traditional federal government funding. This strong commitment to unique projects is shared by our 35 professional staff members at Roxbury who have a cumulative 348 years of service to the elderly.

The Problem: Fragmented Services and Multiple Vendors. In five years, a population tsunami of "Baby Boomers" will enter the ranks of the elderly. The latest statistics available indicate the older population — persons age 65 or older—numbered 36.3 million in 2004 (Administration on Aging, 2004). In 2000, people ages 65+ represented 12.4% (about one in every eight Americans) of the population but are expected to grow to be 20% of the population by 2030, where there will be about 71.5 million older persons, more than twice their number in 2000. Further, the Census Bureau data projects a notable increase in the "oldest old" population, persons 85 and older. Specifically, this population will double between 2000 and 2030; it will quadruple between 2000 and 2050. (U.S. Census Bureau, 2004) Over one-half of those aged 85 and older are impaired and require long-term care (American Association of Homes and Services for the Aging, 2005). **More people are living longer, require more intensive care, and consume major health care resources.**

According to the National Center for Health Statistics, 40% of the elderly currently use one or more community health services. The most commonly used services were those provided outside the home rather than in the home. The most widely used service was senior center, then congregate meals, followed by special transportation. **While many elderly patients now see several health care providers, their numbers will increase, especially among women, those with limited education, and minorities.**

Beyond visits to family practice physicians, internists, cardiologists, and oncologists, the elderly experience a growing need for information and referral, legal assistance, counseling, housing and employment services, outpatient rehabilitation and physical therapy, case management, and social and recreational activities. **Gaining access to these specialists involves many trips to different locations.**

The Solution: One-Stop Shopping and a Few Vendors. Current research verifies that the elderly prefer "one-stop shopping" and dealing with only a few vendors. Specifically, about two-thirds prefer purchasing additional products or services from the same vendor rather than dealing with different ones. The goal of this project is to consolidate a broad range of deliverables designed to meet the needs of older adults and their caregivers. The specific objective is to centralize 75% of the elderly healthcare and related services in Memphis under one centralized source within the next three years.

With the full endorsement of the three major area hospitals and the Shelby County Medical Society, one centralized call center will be established and a uniform electronic records system will be implemented that links participating providers. This health information technology approach will improve the coordination of service delivery, as the

REQUEST FOR COORDINATION OF SERVICE DELIVERY

EXHIBIT 32

Institute of Medicine has noted (2005). The delivery of these services will be characterized by consistency of quality, accessibility, and single-source reliability. The composition and utilization of these services will be determined by the needs of the individual. The consumer is advised on the best utilization of the services as a result of an intake evaluation and needs assessment. The program offers flexibility to select from a menu of services. **By establishing a centralized referral system that takes full advantage of available health information technologies, Shelby County will be prepared to cope with the coming Population Explosion among persons age 65 and older.**

Roxbury Elder Institute Credentials: Senior Service Experiences. The Roxbury Elder Institute is uniquely positioned to develop an integrated system of medical and nonhealth services. The Institute was established six years ago with its goal to provide quality health, education, and research services. As a result, it has established a full range of services in response to the seniors' needs. During this time, positive working relationships have been established with all sectors in the Shelby County healthcare community. These working relations will provide entrees to develop the nonmedical component. **This project represents a systematic continuation of prior efforts to establish a diversified continuum of services and the vision to reallocate existing resources to meet the needs of the elderly.**

Budget Request: $250,000 payable over three years. With the demonstrated concern that you have shown in the delivery of senior services, I am requesting a grant in the amount of $250,000, payable in thirds over three years. Quite frankly, this project extends beyond the financial boundaries of the Roxbury Elder Institute. Accordingly we must now reach out to the community for assistance in what surely is a vital service to seniors. In making this investment, the Senior Foundation will be supporting a cost-effective, client-sensitive service that will address major access problems. More precisely, our 50,000 senior citizens average 10 health-related visits per year; **your support represents an investment of 5¢ per patient visit.**

Ms. Beatrice J. Hiccock, Administrative Director of the Roxbury Elder Institute, can be reached at 615-456-7890 to answer questions or give further information.

Sincerely,

Shandel Lear
President

P.S. I can't stress enough how much your support will improve the quality of life for our senior citizens.

REQUEST FOR COORDINATION OF SERVICE DELIVERY

EXHIBIT 32 (Continued from page 81)

proposals to sponsors when they **do** have submission guidelines to be followed.

A growing number of foundations use what is called a "common application form," a phrase that can be used in your favorite search engine to find current examples used in larger cities (e.g., the Association of Baltimore Area Grantmakers—www.abagmd.org), states (e.g., the Minnesota Council on Foundations—www.mcf.org), and regions (e.g., Philanthropy Northwest—www.philanthropynw.org). The common application form typically includes a cover letter, participating funders list, cover sheet, narrative instructions, attachments list, and budget page.

Whether the sponsor requires use of a common application form or has a unique one, you can adapt the letter proposal format described above to serve as a transmittal letter. Sometimes, a sponsor's guidelines may be constraining, not letting you present all of the information you think reviewers need to know. Accordingly, the transmittal letter approach enables you to supplement the sponsor's guidelines with additional important information.

Orienting Observations

Exhibit 33 is an example of a letter proposal adapted for use as a transmittal letter. In this situation, the applicant, a local fire department, was seeking federal funding to improve their services to the frail minority elderly in their community. The grant development team at the fire station found the application form somewhat constraining. They decided to adapt the letter proposal template and use it as a transmittal letter, enabling them to highlight key proposal content and actually include a few summary statements that were not requested in the application guidelines.

Specific Comments

Content. Experienced grant writers consider application guidelines as merely guides, not as limitations. While you want to respond to all of the requested information, include additional information you feel

---

Today's Date

Federal Emergency Management Agency
USFA Grant Program Technical Assistance Center
16825 South Seton Avenue
Emmitsburg, MD 21727-8898

RE: FIRE Grant Proposal
Northshore (WI) Fire District

Dear Colleague:

Northshore Fire District, Milwaukee's suburban community with the greatest population density, invites your investment of $50,000 in a fire prevention project for the frail minority elderly that will save lives—and lifetimes.

Enclosed you will find the required original and two copies of our proposal, entitled PROJECT FIRE. As you review specific details in the accompanying proposal, you will note in particular the following:

- The frail minority elderly represents the most rapidly growing—and most at-risk—segment of our community population.
- The existing firefighting staff have had limited experience in interacting with the target population and their special needs.
- There is a growing need for a culturally sensitive fire prevention program that will decrease exposure of the minority elderly to fire hazards while, at the same time, increase their fire safety.

Accordingly, this proposal offers dual benefits to: (1) firefighters, through customized training and access to essential resources; and, (2) citizens, through installing and training in fire detection devices.

The proposed program is decidedly cost beneficial to firefighters and the community alike. All direct firefighters will participate in PROJECT FIRE at a nominal opportunity cost, while 1000 citizens will benefit at a one-penny per hour cost, amortized over a five-year product life.

NFD is uniquely postured to conduct this project, which is similar to an early project targeting at-risk youth, a project recognized by the Governor of Wisconsin as a "model youth fire safety project." However, given the population size at risk among the frail minority elderly, this proposed project simply extends beyond the financial boundaries of the community. For this reason, we reach out to FEMA in providing essential services to a worthy, deserving, and needy population.

Sincerely,

Matt Hazard
NFD Fire Chief

LETTER PROPOSAL ADAPTED AS TRANSMITTAL LETTER

EXHIBIT 33

RERC Concept Paper

Today's Date

Dr. Melissa Moyer, Program Officer
Rehabilitation Engineer Research Centers
Rehabilitation Services Administration
U.S. Department of Education
400 Maryland, SW
Washington, DC 20202

Dear Dr. Moyer:

This brief letter presents our current concept of an inter-institution, interdisciplinary proposal to create a Rehabilitation Engineering Research Center for Low Vision and Blindness and invites your candid feedback.

Overview: The National Association of Rehabilitation Engineers (NARE), the world's largest organization of engineers serving persons who are blind or visually impaired, seeks $4,950,000 over five year years to launch a Consumer-Based Rehabilitation Engineering Research Center for Low Vision and Blindness. A virtual center binds eight academic collaborators from Massachusetts Institute of Technology, University of Virginia, Florida State University, St. Norbert College, Oklahoma State University, Michigan State University, University of Iowa, City College of Los Angeles, two commercial firms: Sensory Technologies, Inc. and Vision Enhancement Systems, Inc.; and our nonprofit organization: NARE.

Need: Persons who are blind or visually impaired face substantial barriers when accessing information or moving about the environment. More precisely, they encounter major barriers when attempting to identify and evaluate the following:

Visual Displays. The exploding array of consumer electronics exacerbates the challenges the blind face to fully participate in all aspects of society. New technologies can erect information access barriers. At present, technology and marketplace considerations limit options for the blind.

Graphical User Interfaces. Attempts to master graphic information result in early frustration for young blind learners and limited career aspirations for blind adults seeking gainful employment. Assistive technology developers must follow universal design standards and conventions for interoperability. Many constraining factors impede graphical user interfaces for the blind.

Signage. Currently three major technologies have been used to reduce access barriers to signage information: infrared technology, radio frequency identification technology, and global positioning satellite technology. Infrared technology applications are limited and only work best in controlled environmental settings. RFID tags have multiple advantages, although human applications remain underdeveloped. GPS systems need further refinement to be of value as blind persons move about metropolitan areas. These barriers must be reduced from the perspective of the consumers who represent the litmus test of user satisfaction.

Hypotheses/Questions: Eight specific research and development projects cluster into three thematic areas: visual displays, graphical user interface systems, and signage. Each project has specific research hypotheses or questions as well as outcomes indicating what will be different at the end of the project period.

Methods: To address the three primary project areas, eight different research/development teams will concentrate on the following topics: developing accessible environmental systems; a nanobiotechnology approach to a dynamic tactile tablet; Web annotation software; alternative graphical display, RFID tags, sign location and recognition technology; low vision enhancement solutions; and multi-modal I/O systems.

LETTER PROPOSAL ADAPTED AS CONCEPT PAPER

EXHIBIT 34

Training/Dissemination: Multiple training and dissemination strategies include an Online Campus linked to the NARE network, poster sessions, Web sites, conferences, demonstrations, site visits, Web casts, teleconferences, consumer summaries, journal articles, press releases, and conference papers—targeted to consumers, vocational rehabilitation professionals, university professors and students, and clinicians.

Evaluation: Throughout the project period, formative and summative evaluations will be conducted by internal and external evaluators. The Project Director and eight Project PIs will conduct internal evaluations using their measurable objectives and timelines as benchmarks. Additionally, two external evaluator consultants will independently assess (1) the R&D projects, and (2) the training activities and the overall Center functioning.

Outcomes: The project outcomes go beyond reducing barriers in the three priority areas. More importantly, they expedite the transfer of technology from the research laboratory to the marketplace, technologies that are driven by broad-based consumer demands.

Dr. Moyer, thanks for taking the time to see whether this concept paper matches with your program priorities. I'll call you in 10 days to learn your feedback.

Sincerely,

Otto Jaskolski, Ph.D.
Executive Director

P.S. We share your continued commitment to serving people with special needs.

LETTER PROPOSAL ADAPTED AS CONCEPT PAPER

EXHIBIT 34 (Continued from page 84)

essential, even if it is not requested. Frankly, some grant guidelines are not well conceived.

Format. A writing challenge arises when you have to put 10 pounds of information in a one pound package. The solution to squeezing a lot of information in a limited space? Rely on priorities learned from your preproposal contacts and apply your best editorial writing skills, as evidenced in this 289 word version.

LETTER PROPOSAL AS A CONCEPT PAPER FOR FEDERAL GOVERNMENT GRANTS

Orienting Observations

Our final application of the letter proposal template concerns its use with federal government grants. Most government proposals are lengthy and require substantial time and effort in their development. Exhibit 34 shows how the letter proposal template can be modified and used as a concept paper to seek preliminary proposal feedback before developing a full length proposal.

Specific Comments

Content. Exhibit 34 uses the 611 words in this letter proposal template as an economical trial balloon to determine whether the idea merits the substantial energies required to write a full-length federal government proposal.

Format. The persuasive writing challenge is to present enough information so the program officer can see the merit of your idea, but avoid getting bogged down in lengthy details. The solution is to concentrate on the statement of the need, the rationale for conducting this project. If program officers think you have identified a significant problem, then they are apt to encourage submission of a full-length proposal, recognizing that methodological details will be forthcoming in the expanded version. On the other hand, if your proposal idea does not match with program priorities, you have saved valuable time by seeking a different sponsor to support your project. Experience shows that most program officers are willing to review a concept paper—also called a "White Paper" in some mission-oriented agencies—when given sufficient lead time, say, two months before the proposal deadline.

Clip File Action Item # 11
Letter Proposals

Start your Letter Proposals clip file by doing the following:

- Select two letter proposals from this chapter and create electronic copies as models.
- Add an electronic copy of a letter proposal used as a transmittal letter (Exhibit 33).
- Choose sample electronic paragraphs for all seven sections of a letter proposal that can be edited and adapted as you write your next one.
- Re-examine all of the letter proposal examples and notice the different P.S. statements. Psychologically, many people read the salutation, signature and P.S. statement in a letter *before* reading its body. The P.S. helps establish a positive mindset as the reader studies your letter. Make a list of P.S. statements to include in your clip file. Use these as a starting point.

PART III

Writing Government Proposals

OVERVIEW OF PART III

A complete government proposal usually requires substantial detail; most include eight basic sections. The following table lists those sections in the sequence that proposal reviewers typically read them and the sequence that proposal writers usually write them; they are not the same. The sequence which one follows to write a proposal differs from the order reviewers follow when reading a proposal.

The reviewer column shows the way in which most proposals are assembled for mailing and reviewed by specialists; the writer column shows the progression followed when authoring a government proposal. For example, to begin writing your proposal, start with the need section first.

In contrast to proposals to private sponsors, which typically involve two to five pages, a complete government proposal to a local, state, or federal agency may range from 10 double-spaced pages to 100+ single-spaced pages. A few government agencies use a two-tier application process; that is, they initially require a letter of intent or short proposal before accepting a full proposal. Sponsors typically request a letter of intent when they want to know in advance how many full proposals to expect. On the other hand, sponsors may use short proposals as a screening device: only a select number of applicants with projects of the greatest interest are invited to submit a longer and more detailed proposal.

Part III discusses each proposal section and its following elements:

- Purpose
- Key questions to answer as you begin writing
- Examples from successful grant proposals
- Writing tips
- Rejection reasons from actual proposals that were declined

Not all public proposals require all of these sections, so you should follow your grant guidelines. Finally, successful grant writers sometimes include valuable information, even if it was not requested. For example, if no dissemination discussion is requested, include it in your methods section. If no needs statement is called for, include it when you introduce your agency's mission.

Proposal Reviewer Sequence	Proposal Writer Sequence
Abstract/Summary	Need or Problem (Chapter 7)
Need or Problem	Goals, Objectives, Outcomes (Chapter 8)
Goals, Objectives, Outcomes	Methods (Chapter 9)
Methods	Evaluation (Chapter 10)
Evaluation	Dissemination (Chapter 11)
Dissemination	Budget (Chapter 12)
Budget	Appendixes (Chapter 13)
Appendixes	Abstract/Summary (Chapter 14)

CHAPTER 7
Statement of Problem

A problem is a chance for you to do your best.
—Duke Ellington

PURPOSE OF THE PROBLEM STATEMENT

To Duke Ellington, a problem was music to his ears. For grantmakers, a problem statement answers one primary question: "Why do this project?" The emphasis is on the "why." To answer this question, grant writers must (1) define the problem and (2) document its existence. Effective grants produce change. Your statement of problem describes precisely and persuasively why change is necessary.

DEFINING THE PROBLEM

Beginning grant writers typically make three mistakes in defining their problem statement. They may define it from their perspectives, not the sponsors; they may—in reality—end up describing opportunities and not needs; or they may define their project using circular logic. Each grant writing trap is discussed below.

When we ask beginning grantseekers why they want a grant, typical answers include the following:

- "We lack sufficient resources to serve our frail elderly population."
- "Our agency needs sufficient operating support to meet our growing client demands."
- "We want a new roof for our building."

Unfortunately, these problem statements all share one common difficulty: they are written from the perspective of the applicant, not the sponsor.

Experienced grant writers avoid the self-focus and instead concentrate on the sponsor's needs when writing this proposal section. Why? Because seasoned grant writers recognize that sponsors won't fund you because you have a need; rather, sponsors will fund you because you can be a change agent to solve a problem they consider important. Grantmakers award grants when you enable them to do something about a major problem or issue that makes a positive difference. **Sponsors fund their needs, not yours.**

Let's take a closer look at the difference between your needs and the sponsors. In Exhibit 35, the first column lists a few of the reasons why applicants write grants. The second column lists major reasons why grants fulfill sponsor needs. The two columns are quite different. Proposal writers who base their problem statement on the first-column items severely limit their likelihood of getting funded. A more successful approach would be to frame your problem statement from the perspective of the sponsor. When sponsors see you share their "values glasses," you increase your odds for funding success.

A second mistake of beginning grant writers is to describe an opportunity instead of a need. They reason, "Our organization doesn't really have a need. We see grants as an opportunity to expand our outreach into the community, to do more and better things." Such a perspective fails to recognize that sponsors focus on their concerns, not your. To sponsors, your wants and needs are opportunities; sponsors award funds to solve the societal needs that they see. Sponsors fund you when they believe that your project will help them solve their need to close gaps in society. Funding you helps them fulfill their mission. Said differently, there are no solutions to opportunities. When you write your next proposal, be sure you present the sponsor with a problem, not an opportunity. **Sponsors fund needs, not opportunities.**

As a third writing pitfall, grantseekers often use circular proposal logic. To illustrate, grant proposals

Applicant Needs	Sponsor Needs
• Ensure operating support	• Solve a societal need
• Expand services	• Fulfill existing mission
• Acquire new training materials	• Acquire new knowledge
• Make capital improvements	• Apply existing knowledge
• Purchase new technology	• Improve the community
• Obtain endowment funding	• Benefit from tax write-offs
• Support existing programs	• Increase name recognition
• Meet payroll costs	• Ensure a big bang for the buck
• Market services	• Help people
• Acquire new physical space	• Fill a gap in community services
• Run a conference	• Improve public image
• Conduct research	• Avoid loss
• Sustain operations	• Develop new products, systems

COMPARISON OF APPLICANT AND SPONSOR NEEDS

EXHIBIT 35

may seek support for new equipment, e.g., computers or highly technical research instruments. The proposal logic often argues as follows.

> The problem is that our institution lacks (and therefore needs) some new computer equipment. The objective of our proposal is to acquire the computer equipment. Our implementation strategy is to plan to acquire the equipment and put it to good use. Our evaluation plan will be to find out if we acquired and used the equipment.

This example used circular logic to form its problem statement; no real need was established first, the starting point for proposals. A much stronger approach would have been as follows.

> The problem is that our students' failure rate is too high in five key courses. Our objective is to decrease the failure rate from 40% to 30% in the next three years. Our implementation strategy, chosen from among many, is to acquire some new computer equipment. Our evaluation plan will focus on our implementation plan execution and see if the failure rate decreases.

The lack of something does not justify acquisition: that's circular logic. Note the revised example quantifies a problem, thereby creating a need that can be addressed in other proposal sections.

In sum, your statement of the problem should quickly summarize the problem from the vantage point of the sponsor as revealed through your preproposal contacts (Chapter 4), document its frequency and severity, show your familiarity with prior research or work on the problem, reinforce your credibility for investigating the problem, and justify why this problem should be investigated. Do not assume that everyone sees the problem as clearly as you do. Even if the problem is obvious, your reviewers want to know how clearly you can state it.

DOCUMENTING THE PROBLEM

By definition, a problem is a gap, a discrepancy between the way things are and the way things ought to be. To persuade proposal reviewers that you have identified a significant problem, you must present two data points or lines that are separated by a gap. Suppose, for example, that you are a high school principal who wants to upgrade your computer laboratory. What, then, are your two data points?

- **Data Line A:** The increasing need to train computer literate students in the 21st century.
  As educators, you recognize that computers are a means to an end of training computer literate students, a need that has grown over time as evidenced by the increase in such things as iPods, scanning machines at checkout counters, ATM machines at

banks, Internet information explosions, and the deluge of information technology devices.

- **Data Line B:** The growing obsolescence of existing computers in your computer laboratory.

Given the rapid changes in computer technology, machines must be replaced on a regular basis. Computer memories increase and processing speeds accelerate. New software requires increased capacity. Existing machines malfunction over time and through heavy use. Existing computer capacities will decrease over time unless upgrades occur.

Your proposal narrative could document the following:

- The **frequency** of the problem: how often do computer malfunctions occur, how much instruction time is affected, to what extent have student complaints increased.
- The **severity** of the problem: students perform poorer than peers on computerized academic achievement exams, future employment opportunities are affected, parents become disenchanted with the quality of instruction provided at school.
- The **consequences** of not addressing the problem: students have restricted access to information, the computer literacy of students is constrained, the school system is less able to fulfill its instructional responsibilities.

Visually, you could graph your statement of the problem to show how your gap is widening over time, as Exhibit 36 indicates.

Your gap analysis tells your sponsor that the demand for computer literacy grows while the capacity of your instructional tools to meet that demand has been declining over time.

As you write you next proposal, conduct your gap analysis. What is your A Line and your B Line? Consider the following brief problem statements that could be graphed as shown in Exhibit 37.

The A/B gaps may exist for multiple reasons. Perhaps stakeholders are unaware that the problem exists, that it doesn't appear on the "radar" screen of many people. Perhaps stakeholders are aware of the problem but unable to do anything about it because they lack the human, fiscal, or physical resources necessary to solve it. Perhaps stakeholders know about the problem and are able to solve it but are unwilling to do so because of attitudes or beliefs that they hold. Your gap discussions can address the reasons why you think they exist.

As you write your statement of the problem, what are your A and B lines? If you don't have clear answers, then you need more conceptual clarity before you start writing. Reviewing the preproposal contact questions in Chapter 4 may help you defuzzify your problem statement.

Finally, you should regard the statement of the problem as the single most important section of your proposal that influences funding success. The statement of the need is so important in proposals that it should be stressed regardless of the point value assigned to it in the reviewer's evaluation form. That is, the need section may or may not receive the

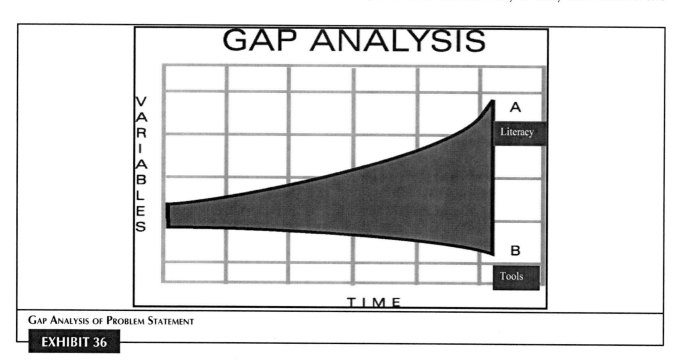

GAP ANALYSIS OF PROBLEM STATEMENT

EXHIBIT 36

Statement of Problem	A Line	B Line
Inadequate healthcare services exist in Eastern Tennessee, despite the fact that access to basic health care is a fundamental right.	Multiple indices show a growth in health problems and a decrease in the quality of life.	The number of healthcare providers has remained constant.
Living conditions in New Orleans' Lower 9th Ward remains devastated due to Hurricane Katrina.	Roads, utilities, and habitable facilities are devastated.	No multidisciplinary comprehensive plan exists for restoring, reconstructing, and resettling the Lower 9th Ward.
Youth suicide is a significant health issue in Wyoming.	State vital records show suicide is the second leading cause of death among teenagers and is growing each year.	The number of schools with suicide prevention programs remains low and has remained constant over time.

EXAMPLES OF A/B GAPS

EXHIBIT 37

highest point total, based on the reviewer's evaluation form. Nevertheless, *you* should consider it as the most important proposal section, since it will weigh most heavily in the minds of reviewers.

KEY QUESTIONS TO ANSWER

As you write your statement of problem, answer these questions. Does your proposal:

1. Specify the conditions you wish to change?
2. Define the gaps in existing programs, services, or knowledge?
3. Include appropriate statistical data about the frequency and severity of the problem?
4. Clarify what will happen if nothing is done about this problem?
5. State the problem in terms of human needs, not your opportunities?
6. Cite pertinent theoretical literature, research findings, or ongoing studies?
7. Convey the focus of your project early in the narrative?
8. Establish the importance and significance of the problem from the sponsor's perspective?
9. Point out the relationship of your project to a larger set of problems or issues?
10. Supply an appropriate and compelling introduction to the rest of the application?

Use this list both as a guide to develop your statement of the need and as a checklist to critique your draft, making sure you have included all essential elements.

EXAMPLES OF PROBLEM STATEMENTS

As you read the following examples, note the repeated emphasis on two points:

1. The frequency and severity of the current problem or need
2. The failure of the status quo to address the need

Example 1

This grant proposal from a social service agency is seeking foundation funding to expand its outreach to underserved people.

> Although the Family Crisis Center is currently operating at near capacity, the Center intends to reach more fully those families who are underserved. This group includes minority citizens, senior citizens, and individuals with disabilities. While approximately 5% of the general population in our catchment area uses the service of the Center, minorities and others do not traditionally use our services. In addition, the newly appointed Coordinator for Community Outreach Services has identified for the first time the community's population with disabilities—a potential new target group for specialized services.

The gap? The Center's disparity between its heavy service demands and its need to serve other clients. This needs statement is unpersuasive because it focuses on the needs of the Center: to add more staffing so it can do a better job of serving underserved families. A more persuasive approach would concentrate on the needs of the underserved, as the following rewritten example indicates.

> Inner city, urban living—what some would call ghetto survival—is stressful. As evidence, all social service agencies report heavy demands for social services, and many have lengthy waiting lists. The primary users of social services are families with more than high school educations and above average socioeconomic status.
>
> Unfortunately, three major community groups are notably underrepresented among social service agencies: minorities, seniors, and the handicapped. Each group faces special stressors that are further exacerbated by their urban environment. Most social service agencies have a monocultural staff, yet serve a multicultural clientele. Seniors face transportation barriers in traveling through what they perceive to be risky neighborhoods to receive various medical services. Minorities often distrust welfare agencies. The handicapped face substantial architectural barriers in moving through urban neighborhoods.
>
> Since the Faith and Justice Foundation and the Family Crisis Center share the same mission of serving the needs of all community residents, we invite your investment in the following project.

This revised need statement refocuses the gap on the inconsistency between the service needs of special populations (A Line) and their ability to obtain those services (B Line).

Example 2

This example is taken from an application for a research proposal submitted to a social and rehabilitation service agency to evaluate the comparative effectiveness of different types of service and income maintenance programs. This short excerpt is included to show you an approach for tying the statement of need at the local level to an interest of the funding agency itself.

> The national investment in social welfare demonstration projects continues to expand, yet the local consequences of these projects on client and family functioning have been only partially evaluated. Without careful assessment, the relative merits of any given project will be lost or incorrectly estimated while errors may be repeated if the project serves as a prototype.
>
> A favorable set of conditions allowing a careful assessment has arisen in a demonstration project jointly sponsored by the Bureau of Health and Family Services and the Department of Public Welfare. The State Department of Public Welfare has created four groups of AFDC clients who will receive various combinations of increased services assistance.

What is the gap in this example? The information void between national activities being provided (A Line) and their impact at the local level (B Line).

Example 3

This research proposal suggests a new way to produce a substance thought to cure certain types of cancer.

> Convincing evidence exists that interferon is a powerful antiviral and antitumor substance. Wide medical application of interferon therapy will depend upon production of large quantities at a price the public can afford. It is doubtful whether the current technology of cell culture will be economical enough to allow mass production of this material. Other alternatives include organic syntheses or productive insertion of the interferon gene into microorganisms. The proposed research offers a lead to both procedures, thereby opening the door to application of interferon therapy beyond a few clinical trials. Success in any one of the steps outlined in this proposal would be a major breakthrough in achieving progress toward eventual use of interferon in the treatment of human disease.
>
> Human interferon has only recently been obtained in preparations approaching homogeneity. The amounts of such highly purified preparations, available only in the laboratories where they have been produced, are exceedingly small. Partially purified preparations of human interferon, on the other hand, are commercially available.

The gap? The growing need for crucial medications (A Line) continually outstrips the capacity of current technologies to produce sufficient quantities (B Line). This proposal need section went on to delimit the specific topic and show its possible contribution. The sentences are short and use simple syntactic structures, making it easy for a reviewer to follow a technical topic.

Example 4

This hospital-based bioethics proposal was submitted to a federal health care agency. Note the use of subheadings to help organize the various dimensions of the overall needs statement.

Overview of Need for Bioethical Sensitivity. While the relevance and rectitude of ethics in medicine are indisputable, their extent and form produce far less agreement. Ethics often has a second-class status in medical school training and subsequent patient management; both situations add to the ethical insensitivity prevalent in the contemporary world. Moreover, the complexities of the human condition require specialized and applied knowledge. The following paragraphs elaborate on the multiple dimensions of the need for this project.

Growing Insensitivity to Ethical Issues. The world has been described as becoming increasingly amoral. The prevalence of major ethical problems in the popular press, such as gambling among athletes, swindles in the ministry, or political sex scandals, underscore a lack of ethical sensitivity. While the mass media has made the public well aware of the ethical problems, the scope of the problems in bioethics is less popularized but more prevalent and includes such issues as the following:

- Use of artificial heart as a bridge to transplant
- Economic dilemmas in ethical decision making
- Involuntary medical detention
- Withdrawal of tube feeding
- Forgoing CPR in elderly patients

In reality, many clinicians encounter these ethical decisions, and others, on a daily basis. Relegating ethics to a second-class status in medical training programs and practice, in effect, contributes to our society's lack of ethical awareness. Certainly, colleges and universities need a more salient and explicit focus on the legitimacy of ethics to nurture the moral sensitivity of its students and of its local community.

Conflicting Trends in Biomedical Ethics. The study of ethics has become increasingly compartmentalized and applied, with specialists in such areas as nursing ethics, physician ethics, and patient ethics. These targeted emphases are notably deficient in the study of the theoretical principles of ethical decision making. Ironically, the "technologizing" of ethics education has developed at the same time as a renewed national emphasis on holistic medicine.

In an analysis of trends in ethics, Marcus Singer noted that "The first thing to be said about ethics in this day and place is that it is different—different from what it was and has been and in the process of becoming what it is going to be." Philosophers automatically think of ethics as identical with moral philosophy. But there is a sense of ethics gaining currency in which it is not a branch of philosophy, in which ethics is regarded as a new, independent (yet interdisciplinary) subject, exercising the skills of physicians, psychologists, lawyers, economists, sociologists, scientists, and others who would not normally think of themselves as doing philosophy.

Distortion of Ethics Studies by Specialization. Ethics has a sweeping interdisciplinary nature with a multifaceted relevance to theoretical, characterological, professional, and theological domains. Consequently, the clinical application of ethical principles cannot be limited to a single discipline without producing a restricted and distorted sense of ethics. This constrained focus divorces ethics from its true richness as a central facet of the human experience and from the history of human intellectual and spiritual achievement. As one ethicist recently argued, "Is there one unitary discipline, ethics, somehow involved in these otherwise apparently diverse areas of environment, ecology, science, medicine, biology, engineering, technology, law, government, and business? This is not a question that can be answered merely a priori and in advance; it must wait for reasonable settlement until each of these areas has been explored further and until a better grasp than we have now is achieved of the underlying structure of ethical or moral problems in each of these areas of human endeavors."

Prevalence of Ethics Training in Medical Schools. According to the American Medical School Association (2007), all medical schools recognize the importance of ethics training and include it in their curricula. A closer look, however, reveals a number of training gaps. First, only 18% of the 127 medical schools in the United States offer a specific ethics course. Most medical schools include it as a teaching unit in clinical courses. Typically, one to two hours of ethics training is included in courses taken in each specialization area, e.g., family practice, internal medicine, or radiology. As a consequence, the average medical student receives 20–30 hours of ethics-related training, which is usually taught by a physician with little or no training in philosophy or bioethics. As a result, there is an ever widening gap between the need for bioethics expertise and the training provided in medical schools, which has plateaued for years.

The gap? The growing demand for bioethics expertise resulting from advances in medicine and technology (A line) and the steady-state training provided by medical schools (B line).

WRITING TIPS FOR THE PROBLEM SECTION

1. Describe the problem, its causes, and the consequences, if left alone.
2. Describe the need in human terms. For example, if you want to buy a van for your health clinic, talk about the transportation barriers that patients encounter when getting access to the health care to which they are entitled.
3. Review preproposal contact questions in Chapter 4. They were all focused towards pinpointing the problem. They followed a logical progress from analyzing the baseline position, existing rationale, future expectations, and priorities that lead to the needs.
4. In your literature review, check on currently funded (but unpublished) research-in-progress. Contact the National Technical Information Service. They serve as a clearinghouse for recently initiated projects and can provide you with information at a nominal charge which indicates who might be doing something similar to what you propose. Their Web address is www.ntis.gov.
5. Beyond discussing the importance of the project's topic, you should also demonstrate the need for your methodology; that is, the reviewers should be able to anticipate your solution based upon your analysis of the problem. The ability to foreshadow a solution from the problem statement represents a very logical, fluent writing technique.
6. Don't say "little is known about...," "there is a lack of information about...," or "no research dealt with...." Arguing for something that isn't is a weak need statement; it's circular logic. Go one step further. Explain the consequences of the information void. So you don't know something about this problem. So what?
7. GIS (Geographical Information Systems) can provide new ways of conducting a gap analysis for a strong problem statement on your next grant. Some local counties have qualified staff and software in their planning departments to help you analyze U.S. Census information and other local geographical data. For example, one county grant writer tapped her local Planning and Zoning experts for information on the percentage of the county that required off-road access for emergency response. The GIS experts "lifted" the roads and streets from the county map along with a margin of access along those roads and determined the percentage of the county that required off-road access in case of emergencies. She used this data to build a winning national grant. On a different public transportation grant, she asked her GIS colleagues to calculate the percentage of the land covered in her county that did not have access to the established public transit bus routes. The possibilities are endless for GIS applications and uses of GIS maps that can be generated from the software.
8. Your problem section is the "sad" section of the proposal. Use appropriate "sad" words: almost, barrier, below, bleak, bottom, decreased, deficit, dependent, depressed, desperate, destitute, disadvantaged, discouraged, disheartened, disregarded, disruption, distressed, failed, gloomy, grim, harsh, highest, high-risk, hopeless, hurdle, ignore, impaired, inadequate, increased, infested, lacking, less than, lowest, minimum, miserable, miserable, needy, neglect, obstacle, outbreak, overlooked, pathetic, pitiful, plagued, poorest, poverty, severe, sparse, substandard, trapped, unacceptable, violent, widespread, worst.
9. Five major federal agencies collect, analyze, and disseminate data on virtually all aspects of society and its individuals. Web addresses are provided in Exhibit 38.

The national "fact-finders" in Exhibit 38 are rich with data useful in most proposals. Beyond these federal agencies, consider approaching local and regional health planning councils; city, county, or regional planning departments; vocational rehabilitation agencies; crisis centers in your field; law enforcement and judicial departments; chambers of commerce; universities (libraries, academic departments, computer centers, research offices); national associations; other grantees; United Way (community resource file); and development departments in state and local governments. Don't overlook your state and federal legislators. They survive in large part by providing constituency services. They can help you find government reports on your project topics.

Agency	Web Address
Bureau of the Census—general	www.census.gov
Bureau of the Census—data sets	www.factfinder.census.gov
Bureau of Justice Statistics	www.ojp.usdoj.gov/bjs
Bureau of Labor Statistics	www.stats.bls.gov
National Center on Education Statistics	www.nces.ed.gov
National Center for Health Statistics	www.cdc.gov/nchs

FEDERAL DATA COLLECTION AGENCIES

EXHIBIT 38

REJECTION REASONS

Reviewers have rejected some proposals for the following reasons:

1. The problems to be investigated are more complex than the applicants realize.
2. The applicants need to acquire greater familiarity with the pertinent literature.
3. It is doubtful that new or useful information will result from the project.
4. The basic hypothesis is unsound.
5. The proposed research is scientifically premature; the supporting knowledge is inadequate.
6. The relationship of rationale to regional needs is not clearly delineated.
7. Some significant efforts in the State are not mentioned in the rationale.
8. The rationale is heavily based on local needs rather than regional impact.
9. The demographic analysis is not developed; implications are not explored.
10. Overall rationale is inadequate. Evidence to support training and patient care needs specific is lacking.
11. The project director appears to lack knowledge of published relevant work in this area.
12. The project codirectors fail to present an acceptable scientific rationale for conducting this project.
13. The proposal narrative often relies on State-level data to justify local needs.
14. The "Problem Statement" should be twofold: identify and quantify the healthcare needs of the community, and discuss the inadequacies of the current system to address these needs.
15. Although the proposal targets expansion in year 2 to address mental health services and

transportation issues, there is no discussion of the quantifiable need for such services.
16. This proposal offers no evidence of a formal needs assessment to identify and prioritize community needs. What sources were used to determine and prioritize the most important needs? Did this assessment solicit community input in identifying, defining, and assessing their needs?
17. The proposal does not quantify or support its claim that "The need for mental health services is great within the community."
18. This project doesn't explain why the needs of this subpopulation are greater than the needs of other community residents.
19. The applicants have great theories unsubstantiated by data.

In each case, the reviewers have serious reservations about the credibility of the investigators and/or the chosen topic area. After you write your needs statement in your next proposal, reread these rejection reasons and see if any of them cause you to say "ouch."

 Clip File Action Item # 12 Statement of Problem

Fill your clip file with data documenting the frequency and severity of the problem you propose to solve in ways that meet your sponsor's needs, not yours. Follow these tips:

- Sources of data include surveys, statistical analyses, key informants, community forums, case studies, legislative bureaus and officials, universities, community agencies, professional associations, crisis centers, chambers of commerce, planning commissions, and clearinghouses.

CHAPTER 8
Goals, Objectives, and Outcomes

*Those who cannot tell what they desire or expect, still sigh
and struggle with indefinite thoughts and vast wishes.*
—*Ralph Waldo Emerson*

PURPOSE OF GOALS

Your project goals represent the idealized dream of what you hope to accomplish. They are usually presented in terms of hopes, wishes, or desires. Goals project the "big picture" vision of what you wish to accomplish. They communicate global purposes. Typical goal-oriented words include advocate, analyze, appreciate, behave, develop, empower, enjoy, extend, feel, illustrate, improve, integrate, internalize, know, participate, promote, recommend, and understand. For instance, a recent health education proposal included four goal statements:

- To analyze the special needs of underserved populations and to develop new programs to meet those needs.
- To extend services to underserved target populations.
- To improve the quality of services while experiencing an increased demand for those services.
- To integrate new educational materials for special focus programs.

Although these are valuable goals, they cannot stand by themselves. They need to be followed by concrete, measurable objectives.

PURPOSE OF OBJECTIVES

Your objectives specify the end products of your project. When sponsors fund your project, they are literally "buying" your objectives. That's why it is extremely important to state your objectives in clear and measurable terms.

When you write your objectives, follow the acronymic advice: "Keep them S-I-M-P-L-E." Your objectives should be:

- *Specific.* Show precisely what you intend to change through your project. What will be different when your project is finished? What will people know, feel, or be able to do once the project is completed that they couldn't before?
- *Immediate.* Indicate the time frame during which a current problem will be addressed. Why should the project be acted on right now? How long will it take to achieve your goals and objectives?
- *Measurable.* Specify what you would accept as proof of project success. What qualitative and quantitative data will you gather? What tools will you use to measure project success?
- *Practical.* Point out how each objective is a real solution to a real problem. Are your objectives realistic and feasible? Does your organization have the skill, experience, qualifications, resources, and personnel to carry out each objective?
- *Logical.* Describe how each objective systematically contributes to achieving your overall goal(s). Are you really doing what you think you're doing? Do your objectives relate to your goal and the sponsor's priorities?
- *Evaluable.* Define how much change has to occur for the project to be effective. What are your criteria for success? What impact will your project make? What is the value of your project?

Although these categories are not mutually exclusive, each of your objectives should meet at least several of these criteria.

For instance, given the goal of "improving the quality of life for homeless individuals in our city," a proposal objective might be stated as follows.

> Midwest Home Shelter Agency will reduce the number of homeless [Specific] [Practical] [Logical] during the next 24 months [Immediate] by 15 percent [Evaluable] as noted in the Department of Social Welfare Homeless Survey Report [Measurable].

The following example of a goal and its objectives is taken from a demonstration project submitted to the U.S. Department of Education. The objective has several parts that meet each of the six criteria, with some overlap.

> **Goal.** This program is designed to prepare parents to function independently and effectively in helping their children develop to their own potentials.
>
> **Objectives.** During the next 18 months [Immediate] the parents who participate in the program will be able to [Specific]

- identify the education content in the events that occur in the home [Logical]
- structure sequential and cumulative instructional tasks in the home for the child [Logical]
- observe the child and use checklists to monitor progress [Measurable]
- use available equipment and processes in the home to teach children specific skills [Evaluable]
- use packaged materials prepared by the project or other agencies in teaching specific skills [Practical]

Your objectives represent the yardstick to evaluate your proposal results; that is, if you write your objectives in precise, measurable terms, it is easy to write your proposal evaluation section because you know exactly what will be evaluated.

PURPOSE OF OUTCOMES

Outcomes are the benefits, changes, or effects that occur to the target population due to participation in your project. Outcomes express project results in humanistic terms; they are the desired changes in peoples' knowledge, skills, attitudes, or behaviors. Identifying outcomes means going beyond outlining how the project will operate to describing how participants will be able to think, do, act, or behave differently by the conclusion of your project.

In the increasingly competitive world of grant-seeking, accountability is key. Sponsors want to know that their funds are being spent wisely and that your project is really making a difference in the lives of people; hence, outcomes. Your proposal must balance process and outcome statements. Process statements answer "what?" What are you going to do? Outcome statements answer the question "so what?" What are the benefits of this project to the target population?

Consider the following pairs of statements: the first describes a process, and the second describes an outcome.

Process: Provide firefighters with new communications and personal protective equipment.
Outcome: Firefighters will increase coordinated service delivery to the community and decrease average response times.
Process: Conduct 10 cultural sensitivity training courses.
Outcome: Employees will respect and value diversity.
Process: Enroll 6,000 at-risk youth in summer school classes.
Outcome: Students' academic performance will improve.
Process: Provide 10,000 free meals to low-income senior citizens.
Outcome: Senior citizens are able to remain in independent living.
Process: Have 60 undergraduate university students contribute a total of 3,600 hours to service learning projects at the Hispanic Community Center.
Outcome #1: Students will make real world connections to the local community through service, educational outreach, and employment.
Outcome #2: Continuing education adults at the Hispanic Community Center will earn their GED (General Educational Development) diplomas.
Process: Distribute 25,000 "So You're Having A Baby" educational packets to pediatric physicians' offices.
Outcome #1: Teen mothers will immunize their newborns by age two.
Outcome #2: Teen mothers will understand the value of breastfeeding their babies during the first year of life.
Outcome #3: Teen mothers will not have a repeat pregnancy until after age 18.

The final two examples illustrate that even when projects appear on the surface to be similar, they may in fact target very different outcomes. That's why prior to developing intervention strategies, you must identify outcomes that will be meaningful to your project. Outcomes borrowed from or imposed by individuals external to your organization are unlikely to be valuable to your efforts. Chapter 10 takes a closer look at evaluation and outcomes, including outcome indicators—specific characteristics selected for measurement to demonstrate success in achieving project outcomes.

KEY QUESTIONS TO ANSWER

Answer these key questions as you write your proposal objectives. Does your proposal do the following:

1. Clearly describe your project's objectives, hypotheses, and/or research questions?
2. Signal project objectives without burying them in a morass of narrative?
3. Demonstrate that your objectives are important, significant, and timely?
4. Directly address the chosen problem?
5. State your objectives in a way that they can later be evaluated or tested?
6. Demonstrate why your project outcomes are appropriate and important to the sponsor?
7. Reflect the need for the project and show clearly its purpose and direction?
8. Include one or more objectives for each need discussed in the problem statement?
9. State objectives in terms of outcomes and not methods or activities?
10. State the time by which the objectives will be accomplished?

EXAMPLES OF OBJECTIVES

Example 1

A child safety proposal from a community-based organization to a local corporation. Notice that because objectives are expressed in terms of process activities, a subsequent paragraph is included that defines humanistic outcomes for parents participating in the project.

Misuse of child safety seats is widespread. Although 95% of parents believe they install their child seat correctly, 80% of children are improperly restrained. The goal of this project is to enhance existing collaborative partnerships to prevent injuries to motor vehicle

occupants. By December 31, 2008 we will accomplish the following objectives.

Objective # 1: Offer car seat education to 500 parents attending birthing/prenatal classes at County Community Hospital.

Objective # 2: Train 50 staff members at 10 pediatric offices in our county on the importance of using car seats properly and motor vehicle safety resources available within our county.

Objective # 3: Create 10,000 educational packets to be distributed at birthing/prenatal classes and pediatric offices, promoting car seat safety checks and other community resources.

We will measure the intended effects that this program is trying to produce on parents' knowledge, attitudes, and behaviors. Specifically, the outcomes of this project are to enable parents to better identify, access, and use community resources that will help prevent unintentional childhood injuries. Increasing parents' knowledge of community resources will motivate them to participate in car seat checks at local fitting stations, i.e., police stations, fire departments, and hospitals. Education provided at fitting stations, in turn, will prompt behavior changes so parents continue to install and use care seats correctly.

Example 2

This example is taken from a Blood Center seeking private foundation funding for a hemophilia proposal.

Goal: Modern care for all persons affected by hemophilia, related bleeding disorders, and complications of those disorders or their treatment, including HIV infection. By the target date of July 1, 2010, four objectives will be met.

Objective 1: 90 percent of the identified persons with hemophilia at risk of HIV infection enrolled in comprehensive care programs will be tested for HIV status with appropriate pre- and post-test counseling, with maximum consideration to confidentiality.

Objective 2: 80 percent of persons with hemophilia, all their identified sexual partners, and their families will be provided with comprehensive risk-reduction information and psychosocial counseling and support.

Objective 3: 100 percent of the hemophilia treatment centers will offer hemophilia and HIV-related medical and psychosocial care to sexual partners and offspring of persons with hemophilia, with consideration given to their independent needs.

Objective 4: 90 percent of persons identified with severe hemophilia will have access to medically supervised home therapy.

Example 3

A recent wastewater management RFP (Request for Proposals) from the Environmental Protection Agency asked for a distinction between primary and secondary objectives. Further, it wanted objectives to be classified by type. A local community-based organization submitted a proposal for a decentralized wastewater demonstration project. Their proposal presented the objectives in a table format as indicated in Exhibit 39.

Work Plan Objectives	
Primary Objectives	
Type	**Objective**
Needs Assessment and Analysis	By January 2009, identify and prioritize wastewater management needs responsive to local deficiencies
Planning	By February 2009, develop a local model for addressing rural wastewater management needs
Financing	By March 2009, secure project financing
Community Capacity Development	By April 2009, develop local capacity to effectively administer rural wastewater management systems
Project Management and Coordination	By May 2009, maximize project administration through shared local governance
Construction	By June 2009, implement designs resulting from local needs assessment
Education and Outreach	By July 2009, report local project accomplishments and management model to state and national audiences
Evaluation (Outcome)	By August 2009, complete the assessment of the benefits and changes to local public health and environment as the project ends

Secondary Objectives	
Type	**Objective**
Financing	By September 2009, identify and assess public and private financing options
Community Capacity Development	By October 2009, develop local capacity to design, construct, operate, inspect, maintain, and repair rural wastewater treatment systems
Project Management and Coordination	By November 2009, develop and maintain a process to manage and coordinate the project with maximum local community involvement
Construction	By November 2009, develop design alternatives and create a local construction plan
Education and Outreach	By December 2009, create an education and outreach plan for local residents to encourage further installations
Evaluation (Process)	By December 2009, monitor local progress in evaluating repairs and installations of wastewater treatment

SAMPLE WORK PLAN OBJECTIVES

EXHIBIT 39

Example 4

The following example from a proposal to USAID (U.S. Agency for International Development) presents a goal statement and eight measurable objectives for an international health project targeting individuals (called internally displaced persons) living near camps in Northern Uganda.

Project Goal

Our project goal presents the "big picture" vision of what we wish to accomplish. It communicates our desired long-term outcomes. This project goal matches isomorphically with the purpose of the Request for Application, namely...

To increase the delivery of HIV/AIDS and infectious disease services (Tuberculosis and malaria) with a focus on Internally Displaced People (IDP) living beyond the municipalities in the insecure Acholi and Lango subregions in Uganda.

Specific Measurable Objectives

The project objectives specify the end products of this project. They show what will change in concrete terms over the course of the next five years. The objectives cluster into three categories: training, service delivery, and systemic capacity building, which are listed below for Year One only. Subsequent years will follow the same objectives, although the numbers will likely increase by at least 15%, since out-years will not have the project start-up responsibilities found in the first two months of this project.

1. To prevent HIV infection in 750,000 individuals
2. To prevent HIV mother-to-child transmission in 4,500 individuals
3. To provide HIV and TB counseling and testing to 15,000 individuals
4. To provide palliative care to 15,570 individuals, excluding those with TB
5. To provide palliative care to 1,250 individuals with TB
6. To provide anti-retroviral theraphy (ART) drug services to 1,769 individuals
7. To provide infrastructure support to 15 laboratories
8. To support five local organizations with systemic capacity building

The action items supporting each of these eight objectives are described in detail in the Project Implementation Plan, which is a separate document accompanying this proposal and incorporated herein by reference. The collective outcome of these objectives is that new structures, systems and roles will be defined, thereby providing staff with a new infrastructure to increase their skills to deliver improved HIV/AIDS, malaria and tuberculosis services to persons in Northern Uganda.

This was a large scale, interdisciplinary, intercontinental proposal involving approximately 50 health providers. Because this proposal was going to be read by health specialists in several countries, the proposal writer thought it wise to present an operational definition of "goal" and "objectives" since these terms may not carry the same meaning across cultures.

Example 5

An asthma management project from a community health coalition to a national private foundation.

The **goal** of this project is to develop a sustainable strategy for asthma management in the community. By October 31, 2008, we will accomplish the following key **objectives.**

- Significantly improve asthma-related qualify of life among children participating in coalition intervention activities.
- Reduce missed school and childcare days by 25% among children participating in coalition intervention activities.
- Reduce the number of children admitted for acute asthma at the Midwest Pediatric Hospital by 15%.
- Reduce the number of children making emergency visits for asthma to five area hospitals by 15%.
- Institutionalize the coalition and develop a financially sustainable strategy for childhood asthma control.

We recognize that measuring outcomes for some objectives will be more challenging than others, for example, asthma-related qualify of life among children under age five. Thus, survey tools selected will balance statistical reliability, validity, and responsiveness; cultural relevance and sensitivity; and be minimally burdensome for community members. Collectively, these objectives contribute to achieving our ultimate outcome goal: to control asthma in the county's high-risk pediatric population.

Example 6

A chemistry research proposal to NIH (National Institutes of Health). The application form uses the language "Specific Aims," which means the same as "Objectives."

> **Specific Aims:** Considerable attention has recently been focused on the use of phospholipid bilayer vesicles as a means for encapsulating and delivering antitumor agents to neoplastic cells. Although there have been some encouraging signs, the ultimate therapeutic value of this technique remains unclear. The basic premise underlying this proposal is that carriers of the type currently being examined have limited potential and that new ones need to be developed which are more stable and offer better control over drug delivery. Our immediate chemical objective is to synthesize and characterize four new classes of phospholipid carriers within the next two years. One carrier is based on vesicles whose lipids contain two polar head groups, each of which is covalently attached to the terminal positions of a rigid hydrocarbon chain.
>
> Based on close analogy with surfactant analogs recently described in the literature, these molecules should yield monolayer phospholipid vesicles. A second type of carrier is based on vesicles comprised of phospholipid dimers covalently coupled at the polar head group. The third and fourth classes of carriers we propose are polymerized forms of micelles and vesicles, and are termed, ultrastable micelles and ultrastable vesicles. Each of the above has been specifically designed to equip the drug delivery vehicle with (1) greater intrinsic stability, (2) slower and more controllable time-release action, (3) preferred endocytotic and adsorption modes of interaction with cells, and (4) greater targeting potential.

NIH uses two terms relevant to this chapter: "Broad, long-term objectives" and "Specific Aims." As the terms are defined in this chapter and commonly used in many grant sectors, the phrase "Broad, long-term objectives" is equivalent to "goals" and "Specific Aims" is interchangeable with "specific, measurable objectives." NIH recommends allocating one page to a discussion of Specific Aims. In practical terms, successful NIH grantseekers begin this section with a short paragraph describing the context for the Specific Aims. A fuller discussion of the application background is provided in another NIH proposal section. The Specific Aims describe what the research is intended to accomplish. The discussion should include the hypothesis to be tested and usually avoids methodological details, again a topic discussed in another proposal section.

Example 7

A chemistry research proposal to NSF (National Science Foundation). This writing approach uses questions as a technique for stating proposal objectives.

> The chemistry of molecular oxygen compounds has been studied extensively. Yet a number of basic questions remain unanswered. This reality is particularly true for the electronic and vibrational spectra of these compounds. The questions we propose to address are
>
> 1. What is the range of v(02) and its relationship with the M-02 (M: a metal) bond strength?
> 2. Does v(02) reflect the effect of the axial and equatorial legends?
> 3. Where are the M-02 CT bonds responsible for the embracement of v(02) and v(MO) in resonance Raman spectroscopy?
> 4. Is it possible to prepare novel symmetrical, side-on adducts with large legends such as metalloporphyrins?
>
> The objectives of our systematic spectroscopic study are to examine the effects of molecular oxygen adducts on a number of CO (11) chelates. The techniques employed include UV-visible, enforced, resonance Raman, and C-13 NMR spectroscopy.

Beyond the use of questions, note the last two sentences serve as a transitional bridge to the methodology section. This approach provides continuity in a proposal that flows smoothly between sections.

The NSF application guidelines indicate "The Project Description should provide a clear statement of the work to be undertaken and must include: objectives for the period of the proposed work and expected significance; [and] relation to longer-term goals of the PI's project." The NSF definitions of "goals" and "objectives" are consonant with those used throughout this chapter.

Example 8

Because writing objectives can be a bedeviling experience for some people, in an attempt to level the playing field, the U.S. Department of Education is experimenting with a new approach: fill-in-the-blank objectives. As the following example illustrates, the language of the objectives is prescriptive and cannot be altered; applicants simply write in a number percentage. Subsequently, however, they need to justify why the percentages are simultaneously "ambitious" and "attainable."

____% of participants will complete research and scholarly activities that will directly impact their educational progression each academic year.

____% of new participants served in each academic year will attain a baccalaureate degree within three years.

____% of bachelor's degree recipients will enroll in a post baccalaureate program by the fall term of the academic year immediately following completion of that degree.

WRITING TIPS FOR THE OBJECTIVES SECTION

1. List your specific objectives in no more than one or two sentences each in approximate order of importance.
2. List your specific objectives in expected chronological order of achievement if you are submitting a phased proposal.
3. Avoid confusing your objectives (ends) with your methods (means). A good objective emphasizes what will be done and when it will be done, whereas a method will explain how it will be done.
4. Include goal (ultimate) and objectives (immediate) statements.
5. Limit this proposal section to less than one page.
6. Use action verbs. The following list provides a few action verbs to get you started. Usually, the action verbs are written in the infinitive verb form, e.g., to advocate, to analyze, to anticipate.

- Anticipate
- Arrange
- Assemble
- Assess
- Build
- Categorize
- Classify
- Compare
- Conduct
- Construct
- Contrast
- Coordinate
- Decrease
- Demonstrate
- Describe
- Design
- Detect
- Discover
- Discriminate
- Display
- Distinguish
- Establish
- Estimate
- Evaluate
- Explain
- Illustrate
- Increase
- Investigate
- Measure
- Motivate
- Organize
- Quantify
- Solve
- Stimulate
- Summarize
- Translate

7. As an alternative to use the infinitive verb form, some proposal writers prefer to start out using the word "By" followed by some date, e.g., "By January 2011, such and such will happen."

REJECTION REASONS

These common rejection reasons were noted in actual reviewers' critiques of rejected proposals.

1. The objectives are more like global purposes than specific, measurable, achievable activities.
2. The realism of some objectives is questionable.
3. Some of the objectives are confusing, nonspecific, not measurable, and clearly not appropriate to the purpose of the grant.
4. Objectives are general and stated as "activities"—thus nonmeasurable. It is unclear how activities will relate to the professions involved.
5. The project objectives are more comprehensive than covered by the methods.
6. Project objectives are vague, nonspecific, and difficult to measure. No targets are set in terms of faculty reached, trainees enrolled, disciplines involved.
7. The project outcomes are of limited significance.
8. The project outcomes are nebulous, diffuse, or unclear.
9. The research hypothesis is not testable.

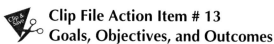

Clip File Action Item # 13
Goals, Objectives, and Outcomes

These suggestions will get you started on building your Goals, Objectives, and Outcomes clip file:

- Collect lists of well-written statements from other proposals, whether or not they are in your interest area. Often, clear statements of goals, objectives, and outcomes can be adapted to other proposal circumstances.
- Beyond successful proposals, many program announcements have carefully worded goal, objective, and outcome statements that can be added to your clip file.

CHAPTER 9
Methods

Vision without action is merely a dream. Action without vision just passes the time. Vision with action can change the world.

—Joel Arthur Barker

PURPOSE OF THE METHODS SECTION

Your methods are your action plan to reach your project goals and eventual dream. Your methods section tells how your project activities will accomplish your objectives, including your project sequence, flow, and interrelationships. It answers one key question: "How will I do this project?" In essence, your methods section—sometimes called "methodology," "plan," "statement of work," "approach," or "procedures"—tells who is going to do what, when it will be done, and how it will be managed. Each of these four components is discussed below, followed by an example, tips for getting started, and common proposal rejection reasons due to methodological errors.

KEY QUESTIONS TO ANSWER

Here are some key questions to answer. Does your proposal do the following:

1. Explain why you chose one methodological approach and not another?
2. Describe the major activities for reaching each objective?
3. Indicate the key project personnel who will carry out each activity?
4. Show the interrelationship among project activities?
5. Identify all project data that will be collected for use in evaluating proposal outcomes?

The Who: Key Personnel

There are three categories of key personnel in most projects:

- The **staff** who will be conducting the project.
- The **subjects** participating in the project.
- The **collaborators** who will join you in conducting the project.

Each should be described in sufficient detail to establish credibility.

Project Staff. Name all key project staff, including consultants and subcontractors, in your proposal. If this is not possible, include job descriptions for the people you propose to hire. At a minimum, describe the major roles each will play, whether they are already onboard or proposed to hire, e.g., responsible for overall project management, liaison with project collaborators, office manager, project fiscal officer, recruiter of project participants, volunteer coordinator, evaluation specialist, and so forth. Your appendixes should contain brief resumes (or job descriptions) that stress prior relevant training and experience that will transfer to the proposed project (see Chapter 13, Appendixes, for preparing resumes). Add the number of years your project staff has worked in this area and mention the total in your proposal.

> Our project staff of six has a cumulative 119 years of experience in dealing with this nagging problem.

Consider this section as a credibility statement about you and your other key project personnel. While your resume is an important credibility statement, particularly in governmental proposals, it may not communicate the fact that you work in an environment conducive to your project. Weave this point into your introduction. Further, tell the reviewer about your track record in similar projects. If you don't have a strong track record in your proposed project area, borrow credibility from other field experts through the use of project consultants, letters of endorsement, and supporting statistics.

Exhibit 40 is from a for-profit corporation seeking funding from a SBIR (Small Business Innovation Research) grant to develop some new technologies for use with persons who have low vision or blindness. It provides a fuller description of the Project Director, followed by briefer descriptions of two key project personnel and a consultant. Resumes for all key project personnel are presented as appendix material.

This proposal section summarizes the key project personnel and the project responsibilities. Collectively, they have the professional training and R&D experience necessary to successfully complete this project on time and budget. They have a track record spanning over 100 years in dealing with wayfinding technologies.

Michele Major, Project Director, has been a pioneer in new product and business development for 24 years. Her current adaptive technology company is Wayfinding, Inc. founded in January 1990 to make location information accessible to the blind. Ms. Major is Principal Investigator on a five year $2.25 million NIDRR funded grant (award number J248A023943) for the research and development of accessible wayfinding technology for blind and visually impaired individuals. The NIDRR Wayfinding grant focuses on navigation for blind people and is distinctly different from this SBIR proposal that focuses on people identification and information transfer.

Ms. Major is directly responsible for the development, implementation, monitoring, and day-to-day supervision of this project. Further, her broad-based networks enable her to stay informed about telecommunication industry trends and for creating products and distributing them to blind users. She works directly with and can rely on support from the various universities involved in the wayfinding field, namely, University of California-Santa Barbara, Western Michigan University, University of Minnesota, Smith Kettlewell Institute, Carnegie Mellon University, and the Department of Veterans Affairs R&D division.

Charles Dakota, Project Engineer, Wayfinding's Chief Technology Officer and lead software engineer, holds a patent for the first commercially available accessible Global Positioning System for blind and visually impaired individuals. He is an electrical engineer with an MSEE from Midwest University whose work has involved the integration of GPS and dead-reckoning technology. He has been a software engineer for four adaptive technology companies, VisuAide, Arkenstone, Benetech, and Wayfinding, Inc. He and Michele Major have a successful track record in obtaining the cooperation of software and hardware manufacturers in order to leverage the development of products for the blind. For example, Wayfinding, Inc. has negotiated low cost and no cost map licenses worth hundreds of thousands of dollars. We anticipate continued cooperation with industry on issues such as these, and we recognize that co-operation with industry and government is essential to accomplishing our specific aims. His primary project responsibility is to develop a working technology prototype of the wayfinding device to be developed.

Casey Malek, Technology Transfer Specialist, is Wayfinding's Training Coordinator and Marketing Manager. She has over 12 years of experience working with accessible GPS systems. Her expertise spans from testing and development to end user training. Ms. Malek also possesses the ability to market using various media—World Wide Web, HTML programming, video, print, and audio presentations. She has a demonstrated track record of leading product from the research bench to the marketplace.

Dr. Paul Vargas, Project Consultant, Department of Blind Rehabilitation at Western California University, will bring his expertise in consumer needs assessment, rehabilitation outcomes, program evaluation, focus groups, and development of technological devices to the project. He has worked with the key project personnel on other similar projects.

SAMPLE PERSONNEL DESCRIPTION

EXHIBIT 40

Project Subjects. Most—but not all—grant projects involve interaction with some target audience, usually called "subjects, " "clients," "patients," or "participants" who are your ultimate focal point. Often these projects involve some research, training, or service delivery that interface with people. Your methods section should answer these basic questions, as suggested in the examples that follow.

1. How will you recruit and retain your subjects?

- All patients between the ages of six and 16 seen in the emergency room during the past 12 months will be contacted to solicit their participation in this project.
- All children with Iowa Reading Test Scores one standard deviation below their grade level will constitute the initial project subject pool.
- Each project collaborator will refer 10 subjects for participation in this study.
- To select the participants for this project, volunteers will be sought from local community welfare agencies. Additionally, a newspaper advertisement will invite interested participants to call our office, where screening questions will determine subject eligibility.

2. What are their basic geographic and socioeconomic characteristics?

- All subjects must live within the four-country area and have access to transportation, to be compensated by the project.
- All participants must have an income level of at least 150% below the federal poverty level.
- To be eligible for participation in this study, the children must have received a grade of D or below in eighth grade algebra within the past 12 months and parental approval for participation in our Math Rules and You're the Ruler Project.
- All volunteers must be members of a community Senior Citizens Center and hold a valid driver's license.

3. How long will they be involved in the project?

- The subjects will participate in three two-hour focus group sessions.
- The participants will participate in a 30-minute checkup once a month for 12 months in the Emergency Room at no cost to them.
- To measure attitudes, the clients will take a 45-minute pencil and paper test asking questions about their opinions regarding spirituality: The Grace Hope Scale.

- Both the experimental and control groups will participate in pre- and post-tests of motor coordination. In addition, the experimental group will receive six one-hour training sessions of eye-hand coordination training.

4. To what extent do special client issues need to be addressed, e.g., compromised health status, transportation barriers, restrictive home environments, unsafe neighborhoods, unfavorable publicity, controversial policies, limited educational opportunities?

- To ensure the clients physical health status is not compromised during the period of intense physical exertion, an emergency room physician will oversee all stress testing.
- Since the After-School Project ends after sunset, our mobile vans will transport the students directly to their homes, rather than risk them walking home in unsafe neighborhoods.
- Our physical facilities comply wholly with the American Disabilities Act; accordingly, our wheelchair clients will face no physical barriers entering the building or negotiating its interior.
- Since our HIV clients could risk unfavorable publicity if they were identified by name, all records will use fictitious first names only, and only the project director will have the master list of record identifier numbers in order to ensure confidentiality and respect individual privacy.

Project Collaborators. Increasingly, sponsors encourage—and indeed expect—collaboration. Collaborations show a large "buy-in" to projects and increase the likelihood of sustainability beyond the granting period as project components are institutionalized.

There are many different types of collaborations. They exist along a continuum from casual to formal relationships. Four common types include informal collaborations, consortia, interdisciplinary teams, and centers or institutes. Regardless of the level of formality, good business practices warrant reducing the understanding and agreements to writing (see Chapter 13 for sample consortium agreements). Picking collaborators is like picking a mate: you want to do it carefully, for it has long-term relationship and financial consequences. In essence, project collaborations are valuable for informing people, solving problems, and creating support.

Successful collaborations often entail many hours of meetings. Experienced grantseekers have learned through trial and error these tips for conducting effective grant collaborations:

- Limit the meeting to no more than 1.5 hours.
- Invite no more than nine people.
- Include the key players in the meeting; if they can't attend, reschedule.
- Provide a two-week advance notice of the meeting.
- Distribute a detailed written agenda one week in advance of the meeting.
- Take thorough minutes.

The What: Project Activities

Justification of Methods. Each project will have its own unique set of methods, activities, tasks to accomplish the stated objectives. Whatever methods you deem appropriate for your project, justify their selection. You had choices and reviewers will want to know why you chose this approach and not some other alternative. A few sentences of methodological justification prior to describing specific project activities will anticipate and answer an important question in the minds of the reviewers: "Of the universe of possible methodologies, why did you pick this one?"

- The method of choice is to use a double-blind study; it is the only experimental design available that can isolate the effects of the independent variable on the project outcomes.
- This project is using the Grace Hope Scale to measure spirituality since it is, according to the Buros's *Yearbook of Mental Measurements*, the only instrument with acceptable reliability, validity, and normative data for our target population.
- Because no psychometric instrument exists to measure teenage attitudes toward learning a foreign language, according to the Buros's *Yearbook of Mental Measurements*, it is necessary for us to develop our own measurement instrument; Dr. Don Sprengel from the Department of Research Methodology at the local university has agreed to serve as a project consultant in this regard.

- Since it is imperative that we have the broadest possible community input in the most cost-effective manner, our approach relies on the time-proven benefits of using focus groups, a survey procedure that the project director has used successfully in similar past situations.
- Since research over the past 15 years documents that mentoring is the most cost-effective approach to integrating individuals with severe physical disabilities into the workplace, it is our preferred method to solve the existing needs.

Data Collection. You will probably need to collect some data as a part of your project. Common types and sources of data collection include those listed in Exhibit 41.

You can either construct your own data-gathering instruments or use existing ones. To find out if an appropriate instrument already exists (and avoid reinventing the wheel), consider looking through Buros's *Yearbook of Mental Measurements*, a two-volume listing of available tests in many different fields. More specifically, the Buros's volumes review the various attitude, behavior, and motor tests that are commercially available. Each review includes a description by the test author(s) and critiques by several experts in the field. The descriptions include the purpose, statistical characteristics, and, when available, the test norms. For example, if you are studying the relationship between spirituality and wellness, you could look in Buros's to see if any attitudinal measures of spirituality exist. The Buros's reference can be found in most libraries or on the Internet at www.unl.edu/buros.

Relationship of Objectives and Methods. Your objectives tell your reviewers **what** you propose to do. Your methods tell your reviewers **how** you will accomplish each objective. Put differently, you should include one or more methods for each objective. Use transitional language in your proposal to signal to reviewers

---

• Achievement tests	• Government records	• Referral forms
• Archival information	• Historical program records	• Reviews of literature
• Attendance records	• Interviews	• Role-playing exercises
• Case histories	• Personal diaries or logs	• Searches of news media
• Clinical examinations	• Physical tests	• Surveys
• Controlled observations	• Psychological tests	• Telephone logs
• Daily program records	• Questionnaires	• Tracking slips
• Focus groups	• Ratings by program staff	• University Research Offices

COMMON DATA COLLECTION TOOLS

EXHIBIT 41

the relationship between your objectives and your methods, as this example does.

To address the first objective, developing an Internet-based geriatric dentistry program, the following action items will occur:

- An Internet service provider will be selected, one with prior experience in mounting distance learning programs.
- The instructional modules will be storyboarded to flush out content.
- The instructional designer will take our content and develop visually literate formats.
- The first draft will be checked for content accuracy and user-friendliness.
- The revised draft will be tested out with 10 geriatric dentists around the country.
- Appropriate revisions will be made.
- The service provider will market the resulting distance learning program.

The following example is from a proposal targeted to a private foundation seeking funding to develop a geriatric education curriculum for use in a medical school. Note the approach taken in this persuasive writing segment. The specific measurable objective is restated to remind the reader, following by the specific activities, their purposes, and the processes to be followed.

Activities for Objective 1
Objective 1: By June 30, 2009, develop three geriatric eLearning curriculum modules for the evaluation and management of frail and minority elderly patients to age in place.
Activity 1.1: Develop Module One: Approaches to Frailty
Purpose of 1.1: This module presents the fundamental techniques for the prevention, screening, assessment, and management of frail health.
Process Tasks for 1.1: Review literature, survey practitioners, survey healthy elders, determine learning objectives, develop pre- and post-evaluation measures, finalize content (Curriculum Development Team led by Dr. Simon), finalize instructional levels (Curriculum Delivery Team led by Dr. Schuster), technologize module, critique by Oversight Committee and Geriatric Advisory Board, revise and resubmit as appropriate.
Outcome Tasks for 1.1: By June 30, 2008, this module will be developed as a case-based, small group activity in Clinical Medicine 1 and will be supplemented with a Web-based assignment. It will introduce the concept of frailty along with the concept of healthy aging.

Activity 1.2: Develop Module Two: Aging Successfully in Place
Purpose of 1.2: This module describes the concept of aging successfully in place and its role in home health care services.
Outcome Tasks for 1.2: By December 30, 2008, this module will include a Web-based assignment that describes the stages of aging successfully in place.
Activity 1.3: Develop Module Three: Continuum of Care for the Elderly
Purpose of 1.3: This module broadens the concept of elder care and identifies paramedical services that enhance the quality of life and its longevity.
Process Tasks for 1.3: Same as Tasks for 1.1.
Outcome Tasks for 1.3: By March 31, 2009, this module will cover the continuity and continuum of care throughout the elderly years, including the role and identification of essential support services.

In sum, the Curriculum Development Team and the Curriculum Delivery Team will work in parallel to ensure that the content and technology meet the highest standards for each of the nine modules. The specific team members are listed in Attachment Five.

The When: Project Timelines

Time and Task Charts. The use of a time and task chart represents one common and successful means of clearly communicating the methods section in your proposal. This visual device segments your total project into manageable steps and lets your reviewers know exactly who will be doing what and when. It tells reviewers that you are organized and have thought out the major steps of your project. This way, your reviewers know you have done significant planning and are not just proposing a wild whim. With a time and task chart, they can look at a road map of the territory you plan to cover. Finally, the time and task chart represents a clear, one-page, visual summary of the entire methodology section. It would, for example, be a logical addition to the end of the bioethics methodology section described in the example below.

Many different types of time and task charts can be used. Which type you use is not as important as the fact that you do include one that the reviewers can easily grasp. Some grant writers like to include it at the beginning of the methods section to provide the reviewers with an orientation to the narrative that follows. Others like to put it at the end of the methods section as a visual summary of the preceding verbal narrative. The choice is yours. Successful grantseekers often include their favorite time and task chart—whether or not it is requested in the application guidelines.

As you study the time and task chart in Exhibit 42, notice that it includes goals and objectives with pertinent activities, including beginning and ending dates as well as the responsible individual. In essence, it is a comprehensive work plan seeking funding for a preschool curriculum development project. Mechanically, it is merely a four-column table generated from your favorite word processing program.

The second example of a time and task chart, Exhibit 43, is sometimes called a project planner. Also prepared in a four-column table format using word processing software, it outlines the major activities of the project and the key individuals responsible for conducting the activities. In addition, it lists the duration of each activity; rather than name specific calendar months, it identifies project months. The final column contains a budget for each activity. While it requires extra effort to determine costs for each activity, this information is useful in those instances when agencies ask you to reduce your budget. If you must reduce your budget by, say, $10,000, which project activities will you eliminate? The program survey? The final publication? Neither makes sense for this project, which is the Project Planner for Exhibit 26 in Chapter 5, Letter Proposal Template. Once sponsors realize how thoroughly you have planned your project, they may show more flexibility in funding your full budget request.

Another approach to developing time and task charts involves the use of computer software specifically designed for such purposes. The following example from a software product called Microsoft

Work Plan for June 1, 2008 through December 31, 2010			
Goal: To enable 200 children between the ages of six weeks and four years the opportunity to maximize their cognitive, social, and emotional potential through participation in a state-of-the-art early childhood learning experience.			
Activity	Begin Date	End Date	Responsibility
Objective # 1: Train 200 children on Houston's northwest side in a culturally competent early childhood program.	Jun 2008	Dec 2010	Executive Director
• Activity 1.1. Develop and field test a modular early childhood enrichment curriculum based on early brain development research.	Jun 2008	Nov 2008	Curriculum Consultant, Health Education Center
• Activity 1.2. Train 10 trainers in the curriculum modules.	Aug 2008	Aug 2009	Curriculum Consultant
• Activity 1.3. Establish formal collaborations between White's Child Development Center, Multicultural Family Services, Silver Lake Neighborhood Center, and affiliate family care.	Jul 2008	Dec 2010	Project Manager
• Activity 1.4. Disseminate project findings through regular monthly meetings with collaborators and quarterly newsletters.	Sep 2008	Dec 2010	Project Manager
Objective # 2: Coordinate education, training and supportive services for parents of at least 200 young children.	Dec 2008	Dec 2010	Executive Director
• Activity 2.1. Explain curriculum to 50 parents.	Aug 2009	Dec 2010	HEC, Project manager
• Activity 2.2. Show 25 parents ½-hour training video.	Sep 2009	Dec 2010	Project Manager
• Activity 2.3. Train 10 parents of special needs infants and toddlers, and link them with support services.	Dec 2009	Dec 2010	Curriculum consultant
• Activity 2.4. Stimulate parental involvement in education sessions, parent-teacher meetings, and class volunteers.	Jan 2009	Dec 2010	HEC, Project Manager

TIME AND TASK CHART

EXHIBIT 42

PROJECT includes specific project tasks, start and end dates, and personnel responsible for each task; additionally, a bar graph indicates the duration of various activities. The example in Exhibit 44 deals with the process to develop a training module to prevent the mother-to-child transmission of HIV, a problem that accounts for roughly 20 percent of all HIV cases in sub-Saharan Africa. This software also contains a number of other features, including resource allocations, activity costs, and adjustments for time slippages, that are not reflected in this example.

The How: Project Management

Your project management approach represents a disciplined way of organizing, allocating, and managing your human, fiscal, and physical resources so that your project successfully meets its objectives on time and within budget. More specifically, your resources include money, people, materials, energy, space, supplies, equipment, communication, quality control, and risk management. Your project management

section in your proposal describes how you will administer your grant.

The following example comes from a proposal that is seeking to empower inner city, low income women with young children by providing them training in securing housing, finding jobs, and gaining an education. Note, in particular, the organizational chart of the project management team and their communication plans, an essential component of project management.

Our Project Management Team (PMT) represents the governance body that provides project leadership and oversight. The PMT bears the ultimate responsibility for ensuring successful project completion. The PMT includes the Project Director (Mike Johnson) and Team Leaders in our three program areas: housing, jobs, and education. Collectively, this four person PMT will be responsible for the successful integration of combination of services to empower inner city single mothers and their families. All teams must rely on

Activities	Responsibility	Duration	Budget
• Identify Target Urban Areas	• Jane O'Connor, Project Director	• Month One	• 3,345
• Design Evaluation Tools	• Jane O'Connor	• Month One	• 2,845
• Survey Program Practices	• Audra Hill, Assistant Director	• Months One and Two	• 8,976
• Analyze Survey Data	• J.O'Connor, A. Hill	• Months Three and Four	• 5,190
• Draft Preliminary Report	• Tera Maki, Technical Writer	• Months Five and Six	• 4,690
• Publish Preliminary Report	• Wise Publishing Company	• Months Seven and Eight	• 7,345
• Disseminate Report	• T. Maki	• Month Nine	• 3,238
• Seek Report Feedback	• J.O'Connor	• Months Nine and Ten	• 4,345
• Revise Preliminary Report	• T. Maki	• Months Eleven and Twelve	• 5,805
• Publish Final Report	• Wise Publishing Company	• Months Thirteen and Fourteen	• 11,690
• Distribute Final Report	• T. Maki	• Month Fifteen	• 3,476
Total Direct Cost			• $57,600
+Administrative Cost			• 11,520
=**Total Project Cost**			• $69,120
-Cost Sharing			• 2,888
=**Amount Requested**			• $66,240

PROJECT PLANNER

EXHIBIT 43

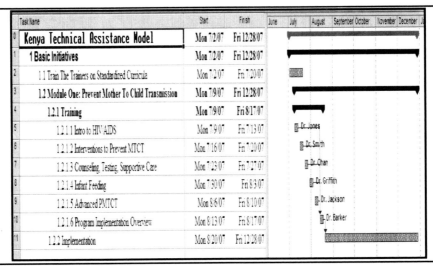

Task Name	Start	Finish	June	July	August	September	October	November	December	J
0 Kenya Technical Assistance Model	Mon 7/2/07	Fri 12/28/07								
1 Basic Initiatives	Mon 7/2/07	Fri 12/28/07								
2 1.1 Train The Trainers on Standardized Curricula	Mon 7/2/07	Fri 7/20/07								
3 1.2 Module One: Prevent Mother To Child Transmission	Mon 7/9/07	Fri 12/28/07								
4 1.2.1 Training	Mon 7/9/07	Fri 8/17/07								
5 1.2.1.1 Intro to HIV/AIDS	Mon 7/9/07	Fri 7/13/07		Dr. Jones						
6 1.2.1.2 Interventions to Prevent MTCT	Mon 7/16/07	Fri 7/20/07		Dr. Smith						
7 1.2.1.3 Counseling, Testing, Supportive Care	Mon 7/23/07	Fri 7/27/07		Dr. Chan						
8 1.2.1.4 Infant Feeding	Mon 7/30/07	Fri 8/3/07		Dr. Griffith						
9 1.2.1.5 Advanced PMTCT	Mon 8/6/07	Fri 8/10/07			Dr. Jackson					
10 1.2.1.6 Program Implementation Overview	Mon 8/13/07	Fri 8/17/07			Dr. Barker					
11 1.2.2 Implementation	Mon 8/20/07	Fri 12/28/07								

MICROSOFT PROJECT AS TIME AND TASK CHART

EXHIBIT 44

collaboration with community partners and the various resources they offer to our target population, as the follow PMT organizational chart indicates.

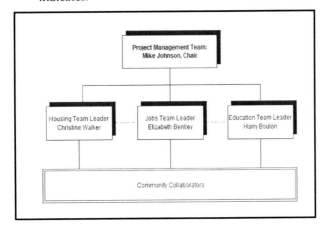

The PMT will meet regularly to monitor project progress and ensure the technical objectives are met on time and budget. Communication is a core value for the PMT as they connect with various external audiences (e.g., community partners and project participants) and internal audiences (e.g., field managers, evaluation personnel). At a minimum, the PMT will address the major project issues and communicate outcomes, including the following:

1. Appropriate deployment and use of resources
2. Project progression and status reports: administrative, programmatic, and fiscal
3. Interim and final process and outcome evaluations
4. Project deliverables

5. Accountability for project human resources
6. Changes in project processes, procedures, and policies
7. Critical incidents
8. Major milestones

The intended results of the PMT's communication efforts are to affect the knowledge, attitudes, and behaviors of key internal and external project stakeholders. Among the timing for the various messages to be disseminated are the following.

• Monthly written status reports: accomplishments, timelines, budget, and risk management
• Ongoing face-to-face communications
• Biweekly teleconference PMT meetings
• Quarterly written quality assurance Status Reports
• Quarterly teleconference Best Practices Meetings
• Biweekly project management Coordination Meetings
• Personal on-site orientation, as needed
• Semiannual site visits by PMT
• Press releases by PMT to mass media, as appropriate
• Journal articles and convention papers by key project personnel, as appropriate
• Monthly electronic project newsletter
• Written minutes of all meetings
• Evaluation reports of training sessions by provider and consumers

The PMT has over 12 years of experience in working together on similar past projects and is familiar with the management style of each person. Collectively, the PMT has spent more than 50 years working on empowerment projects of young women.

Getting Started

Begin with your objectives. Describe the precise steps you will follow to carry out each objective, including what will be done, who will do it, and when it will be done. If you have trouble writing this section, assume the sponsor's check just arrived in the mail. What is the first thing you would do? Hire additional staff? Order equipment? What would you do next? Keep asking and answering the "What's next?" question and you will lead yourself through the methodology section.

EXAMPLES OF METHODS

Example 1

Exhibit 45 contains the key methodological section in a proposal from a nonprofit organization that submitted a proposal to a federal agency seeking support to hold a statewide conference alerting healthcare providers to the problem of perinatal depression. The applicant placed this proposal in a larger context of its long-term initiatives; specifically, this request for conference support represented Phase IV of a five-phased initiative. The methodology section of this proposal concluded with a time and task chart that identified the specific people who would carry out the four different activity areas cited above along with targeted time frames.

Example 2

An example from a hospital seeking federal funding to establish a bioethics center.

Bioethics Center Approach and Methods.

Overview. For each of the three major Center goals described above, this proposal section details precisely what will be accomplished, methods of choice, task sequences, responsible individuals, time frames, and expected outcomes.

Organization. From the objectives, it is apparent that the Center has a tripartite focus: clinical, educational, and administrative. The Center organization chart (see table 1, following page) reflects this service aim. The Center Project Director, Dr. David Schwartz, is a full-time staff member at the Jones Memorial

Hospital. Additionally, Associate Directors in each service area will be appointed: Dr. Marvin Todd, Associate Director for Clinical Affairs, Jones Memorial Hospital; Dr. William Ashmore, Associate Director for Administrative Affairs, Medical University; and Dr. Robert Starr, Associate Director for Educational Affairs, Midwest University. Brief personnel descriptions are provided in the institutional overview statements beginning on page 13. Complete curriculum vitae are appended.

Mechanisms of Commitment and Cooperation. The three core institutions will sign the Consortium Agreement specified in Appendix 1. The agreement describes the programmatic, fiscal, and administrative protocols that form the foundation of the Center. Additionally, the Center will want to quickly expand its affiliation with other medical centers and universities who share a mutual interest and concern in clinical ethics. Those institutions will be actively encouraged to quickly sign the Affiliation Agreement listed in Appendix 2. This formal affiliation will give them early access to the Center and quickly build a national base of operation. Finally, some institutions may not be prepared to make a full affiliation commitment, but they may want to be formally identified with and participate in Center activities. Those institutions will be urged to sign the Participant Institution Agreement listed in Appendix 3.

The lengthy methodology section in this proposal went on to restate each specific objective and describe what specific actions would be taken to carry out each objective. Because the central focus of this proposal was to establish an ethics education program for health and allied health professionals, the methodology section then concluded with the following discussion of a Clinical Ethics Education Program.

Clinical Ethics Education Program. To promote ethics education programs, the Center proposes to establish a program in Clinical Ethics Education (CEE). The CEE program assumes that (1) ethics is appropriate for all health care providers and (2) instruction in clinical ethics demands a novel curricular implementation. Central to the program are two clinical institutes that will provide the groundwork for developing a strengthened interdisciplinary, hospital-wide curriculum in clinical ethics education and for training health care professionals to teach clinical ethics within the hospital. The CEE program also will

Request for Regional Conference Support

This proposal identifies two major goals and subsequent measurable objectives, along with appropriate *dissemination* and *integration* activities.

Goal #1: To disseminate best practices to constituents

Objective 1.1: By March 2009, develop an information architecture for disseminating best practices.

Activities for Objective 1.1

In order to disseminate best practices, an information architecture must exist to provide the key intellectual content and delivery systems for transferring research knowledge to practitioners. Information architecture, in this case, represents the knowledge base generated from the Symposium Proceedings (Phase II) and the Blueprint for Action (Phase III). In essence, the approach of choice establishes the communication infrastructure for disseminating knowledge. To accomplish this, the knowledge base for the information architecture will come from Phase II, the Best Practices Conference and Phase III, the Blueprint for Action. Electronic (Web-based) proceedings will be hosted on the Perinatal Care Group Web site. The deliverable for this objective is to collate, print and bind the Blueprint for Action that will be distributed to an estimated 300 symposium attendees in advance of the regional conferences.

Objective 1.2: By June 2009, disseminate select prenatal and postpartum depression information throughout seven regions in the state.

Activities for Objective 1.2

Once the information architecture is built, the host information will be widely disseminated to targeted consumers and prenatal and postpartum practitioners throughout the state using two different approaches. First, the Phase I mailing campaign identified 15,000 prenatal and postpartum healthcare providers who will be notified by a third postcard (earlier ones sent on November 2007 and January 2008) about access to an electronic version of Symposium Proceedings/Blueprint for Action (15,000 distribution). Second, beyond the symposium participants, electronic (Web-based) and bound printed Symposium Proceedings and a Blueprint for Action will be distributed to an estimated 350 conference professionals who will participate in the regional conferences, described below.

Goal #2: To integrate best practices among constituents

Objective 2.1: By August 2009, conduct seven regional conferences: Integrating Best Practices.

Activities for Objective 2.1

Seven regional constituent-based conferences will be convened to encourage and support the exchange of effective implementation strategies; Appendix Six contains a map of regions and probable site locations. The regional conferences will identify culturally sensitive topics, define best practice models relevant to each region, present an overview of Symposium Proceedings and a Blueprint for Action, define cultural and/or systemic barriers that hinder integration into clinical practice, identify criteria for regional customization, and generate customized regional integration strategies.

Objective 2.2: By August 2009, promote partnerships that will stimulate the integration of best practices.

Activities for Objective 2.2

The following actions will promote the development of new strategic partnerships. (1) Expert clinicians, as conference presenters, will establish communications with regional leaders at the seven regional conferences. (2) Practitioners at the local level will identify clinical and systems opportunities of mutual interest as a result of networking. (3) Strategic partners will identify interventions and topics for multiregional clinical research through networking.

SAMPLE PROPOSAL METHODOLOGY

EXHIBIT 45

include ethics seminars, speaker programs, and guest lecturing clinicians and ethicists.

The guiding vision of the CEE program will be to focus the attention of health care professionals upon the principles of ethical theory and their practical application to a broad range of health care matters in other disciplines. Each participating hospital will gain newly energized clinicians, an increase in ethical sensitivity, and relevantly revised training programs in clinical ethics. Moreover, health care providers will gain a new interdisciplinary perspective on ethics and will receive varied supports for collegiate collaboration.

In essence, the major Center outcome will be to provide this cadre of health professionals with focused training in ethics theory and crosswalks that foster interdisciplinary communication. This focus will allow the Center to more fully centralize its clinical ethics curriculum around fundamental philosophical and theological ethical models. Clinicians who are versed in the basic principles of the theoretical study of ethics are better able to see how these principles converge with applied practices.

Rather than allowing ethics to be learned in isolated fragments from different disciplines, the CEE program would coordinate the resources of different disciplines under one umbrella to provide clinicians with a more organized and integrated exploration of ethics. Ethics will achieve a first-class status within the participating hospital as a result of the CEE program. All clinicians will benefit from the increased excellence in the study of ethics.

CEE Program Administration. The Associate Director for Educational Affairs will administer the CEE program with extensive consultation from the Advisory Board of the Center for Ethics Studies at Midwest University, and a broad network of hospital affiliates. Specifically, Professor Starr, of Midwest's theology department, will serve as Program Coordinator. Professor Johnson, of the philosophy department, will function as Associate Coordinator. As shown in Appendix 5, both the Program Coordinator and Associate Coordinator have strong professional records in the field of ethics and are oriented to interdisciplinary ethics education. In general, the program administrators will be responsible for directing the functions of the program and for assessing the success of these activities.

CEE Program Functions. The CEE program will include the following three major functions:

- *A Series of Two Summer Clinical Institutes*
  These institutes will bring together clinicians from different specialties interested in ethics (a) to provide an organized seminar in basic ethical theory, (b) to explore the application of this theoretical framework to the various specialties, (c) to plan curricular changes in medical education at each affiliated hospital, and (d) to provide training for implementing the revised curriculum. Specifically, the first summer institute will concentrate upon the key elements of the theory of ethics. The following summer institute will explore curricular changes that incorporate the theory into practical situations.
- *Development of the Interdisciplinary Curriculum in Ethics*
  As previously described, the ultimate objective of the CEE program is to develop an explicitly highlighted interdisciplinary curriculum in clinical ethics. In light of the natural enrichment generated by interaction of ethicists and clinicians in diverse health care disciplines, proposals will be developed and implemented for incorporating clinical ethics components throughout the hospital system.
- *A Series of Sponsored Programmed Meetings*
  Interested clinicians and medical students will attend a regularly scheduled forum on clinical ethics to share their respective insights and efforts in the study of ethics. These seminars, administered jointly by the Associate Director for Clinical Affairs and the Associate Director for Educational Affairs, will address issues in ethical theory and the application of that theory to problems in the applied fields.

Example 3

A health education center seeking funding from a local private foundation to develop a video on early brain development for childcare providers.

This program will be made available to communities throughout the Center's current service area. This includes 13 counties in southeastern Wyoming and two in northern Arizona. The intended audience for this program would be the parents, grandparents, guardians, public health nurses, parish nurses, home visitors, and child care providers. It is anticipated that approximately 30 people will participate in each session of the program. Twelve presentations will be made during the project period, thereby directly targeting 360 people.

The content of the program will address the healthy growth and development of a child socially, physically, emotionally, and cognitively. A variety of learning formats will be employed, including lecture, small-group discussions, role-playing, interactive videos and models, and group participation. Among these training techniques, the research literature shows that interactive videos are particularly effective in producing long-term behavioral changes. This program will provide participants with the ability to model healthy adult-child interactions for each other. Most important, adults will learn skills that promote healthy brain development and relationship building from 0–3 years of age.

WRITING TIPS FOR THE METHODS SECTION

1. Justify your selection of methods.
2. Tell what is unique about your approach. Have others used your procedures? Is there solid reason to believe they will work? If you use experimental methods, indicate why you chose them over others.
3. Segment your methodological approach into activity areas; this organization makes the project design easier to understand. Note the use of subheadings in Example 2.
4. Discuss the risks with your methods and why your success is probable.
5. Include a time and task chart. Including the names or titles of personnel who will carry out each activity foreshadows for the reader the role each person plays in your project budget.
6. Restate or summarize your objectives at the beginning of each major activity area.
7. If you are generating data, explain how you will collect, analyze, and interpret it. Describe the survey tools that you will use, including reliability and validity characteristics.
8. Explain how information collected will be used to monitor program progress and indicate when final reports and outcomes will be available.

REJECTION REASONS

This chapter concludes with 15 statements from rejected proposals; these methodological shortcomings

are clustered into three categories: Project Personnel, Project Methods, and Project Timelines.

Project Personnel

1. The project appears to incorporate little personnel expertise in the disciplines involved.
2. This proposal seems premature. Not until an interdisciplinary group is in place can this project be expected to operate effectively.
3. Project staff is not specified in the narrative, i.e., job descriptions are not included and prior relevant work experience is not explained.
4. The project director lacks experience in the essential methodology.
5. The applicant does not provide any indication of the number of clients to be served.

Project Methods

1. There is insufficient experimental detail to approve the project.
2. The methodology is diffuse, superficial, and unfocused.
3. The proposal narrative does not describe why the target population of the homeless was selected over other needy populations. Are the homeless disproportionately represented compared to other groups, e.g., frail elderly, battered women, or drug abusers?
4. There is a gap between the "problem" identified in the opening section of the proposal and the "solution" presented here. The "problem" focuses on the needs of uninsured patients. The "solution" focuses on meeting the needs of the providers.
5. It would have been helpful if the applicant had delineated the existing activities versus the proposed program activities as directed in the application instructions.

Project Timelines

1. Greater care in planning is needed. It is highly unlikely that the methods can be accomplished within the specified time frame.
2. No timelines are provided for the major tasks; this represents a serious planning gap on the part of the applicants.
3. While major time frames are provided for each milestone, the applicants do not indicate who is responsible for carrying out each activity.
4. The timelines are extraordinarily ambitious.

5. The sequence of project activities needs to be reexamined. It does not appear that the requisite resources will always be in place to complete the individual activities.

Clip File Action Item # 14
Methods

The following action items will help build your Methods clip file:

- Gather examples of time and task charts from other proposals.
- Collect details on data collection instruments of interest in Buros's *Yearbook of Mental Measurements*.
- List your resources that might support upcoming projects: computers, equipment, and instruments; laboratory, clinical, and animal facilities; clerical, technological, financial, fundraising, and office personnel.

CHAPTER 10
Evaluation

True genius resides in the capacity for evaluation of
uncertain, hazardous and conflicting information.
—Winston Churchill

PURPOSE OF EVALUATION

Evaluations pinpoint what is really happening in your project so you can improve its efficiency, effectiveness, and equity. That is, you can ensure project funds are being spent wisely, the project is making a difference, and project benefits are being distributed across the target population or community. Based on evaluation information, you can better allocate resources, improve your services, and strengthen your overall project performance. Beyond these immediate benefits, a good project evaluation can discover needs to be served in your next proposal as well as make it easier to get and sustain funding. As Churchill notes, grantseekers conduct their evaluation to resolve ambiguous or conflicting information.

In essence, evaluations are conducted for a combination of internal and external reasons. Externally, sponsors may require it to make sure that their project funds are having the desired impact, or as a prerequisite for renewed funding. Conceivably, sponsors may use evaluation information to deal with radical funding cutbacks; applicants without a strong evaluation component are particularly vulnerable to funding cuts.

Beyond these external reasons, many internal reasons exist for conducting an evaluation. You may not have a firm grasp of your project strengths and weaknesses or socioeconomic implications. You may wonder if you need to improve your project effectiveness or to eliminate some duplication of effort. Perhaps, your project is getting little publicity or, worse yet, negative publicity. Maybe your staff feels ineffectual, frustrated, or in need of guidance. A comprehensive evaluation can provide answers to these important project questions.

If you want to include an evaluation component in your proposal but know nothing about the subject, consider borrowing ideas from the evaluation plans developed for other similar programs, or ask a colleague or consultant to review your proposal and develop an appropriate evaluation strategy. Too frequently, proposal writers don't explain how they will evaluate their projects. At best, they may mention some vague process such as conducting a group discussion or assigning the evaluation to an expert, with no specifics on how the evaluation will be conducted or what will be learned from it.

TYPES OF EVALUATION

You may engage in different types of evaluations to assess the effectiveness of your proposed project during, at the conclusion of, and beyond the granting period. Three types of evaluations include, process, outcome, and impact. Public and private sponsors sometimes use different terms to describe the same types of evaluations. For instance, the U.S. Department of Education uses the terms formative and summative evaluations, whereas the W.K. Kellogg Foundation uses the terms process and outcome evaluations; they are synonyms.

A few sponsors, however, have refined distinctions in the types of evaluations they expect. For example, one program in the Health Resources and Services Administration requires you to distinguish between outputs (products) and outcomes (humanistic benefits) that will accrue by the conclusion of the grant period. Preproposal contacts (Chapter 4) will help you to identify the types, levels, and degrees of evaluation strategies you will need to include in your proposal. The sponsor may well require different types of evaluations during different time periods in the grant. Exhibit 46 lists some of the common evaluation terms used during different grant periods.

Note that some evaluation terms overlap; that is, one term can have more than one meaning. For instance, "process" is the umbrella name given to evaluations conducted during a grant; it is also the name of one facet of that evaluation, along with "structure." The semantics of evaluation terminology are not consistent among grantmakers; the following discussion attempts to defuzzify the different evaluation terms.

Process Evaluation

Process evaluations generate information that will improve the effectiveness of the project during the granting period. They systematically examine internal and external characteristics associated with the delivery and receipt of services. This may include evaluating structure, the environment and settings in which services occur. Understanding the strengths and weaknesses of the structure of your organization, the target population and their community environment, and the procedures your organization is using to interact with the community will provide immediate feedback to help you in the process of meeting project objectives. When writing a process evaluation, you'll need to consider the following types of questions.

- **Your Organization.** Are sufficient numbers of key personnel adequately trained to carry out the project? Do staff members reflect the ethnic, cultural, and linguistic makeup of the community? Are suitable facilities and equipment available? Do current services respond to the needs of the target population and community? What is your relation to other organizations that provide similar types of services?

- **Target Population & Community Environment.** Have individual and community needs been identified through a formal needs assessment or an informal survey of perceived needs? Has the community's knowledge, attitude, and behavior toward the problem been assessed? What is the prevalence and distribution of physical, social, and economic risks in the community? Does the community face any geographic, cultural, or linguistic barriers to overcoming the problem? Does the target population have access to additional personal, family, or community resources that will help your project succeed?

- **Organization & Community Interaction.** What types of services are being provided to whom and how often? Who from your organization is collecting what type of evidence to document the quality and quantity of interactions? Is the target population satisfied with services? Are your staff members satisfied with their experiences? What barriers still need to be overcome in order to improve participant satisfaction?

Evaluation indicators are specific characteristics that you will track and measure to gauge project success. Process-level indicators may examine features such as the intensity of the intervention, the quality of service provided, and the cultural competence of the intervention. Structure-level indicators may assess elements such as who provided the intervention, what type of intervention was used, where the intervention occurred, when and how long the intervention took place, and the length of participant involvement.

During the grant period	*Conclusion* of grant period	*Beyond* the grant period
Process	Outcome	Impact
• Structure	• Outputs	
• Process	• Outcomes	
Formative	Summative	Impact
Immediate Outcomes	Short-term Outcomes	Long-term Outcomes
Initial Outcomes	Intermediate Outcomes	End Outcomes

EVALUATION TERMINOLOGY AT DIFFERENT GRANT TIME PERIODS

EXHIBIT 46

Outcome Evaluation

Outcome evaluations examine the end result of an intervention. The goal here is to document the extent to which the project did what it was designed to do. Outcomes are the benefits, changes, or effects that occur to the target population due to participation in your project. Outcomes are generally expressed in humanistic terms, e.g., improved health status, increased knowledge of parenting skills, decreased youth violence. Some sponsors may also ask you to identify outputs, products generated as a result of program activities, e.g., a curriculum to teach oral health to middle school students, the number of conflict resolution classes taught, the number of volunteers recruited. Keep in mind that "ideal" outcomes can vary with perspective: your organization, the target population, and potential sponsors may value different outcomes. Your project might need to evaluate several types of outcomes simultaneously.

The core of outcome evaluations is measurement: collect data to document the extent to which project objectives were accomplished. Outcome indicators—specific characteristics selected for measurement—must best describe an associated end result. For instance, a program whose desired outcome is to improve asthma-related quality of life could measure "improvement" through participants having a written asthma action plan; using anti-inflammatory inhalers, spacers, and peak flow meters; reducing the amount of sleep, exercise, school days lost due to asthma; and reducing the number of hospital admissions and emergency room visits for asthma. Participants who demonstrate these behaviors are the indicators of the project's success in achieving this outcome.

Or, for example, a project whose desired outcome is to improve academic mastery of key science concepts by undergraduate students could use indicators such as results from Web-based polls administered during class; midterm and final exam results compared against classes taught in previous years and against course sections taught in traditional formats by other instructors; performance on standardized exams (e.g., major field tests) compared against other course sections and against national norms; and electronic portfolios that track performance from freshman to senior year.

Three common types of outcome indicators include, functional status, humanistic, and economic. Collecting data to evaluate all aspects of each type of outcome indicator would be extremely difficult and prohibitively expensive. Instead, do like successful grantseekers do: identify a few outcome indicators that will demonstrate meaningful end results to your organization, the target population, and the sponsor.

Functional Status. Performance measures such as physical, mental, social, and spiritual well-being can be used to demonstrate individuals' functional status. Performance measures are generally evaluated at set intervals—for example, prior to intervention, six and twelve months postintervention. Functional status indicators demonstrate that, as a result of the intervention, the client's quality of life improved in a meaningful way.

Humanistic. Humanistic indicators tell you how clients feel about the intervention and reflect how well the project is working. Measures tend to be subjective in nature, for instance: awareness of program services, access to services, convenience of services, quality of services, satisfaction with services, and individual perceptions of well-being. Client satisfaction is a key outcome measure because those who are satisfied with their experiences are more likely to continue participating in an intervention.

Economic. Five measures typically used to calculate the costs and consequences of project interventions include cost-benefit analysis, cost-effectiveness analysis, cost-minimization analysis, cost-utility analysis, and return on investment analysis. Each type of analysis values costs in dollars but differs in the outcome measures used. Sponsors value project outcomes that demonstrate the greatest benefit at the lowest cost.

- *Cost-benefit analyses* identify the most favorable cost-to-benefit ratio of two or more alternatives that have similar or different outcomes for the target population; that is, given finite resources, which project intervention gives the best return for the dollars invested?
- *Cost-effectiveness analyses* compare two or more approaches to a specified outcome, assuming that members of the target population value the outcome equally and that adequate financial resources are available to pursue the most beneficial strategy.
- *Cost-minimization analyses* identify the least expensive of two or more alternatives that have identical outcomes for the target population.
- *Cost-utility analyses* compare the costs of two or more approaches to an outcome, adjusting for preferences of the target population. That is, a child with mild asthma may not value an additional year of life as much as an adult with an advanced stage of the AIDS virus.

- *Return on investment analyses* look at projected benefits or revenue generated by the intervention over a period of time compared to the initial investment and operating costs.

In the public arena, the fundamental method for formal economic assessment is cost-benefit analysis. Cost-benefit analyses attempt to identify the most economically efficient way of meeting a public objective, particularly when measurable benefits or costs extend three or more years into the future. You can find federal guidance for this analysis in the U.S. Office of Management and Budget's "Circular A-94 Guidelines and Discount Rates for Benefit Cost Analysis of Federal Programs," available at www .whitehouse.gov/omb/circulars/a094/a094.html.

Impact Evaluation

Impact evaluations generate information to measure the overall worth and utility of the project beyond the granting period. An impact evaluation goes beyond assessing whether goals and objectives were achieved and focuses on the project's larger value— long-term, fundamental changes in participants' knowledge, attitudes, or behaviors. That is, improving outcomes at the program level may impact change over time at the community level. By their nature, many outcomes are delayed, occurring beyond the granting period. Impact evaluations attempt to attribute outcomes exclusively to an intervention, although data may be difficult to obtain over the long term.

You can demonstrate impact at several levels: the target population, the community at large, and beyond. Lasting changes in the target population demonstrate the project's overall value. Inclusive participation by the community may contribute to long-term project sustainability. Regional and national buy-in for targeted interventions and outcomes can promote large-scale project replication. Consider the following types of questions when writing an impact evaluation.

- **Overall Value.** What enduring changes will occur in participants' knowledge, attitudes, or behaviors as a result of this project? Over the long term, will you be able to demonstrate that the project's impact extended beyond the target population to the entire community, area, or region? Will this project serve as a catalyst for other related community actions, services, and programs?
- **Sustainability.** Will project activities continue beyond the granting period? Will you be able to

mobilize continued support for the project internally and/or externally? Will your organization institutionalize strategies deemed effective? Will key champions for the project be able to increase levels of community involvement and fiscal support? Will your project influence changes at provider, policy, or system levels?
- **Replicability.** Will key findings be disseminated to local, regional, and national stakeholders so that the project can be replicated? Does the project's design have flexibility to be adapted to other populations or topics? Could your organization serve as a national clearinghouse to educate and train other communities about implementing your program? Does your project have the potential to serve as a public policy model?

Collectively, conducting process, outcome, and impact evaluations is a strategy to achieve a competitive grantseeking advantage by increasing project accountability. These assessments also provide essential information about the direction that the project should take in the future and if additional public and private funding will be needed. As evaluation data are generated, be sure to disseminate relevant findings to key constituents.

CHOOSING AN EVALUATOR

Evaluations can be done using someone within or outside of your organization. An individual from within your organization conducting an internal evaluation has great intuitive knowledge of your program and is less likely to be seen as an intruder. Evaluation costs are usually less expensive when the evaluations are conducted in-house. The ability to communicate useful information is high. On the other hand, the internal evaluation may be biased because of involvement with certain program aspects. Evaluation findings may be ignored or not seen as professional enough; that is, the evaluation may not be taken seriously.

Using external evaluators offers considerable objectivity. They often have a fresh perspective and can see things not noticed before. They have a high autonomy and freedom and specialized training. Outside evaluators usually have high professional and scholarly competence. They can mediate and facilitate activities with staff and management while ensuring public confidence in evaluation results. On the other hand, they may be perceived as a threat by the staff and may require extra time to understand the program rationale. Outside evaluation costs may be high. The findings may be ignored because the evaluator doesn't really know the program and can miss essential issues or because the staff perceives this to be the case. Evaluation energies may distract from program activities.

USING EVALUATORS EFFECTIVELY

Whether you use an internal or an external evaluator —or both—be sure to include an evaluation section in your proposal. A common proposal-writing mistake is to budget an amount for evaluation costs and worry later about the evaluation procedure. Instead, involve the evaluators in the proposal writing. Be sure to give them a copy of your project objectives. Recall that pointed objectives will simplify the evaluation process.

Evaluators should provide you with important information to strengthen your proposal. Specifically, ask your evaluators to identify precisely the following:

- What will be evaluated?
- What information will they need to conduct the evaluation?
- Where will that information be obtained?
- When will the information be collected?
- What data collection instruments will be used to get that information?
- What evaluation design will be used?
- What analyses will be completed?
- When will reports be available?
- What questions you will be able to answer as a result of the evaluation?

If you are looking for a good evaluation consultant, contact the grants office at a nearby university. That office is familiar with its faculty expertise and often finds an appropriate evaluator for area organizations and agencies.

KEY QUESTIONS TO ANSWER

As you write this section of the proposal, ask yourself if it does the following:

1. Provide a general organizational plan or model for your evaluation?
2. Identify the type and purpose of your evaluation and the audiences to be served by its results?
3. Demonstrate that an appropriate evaluation procedure is included for every project objective?
4. Demonstrate that the scope of the evaluation is appropriate to the project? To what extent is the project practical, relevant, and generalizable?

5. Describe the information that will be needed to complete the evaluation, the potential sources for this information, and the instruments that will be used for its collection?
6. Define standards that will be used in judging the results of the evaluation?
7. Summarize any reports to be provided to the funding source based on the evaluation, and generally describe their content and timing?
8. Discuss who will be responsible for the evaluation?
9. Establish the credentials of your evaluator, including pertinent prior experience and academic background?
10. Describe mechanisms to disseminate the results of your evaluation?

EXAMPLES OF EVALUATIONS

Example 1

This example presents one type of model that can be used for a project evaluation. It was a portion of a university-based proposal to a federal agency seeking funding to train vocational rehabilitation personnel how to work effectively with hearing impaired youth who are job hunting. Exhibit 47 illustrates process and outcome evaluation questions, outcome criteria, and information collection and reporting plans for one project objective. The remainder of this proposal section went on to list the evaluation approach for other objectives, using this same model format.

Example 2

A geriatrics education proposal submitted to a federal agency that trains health care personnel.

> **Process.** Evaluation is a multifaceted term. In a general sense, the term "evaluation" means to gather information to judge the effectiveness of the project. However, more precise types of evaluation are warranted for this proposal. Specifically, we envision the following evaluation categories:
>
> **Formative Evaluation:** Generating information to improve the educational effectiveness of the Center during the grant period. This evaluation will help determine whether the processes and procedures are working, whether the participants are satisfied with their instruction. This approach represents a good management tool for making "mid-course corrections," providing

Project Evaluation Protocol. To ensure the appropriateness and comprehensiveness of evaluation methods and the use of objective performance measures to produce quantitative and qualitative data, this project follows an evaluation model (Brinkerhoff et al., 1983). This evaluation model makes certain that specific questions are posed for the evaluation, that objectives and outcome criteria are clearly stated, that an information plan is in place and there are plans for data analyses, interpretation and reporting of results. The following table depicts the relationships of the major elements in this evaluation model for all project objectives, which arise from the one major project goal, namely, to increase the number of qualified personnel trained to provide rehabilitation services to transitional youth who are hearing impaired.

Objective 1: By June 2006, develop an O&M curriculum for transition-age youth *(Baseline: No comparable curriculum exists)*

Process Evaluation Questions	Outcome Evaluation Questions
Has pertinent literature been reviewed? Has adequate input been sought from training program directors, vocational rehabilitation professionals, and transitional youth who have recently entered the workforce? Have interviews been held with a convenience sample of youth who failed to gain employment?	Has a curriculum manual been written that includes objectives, materials, procedures, and evaluation for each educational activity? Has the curriculum manual been critiqued by three senior educators and three rehabilitation professionals? Have at least 125 students been successfully trained using this curriculum?

Outcome Criteria Associated with Specific Strategies

1. The resulting curriculum will be developed and independently evaluated.
2. The resulting curriculum will be integrated with the existing curriculum on Individuals with Disabilities Education Act (IDEA) legislation.
3. The "Consumer-Based Model" principles will be applied to "School-to-Work" initiatives.
4. The existing child development course will be modified to include increased emphasis on adolescent behavior and development.

Information Collection Plan	Interpretation and Reporting Plan
Methods and Instruments Literature review of existing curricula. Focus groups with training program directors, Vocational Rehabilitation professionals, and recent youth entering workforce. Interviews with youth who failed to secure jobs. *Types of Data* Curriculum manual. Focus group reports. Interview reports. Curricular evaluations.	The resulting data will be critically reviewed internally and appropriate revisions will be made before reporting outcomes to the appropriate educational and rehabilitation communities through the use of a Web site, www.midwest.edu/transitionalyouth, conference presentations, journal articles, and White Papers to all directors of training programs and state agencies serving the hearing impaired.

EVALUATION MODEL

EXHIBIT 47

the center director and governance council with immediate feedback to make constructive revisions in the training, resource development, and technology transfer activities of the Center.

Summative Evaluation: Collecting data necessary to judge the ultimate success of the completed project. The goal is to document the extent to which the project objectives were achieved; that is, to what extent did the proposal do what it was designed to do? Evaluation feedback will be used for formulating or modifying the sponsor's policy and organization structure, which will improve the likelihood of successfully accomplishing program goals.

The Midwest Geriatric Education Center is not only a structure developed to provide multidisciplinary training, resources, and technology for staffing and service delivery objectives, but it is also a structure that serves as an administrative mechanism to achieve such objectives in the Urban Corridor, which is its geographical focus. This administrative mechanism is designed to be a catalyst and facilitator for change among the educational institutions, the elements of the service delivery system, and the organized professions that also serve the geographic region of the Urban Corridor. Therefore, particular attention will be paid in the evaluation plan to the effectiveness of the Center as an administrative mechanism for achieving professional and institutional change.

To achieve the evaluation goals of this project, the Assistant Directors of Geriatric Education Services will collaborate on the development of data-gathering instruments. This collaboration will express itself in the creation of an Evaluation Steering Committee that the assistant directors will chair. To this committee, the MGEC program director will name seven additional individuals representing the affiliate institutions, agencies, and professions.

The Evaluation Steering Committee shall be charged to agree upon specific measures and data-gathering strategies for each of the variables in the program evaluation protocol. The Evaluation Steering Committee will also review and recommend approval to the Program Director for requests to use data, programs, and products of the Midwest Geriatric Education Center for research, and will assure that the evaluation of the Center is not compromised or contaminated. Finally, the Evaluation Steering Committee will review evaluation activities in progress to identify suggestions that should be made to the Program Director concerning program, structure, or policy that seem warranted on the basis of interim or final results obtained in either the process or outcome evaluation activities. Members of the Evaluation Steering Committee must be appointed in such a way that they are representative of the affiliates and target constituencies, but external to the operations of the MGEC. Thus, the Evaluation Steering Committee will assure objectivity to the evaluation, while permitting maximum feedback to the Center's operations.

Each of the four MGEC goals and the associated objectives are expressed in measurable terms. While the Evaluation Steering Committee bears the responsibility for specific evaluation methodology, their approach will seek,

as a minimum, answers to the following questions for each MGEC goal:

1. *To increase the number of highly trained geriatrics educators*
Determine the number of health professional training institutions in the Urban Corridor. What percentage are consortium members? What are the characteristics of the decision makers within the institutions that joined the consortium? What reasons are given for not joining the consortium? How many geriatrics health care providers exist in the Urban Corridor? How many have links with the consortium academic faculty?

2. *To practice a multidisciplinary approach to geriatric health care*
To what extent was each faculty lecturer able to make an effective and pedagogically sound presentation as evidenced by trainee evaluations? To what extent will trainees be able to utilize multidisciplinary approaches to identify the need for effective patient training packages?

3. *To develop geriatrics education materials*
To what extent will trainees be able to effectively evaluate educational materials in concurrence with peer evaluations? To what extent will the faculty be able to produce and evaluate effective educational packages?

4. *To establish a geriatrics education resource center*
During the grant period, how many requests were received for information, technical assistance, instructional materials, and consultations?

Example 3

A proposal to a federal science agency seeking support for minority students.

The program evaluation process serves two purposes: (1) to provide feedback during program operation, and (2) to provide quantifiable data regarding the short- and long-term effectiveness of the program.

Near the end of the first and second semesters of each program year, each minority fellow and faculty mentor will complete a questionnaire, ending with a section of free commentary. The questionnaires will be prepared and evaluated by the Evaluation Advisory Committee and the project director, who will use the feedback obtained from student and faculty participants to "fine-tune" and improve the operation of the program.

In addition, upon completion of the program, each faculty mentor will complete a student evaluation survey. Additionally, the student fellows will agree in writing to maintain current addresses on file with the department for six years following completion of the Minority Fellowship Program, and to complete an existing evaluation survey upon receipt of their doctorates, a three-year follow-up survey, and a six-year follow-up survey. The data obtained from these surveys will be compiled and analyzed to evaluate the effectiveness of the program in meeting the primary objective of increasing the number of minority individuals entering university teaching and research in electrical and computer engineering.

Observations of the participants would be valuable to the Science Agency in establishing similar programs in the future. Further, comparing national and departmental data can assess the program. The success of the program will be determined based on the grade point averages of the minority fellows, the quality of their dissertation research, the number and quality of their publications, the percentage of minority fellows completing the program, the number of minority fellows actually beginning university teaching careers, the starting salaries of the minority fellows, the quality of the institutions they join and, finally, the progress of their careers after three and six years in the profession. The results of these studies will be reported in the literature after completion of the program, and again after three and six additional years.

Example 4

A childcare development proposal submitted to a private foundation.

> **Evaluation.** An outcomes-directed evaluation plan means collecting data to document the extent to which objectives and activities were achieved. Evaluation feedback will be used to modify childcare programming, trainings, and technical assistance to improve the likelihood of accomplishing project goals. To ensure that the evaluation is objective, meets rigorous standards of research, and is sensitive to ethnic and cultural differences, we will subcontract with external evaluation consultants, Dilworth & Associates, Inc. Methodologically, they will set up appropriate systems to collect, analyze, and report progress on:

1. **Structural measures:** the environment and settings in which services occur, e.g., licensing, accreditation, group size, adult-child ratio, staff experience and turnover.
2. **Process measures:** the type, intensity, and frequency of services provided, e.g., nurturing caregiving, length and quality of teacher-student interactions, responsiveness to children's needs, and cultural- and age-appropriate materials and activities.
3. **Outcome measures:** the effectiveness in achieving goals and end results, e.g., cognitive, social, emotional, physical, and language development improvements in children.

Dr. Katrina H. Davidson, Director of Outcomes Evaluation, will assess the program for usability, satisfaction, and efficacy, including a sophisticated return-on-investment analysis for the community at large and individual participants. Evaluation measures will be practical, efficient, consistent with NAEYC Accreditation Standards, and mirror the Healthy Children Foundation's national evaluation of "Excellent Childcare Centers."

Dissemination is essential to project success because education has a multiplier effect. Consistent monitoring and reporting of evaluation measures will improve children's development, help shape program direction, ensure sustainability, and promote program replication. The intended outcomes of dissemination effort are to affect the knowledge, attitude, and behavior of parents and providers relative to childcare principles and practices.

Example 5

Exhibit 48 shows another graphic technique for portraying project evaluations. The specific example deals with a government proposal to develop some wayfinding technologies for persons with low vision and blindness. In succinct form, it shows the major project components: work planned, intended results, primary assumption, and formative and summative evaluation domains. The missing information pieces, of course, are the who and when, which presumably are indicated on a time and task chart (see Chapter 9).

Further discussions of logic models are found at:

- W.K. Kellogg Foundation www.wkkf.org/Pubs/Tools/Evaluation/Pub3669.pdf
- National Science Foundation www.nsf.gov/pubs/2002/nsf02057/start.htm

Assistive Technology Logic Model

INPUTS	Activities	Outputs	Outcomes	Impacts
Human Resources	**Technical Process: Wayfinding & Info Transfer**	**Project Outputs**	**During Project** *SMART Software Developed and Tested	**After the Project**
*Project PI *Software Engineer *Consumer Advisor *National Subject Pool *National Network with Consumer-Based Organizations	*Requirements *Specifications *Design *Software Development *Hardware Installation	*R&D Strategizing *Meetings *Conferences *Journal Articles *User Satisfaction Data * Formative, Summative Evaluation Data	*Capability to Determine Presence of Individual *Capability to Locate Individual *Capability to Receive Kiosk Information	**For persons with low vision or blindness:** Increased capacity to find people, access information, and move in the environment
Physical Resources	**Administrative Processes**	**Participant Outputs**	*Capability to Manage the Transfer of Text Information via Cell Phone or PDA *Improved Technological Responsiveness to Consumer Communication Needs	**For rehabilitation professionals:** New tools and techniques to foster self-sufficiency, and functional and economic independence
*Sendero Research Laboratories *Benetech Research Laboratories *NFB Jernigan Institute	*IRB Approval *Focus Group User Feedback *Results to Engineering *Final Technical and Fiscal Reports	*PI Findings *Engineering Findings *Increased Consumer Interest *Increased Commercial Interest		

←Formative Evaluation→

← Summative Evaluation →

Feedback Loop

Primary Assumption: R&D activies for persons who are blind or have low vision should be consumer driven

LOGIC MODEL SHOWING EVALUATION IN CONTEXT OF PROJECT MILESTONES

EXHIBIT 48

- University of Wisconsin Extension
  www.uwex.edu/ces/pdande/evaluation/
  evallogicmodel.html
- United Way
  http://national.unitedway.org/outcomes/resources/
  mpo/contents.cfm

WRITING TIPS FOR THE EVALUATION SECTION

1. Make sure that you include a separate evaluation component for each project objective. Designing an evaluation section for each objective forces you to examine the clarity of your objectives, the ease with which they can be measured, and the possibility of their being achieved. A free *User-Friendly Handbook for Mixed-Method Evaluations* is available online at: www.nsf.gov/pubs/1997/nsf97153.
2. If outside consultants are used, identify costs, credentials, and experience.
3. Evaluation sections are less likely to be included in NSF and NIH basic science research grants. Therefore, to include an evaluation section in a research proposal may give you a competitive edge. Replicability is the primary evaluation criterion in most basic science research proposals.

REJECTION REASONS

Some reviewers' comments concerning poor evaluation sections include the following:

1. Evaluation strategy is weak; much of it yet to be developed with the help of unidentified consultants.
2. The evaluation section belabors obvious problems in reliability of measurement but is thin on specific procedures directly relevant to the purposes of the proposal.
3. Although evaluation is tailored to individual objectives, specific outcomes are rarely mentioned. Much of the evaluation plan is philosophical, rather than describing methodology.

4. Program evaluation funding, representing 2 percent of the total budget, is inadequately low to carry out a quality evaluation that looks at process and outcome measures across multiple collaborators, and to participate in a national evaluation.
5. The proposal does not describe methods, objectives, and instruments to measure and evaluate clinical quality.
6. The proposal does not identify a specific expert or organization to conduct the evaluation. What are the evaluator's qualifications?
7. The proposal does not describe how data collection will be standardized across partner agencies so that evaluation results will be meaningful.
8. The sample size of subjects is inappropriate to produce reliable and valid results.
9. The design of this project fails to evaluate important gender, age, and racial/ethnic population differences.
10. This project employs a weak evaluation design to be executed by an inexperienced evaluation staff.

Because grantmakers are increasingly insisting on an evaluation component in proposals, you need to have a strong evaluation section in your proposals. Be sure you avoid problems like those cited above. If you lack evaluation expertise, call your nearest university grants office and ask them to help you select a professor with a specialty in your area.

 **Clip File Action Item # 15 Evaluation**

These suggestions will help launch your Evaluation clip file:

- Secure copies of successful evaluation strategies used in other similar proposals.
- Collect names and resumes of potential project evaluators.
- Retrieve examples from projects you have successfully evaluated in the past.
- Explore the Web sites cited above.
- Take an online tutorial on logic models: www.uwex.edu/ces/lmcourse.

CHAPTER 11
Dissemination

A crank is someone with a new idea—until it catches on.
—Mark Twain

PURPOSE OF DISSEMINATION

Dissemination is the means by which you tell others about your project: its purpose, methods, and results. It's also a way for sponsors to get "more bang for their buck." Some grantmaker application forms may treat the dissemination portion as part of the methodology section. Whether separate or a part of the methodology section, give serious consideration to dissemination if you want to construct a highly competitive proposal. Project dissemination offers many advantages, including increasing public awareness of your program or project, soliciting additional support, locating more clients, alerting others in your field to new ideas, and adding to the stockpile of knowledge. You may need to use different dissemination techniques for different audiences. Remember to justify the budgeted costs of dissemination to the sponsor.

KEY QUESTIONS TO ANSWER

As you write the dissemination section, answer these key questions. Does your proposal do the following:

1. Clearly identify the intended results of the dissemination effort?
2. Include a feasible and appropriate plan for dissemination?
3. Succinctly describe any products to result from the dissemination effort?
4. Demonstrate that you understand dissemination principles and practices?
5. Provide sufficient detail to justify your dissemination budget request?
6. Include imaginative and practical dissemination?
7. Specify precisely who will be responsible for dissemination and why they are capable?
8. Discuss internal as well as external project dissemination?
9. Evaluate the effectiveness of the dissemination efforts and products?
10. Indicate how and when the audiences will get the timely and useful information?

DISSEMINATION STRATEGIES FOR GRANT PROPOSALS

Your specific project dissemination strategies can be active or passive. The active/passive distinction refers to your target audiences and the role they play in processing the information you present. To illustrate, if you write up a report on your project results, your reader will respond passively, since reading is a passive process. On the other hand, if you involve your target audience in a hands-on demonstration of a project result, your strategy is active, since your participants are doing things with their hands. While the active/passive distinction is not wholly discrete, Exhibit 49 illustrates how the more common dissemination strategies might be classified.

As a proposal writer, you should write "generic" versions of each dissemination strategy, about two paragraphs long, and store them in your clip file (see Chapter 1), ready for final editing in your next proposal. A "generic" two-paragraph example follows for each of the 24 dissemination strategies in Exhibit 49. Each example can be adapted to your specific situation. The examples arise from the same theme and assume a proposal is being submitted to develop some

Classification of Common Dissemination Strategies	
Active Dissemination Strategies	**Passive Dissemination Strategies**
1. Commercial Distributors	13. Books & Manuals
2. Conferences & Workshops	14. CD-ROMS
3. Courses & Seminars	15. Conference Papers
4. Demonstrations	16. Executive Summaries
5. Displays/Poster Sessions	17. Interim Working Papers
6. Instructional Materials	18. Journal Articles
7. Site Visits	19. National Information Sources
8. Teleconferences	20. Newsletters & Listservs
9. Video Conferences	21. Pamphlets
10. Webcasts & Chat Rooms	22. Press Releases
11. Web Sites, Blogs, Podcasts, & Video on Demand	23. Staff Presentations
12. Webinars & Instant Messaging	24. Text Messaging

COMMON DISSEMINATION STRATEGIES

EXHIBIT 49

training materials in bioethics that would be used to train members of Institutional Review Boards, committees that approve the use of human subjects in research experiments. Obviously, not all examples would be used in any one proposal.

We begin our example with an orienting paragraph:

> Dissemination of project activities is essential because education has a multiplier effect. The intended results of the project's dissemination effort are to affect the knowledge, attitude, and behavior of health care providers within the hospital system relative to ethical principles and practices. Accordingly, the project will use the following strategic mix of active and passive dissemination strategies.

Active Dissemination Strategies

1. **Commercial Distributors** may agree to produce or market project results. Do you anticipate using a commercial vendor to produce and distribute your project products?

> All resulting tangible products—Training Manual, Demonstration Video, and Training Video—will be produced and distributed by Woodgrain Publishers, who has a 25-year history of successful marketing of biomedical training materials. A preliminary draft of a marketing and licensing agreement has been approved in principle by all parties and now awaits formal completion of the Training Manual.

> One key feature of the marketing agreement sets minimum sales thresholds. Should Woodgrain fail to meet those minimums for whatever reason, we have the option to cancel our agreement and change distributors. While this seems unlikely in actual practice, it is an important contract mechanism to ensure widespread distribution of the intended project results.

2. **Conferences and Workshops** are hosted for individuals or groups that might be interested in project results. What regular forums exist that would be attracted to your project findings?

> During the final quarter of the project period, we will sponsor a Midwest Regional Conference on Bioethics, tentatively titled "Managing Change with Fewer Resources: How to do More with Less—Ethically." Dr. Roberta Griff from the Kennedy Bioethics Institute, a nationally recognized expert in Bioethics, has tentatively agreed to present a keynote speech titled "Application of Ethical Principles to Bioethical Decision-Making." Concurrent breakout sessions will use the case study approach to apply ethical principles in specific patient situations.

> Conference invitations will be sent to all central hospital administrators, all department

heads, and Institutional Review Board members in a five state area, representing approximately 2,500 health professionals; a minimum audience of 250 is anticipated. No registration fees will be charged, although participants will be asked to pay $25.00 for two luncheon meals during the two-day conference, which will be held at the Wingspread Conference Center. Dr. Howard Thornberg will serve as conference observer and write a conference evaluation report, a role that he has repeatedly fulfilled over the past decade. Resumes for Drs. Griff and Thornberg are included in the proposal appendix.

3. **Courses and Seminars** show how the information resulting from the project can be explained to others in a formal instructional setting. Does the nature of your project warrant creation of a special course?

The instructional materials that result from this project form the basis of a continuing education course that could be presented either in person or via the Internet. If presented as a course or seminar, the project director would, working in conjunction with the hospital Director of Continuing Education, arrange for Continuing Medical Education credits (CMEs) to be awarded, thereby counting towards certification requirements. An all-day (eight hour) seminar would permit sufficient coverage of the topic. The hospital administers approximately 75 CME programs per year and brings a prior history of success in coordinating similar seminars.

If the seminar proves successful after several presentations, then it would be converted to a Web-based format and be available online, on-demand so that health professionals could view the training program over the Internet at their convenience. The Office of Continuing Education has instructional designers and Web technology experts who can adapt the content of the training materials to this electronic format that allows for self-paced learning.

4. **Demonstrations** illustrate techniques and materials developed by the projects. Will you develop instructional materials requiring demonstrations?

To increase distribution of the *IRB Bioethics Training Manual*, a 10-minute video demonstration will be prepared to highlight its contents and applications. More specifically, typical clinical scenarios will be presented to show the complexity and impact of bioethical decision-making. Appealing to adult learning

styles, the demonstration video will emphasize the practical applications of ethical theory. In essence, the demonstration video becomes a marketing tool for Woodgrain Publishers to stimulate sales; Woodgrain will underwrite all costs associated with preparation of the video.

The video will be shot in standard DVD format and be of commercial broadcast quality. Woodgrain will use its production studio to shoot and edit the video, once the script storyboard has been prepared. Woodgrain has used this marketing approach with 10 other products in the past two years and found it very successful. The sponsor's role in funding the entire project will be, of course, properly acknowledged.

5. **Displays and Poster Sessions** can be held at appropriate meetings and conferences. Which meetings? Where and when? How many individuals typically attend?

Besides presenting a paper at the National Bioethics Society Convention on July 1, 2009, we will also conduct a poster display of our major project results. The poster display will be titled "Avoiding the Horns of Ethical Dilemmas: A Case Study at the Midwest Agency." More precisely, a case study will trace the bioethical issues and their effective resolution. Poster sessions offer the advantage of one-on-one interaction with interested convention participants.

Beyond disseminating information about the project results, the poster display represents an opportunity to build our newsletter mailing list and identify new collaborators who share our project values. The convention regularly draws 500 attendees from across the country. In particular, we will be seeking other organizations in different geographic locations who might like to replicate our project results, thereby increasing its generalizability.

6. **Instructional Materials** include such things as films, slide shows, filmstrips, videotapes, CDs, DVDs, PowerPoint presentations, or television programs. Will audiovisual materials be produced internally or commercially?

Beyond the demonstration video for marketing purposes, Woodgrain will prepare and distribute a video companion to the *IRB Bioethics Training Manual*. The video will supplement, not supplant the text. More specifically, it will show typical IRB case studies and invite viewer comments based on pertinent bioethical principles prior to showing the actual IRB result.

The final DVD will be approximately 45 minutes long and of commercial broadcast quality. To ensure the appropriateness of the content, two separate focus groups will view the draft cuts and offer suggestions for final editing. The Training Manual and the video will be marketed as one companion unit and not sold separately. The resulting royalties will be used to continue the project beyond the grant period.

7. **Site Visits** are arranged for representatives of key professional associations or organizations. Could you host a site visit, a special briefing that allows key representatives to capture your enthusiasm and results first hand?

During the final project year, a series of four Bioethics in Action Site Visits will be held for key officials, including central hospital administrators, IRB Chairs, health care advocates, and governmental officials. The objective of the site visits—frankly—is to have the administrators and policy-makers visit us and see the personal and practical consequences of bioethical decision-making. This information, in turn, should have a positive impact on future ethical policies upon which these decision-makers must act.

Each site visit will include the following activities during its day-long schedule: Overview of policies and implementation strategies, brief case history reviews, a grand rounds tour of pertinent patients, observation of an IRB meeting, interviews of select patients and families, and a question and answer session. Preparatory materials will be sent to the site visitors one month in advance of their arrival at our facility.

8. **Teleconferences** are group telephone conference calls. Should you hold a group conference call about your project results?

Teleconferences are one of the most cost-effective and time-efficient dissemination strategies available. Live, real-time interactive audio communications occur no matter where the key participants are located, whether they are participating on their cell phone or in a large group on speaker phone.

One objective of this project is to disseminate the results to policy-makers. The strategy is to hold a teleconference call with the staff members in each congressional office that handles health and aging issues. A one-page Results Fact Sheet will be faxed to the participants one week in advance of the teleconference. At the agreed upon conference hour, participants will dial in to the central number and be connected so all parties can hear each other. The project director will present a 10-minute summary of the major project results that have significant policy implications. Next, a 30-minute question and answer period follows. Finally, a 20-minute list of potential legislative policy action items will be generated and subsequently shared with all federal legislators in the state through their key staff members.

9. **Video Conferences** are televised versions of telephone conference calls. It is particularly useful in those instances when participant visual feedback is important to disseminating information. Will a video conference expand the reach of your project?

Video conferencing uses television to join people in live interaction. Its applications range from live video lecturing to large audiences, to a point-to-point, individual-to-individual desktop PC chat. In essence, it integrates the best of distance and conventional information exchanges as participants get together on a "virtual" basis.

One of the target audiences for the project results is health professionals and bioethicists in the 147 Veterans Administration Medical Centers located throughout the country. Accordingly, a two-hour teleconference, titled "Bioethics: Nice Solutions to Nagging Problems," will be held for this audience. A satellite relay system involving one-way video and two-way audio will connect all VAMC locations; each has the necessary send-and-receive technology and indeed, has been involved in video-conferencing for the past six years. The teleconference will focus on three main topics: major project findings, clinical applications, and two case studies, including a question and answer period, all coordinated by the Project Director.

10. **Webcasts** are similar to TV broadcasts over the Internet. Could you broadcast your project results over the Internet? The Web site www.webcast academy.net/faq offers suggestions regarding conducting Webcasts, which are often followed-up with a live **Chat Room.**

The widespread use of the Internet offers new dissemination strategies. One novel technique growing in popularity is Webcasting. With this approach, one literally broadcasts a program over the Internet much like a television show is broadcast. The technological requirements are minimal. At the broadcast end, a camera is attached to a personal computer, which, in turn, is logged on to the Internet. At the receiver end, one only needs a free software program to receive the broadcast, e.g., Real-Player.

Our broadcast, Bioethics 101, will be available to anyone worldwide who can access the Internet. Simple instructions for accessing the broadcast will be posted on our Web site two weeks in advance of the broadcast. Participants can download handouts in advance of the presentation. An e-mail address will be used for participants to send in questions and receive answers during the broadcast. A Chat Room will be created so participants can continue their electronic discussions in real time after the Webcast.

11. **Web Sites** are international electronic libraries with collections of pages, images, and videos. Pre-recorded audio and video files can be distributed as **Podcasts** or **Video on Demand,** and Web site visitors can chronicle their thoughts, opinions, and reactions in a **Blog.** Can your project results be filed in the world's electronic library—the Internet?

It is axiomatic that the project results will be filed on our Web site. A recorded version will also be made available for viewing as video on demand. This offers multiple advantages. The Web site is not appreciably constrained by length. It can easily be updated. It represents the latest technology trend in information dissemination. It can be shared with anyone in an asynchronous format. It is a familiar and friendly communication tool for the end users.

Hosting the report in text and video formats on our Web site is a necessary but not a sufficient condition of information dissemination. The blog feature will allow site visitors to interact with each other, making notes of the report elements they found most useful. Equally important, the report will be structured to attract the major search engines, e.g., Google or Yahoo! This is done by registering the site with the major search engines and loading the report with key words that will facilitate search engine identification. Without belaboring details, we have the technological expertise to attract top search engine hits.

12. A **Webinar** is an interactive multimedia presentation that is transmitted over the Web. Participants view PowerPoint (or Word, Access, or Excel) presentations through their Web-browser and listen to the instructor through a telephone conference call. When participants have questions, they can ask directly on the phone or via **Instant Messaging** on the web. Does your project warrant a presentation to a disparate audience of professionals?

Webinars are a cost-effective and efficient way of using technology to disseminate information on a nationwide scale. Two 90-minute webinars will be offered during the course of the year to the 2,500 nationwide members of the Bioethicists of America. The first webinar, "A Primer on Bioethics," will target professionals new to the field and the second webinar, "Bioethics: Turing Theory into Practice," aims to reach seasoned veterans who are ready to take their programs to a new level.

Not only will participants be able to view the PowerPoint presentation from the comfort of their own offices (and thus save their limited travel dollars), but they will be able to participate in instant polls and ask questions via instant messaging. Web-based polling allows information to be processed immediately and provides instructors with a simple way to gauge participant learning and, in response, incorporate results into the presentation. Both instant polls and instant messages can be set up to ensure a level of anonymity and, as a result, help to create a positive environment where there are no "dumb questions."

Passive Dissemination Strategies

13. **Books and Manuals** are either issued by your organization, the sponsor, or commercial publishers. Do you anticipate textual material to be published for public consumption?

The primary result of this project is to produce a training manual for use with Institutional Review Boards as they consider complex bioethical issues. The leading publisher in the field is Woodgrain Publishers, who has expressed strong conceptual interest in publishing our *IRB Bioethics Training Manual* after review of two initial chapters and the table of contents. Because of their national reputation as a publisher of biomedical books, they have the marketing distribution channels and networks necessary to ensure a reasonable market penetration.

A 200-page training manual is envisioned and will consist of three parts: Ethical Principles, Biomedical Applications, and Case Studies. We will provide appropriate text and references, while Woodgrain will handle graphics and illustrations in addition to marketing. In the event Woodgrain decides against publication, three other publishers in the bioethics field will be contacted. A text delivery date of November 2009 is anticipated.

14. **CD-ROMs** can be used to disseminate project reports instead of the more traditional printed reports. Could you prepare an electronic report that could be produced inexpensively and shared with other computer users?

We propose taking a cost-effective approach to the dissemination of our final project report. Rather than spend valuable project dollars printing a more traditional, four-color report with fancy graphics, we propose to prepare our report on a CD-ROM that can be widely disseminated at low cost. The final report consumers are extensive computer users and will find great convenience in being able to read and search the report for items of special interest to themselves.

Because the report consumers have different electronic platforms—some have IBM personal computers while others are Macintosh users—it is important to prepare the final report in a universal electronic format. Portable Document Format (PDF) files satisfy this requirement. Accordingly, the final report will be prepared using PDF files and a link will be included to a Web site where the latest version of Adobe Reader software for viewing the files can be downloaded for free. The final project report cost will be approximately 30 cents per disc.

15. **Conference Papers** are delivered at regional or national conferences, conventions, trade shows, or professional society gatherings. Which conferences? Where and when?

The project results will be presented at the National Bioethics Society Convention to be held in San Diego on July 1, 2011. The convention has an average attendance of 1,500 bioethics professionals from throughout the United States. The tentative working title of the conference paper is "Avoiding the Horns of Ethical Dilemmas: The Midwest Agency Experience."

The main thrust of the paper is to disseminate project results to the leading national bioethicists. Through the case study method, we will explain how the rather abstract principles of ethical decision-making apply in some very concrete ways to people with seriously impaired health status. Copies of our paper will also be placed on our Web site at www.artseducation.org for those individuals wishing copies; our Web site home page receives approximately 1,300 hits per month. A Web counter will tally the number of hits on the conference paper page, and we will include this information in our final project report to the sponsor.

16. **Executive Summaries** of project results can be faxed to appropriate persons. Are there significant professionals who would appreciate a brief but very timely abstract of your project results?

The ubiquitous fax machine is an ideal communication tool to disseminate executive summaries of project results. Timely project summaries will be distributed to top hospital administrators, IRB chairs, and policy-makers. Taking advantage of skim reading techniques—bulleted lists, bold headings, and short sentences— the executive summaries are intended to keep the project and its results foremost on the minds of executives.

To meet this goal of high visibility, the content emphasis has to focus on how the project results impact the daily lives of executives, e.g., selection of members to local IRBs, ethical treatment of patients, mediation of ethical disputes, and new regulatory agency requirements. The overarching principle is to add value to the executives' understanding of bioethics.

17. **Interim Working Papers** can be used to describe those portions of project findings of most immediate interest to other audiences. Do you have significant provisional findings to share with various publics?

Because our project work progresses in distinct phases, we plan to issue interim progress reports—to be called White Papers. These White Papers will briefly summarize project results to date and concentrate on the findings from each ethical principle and its application; that is to say, since the project involves six different ethical principles, six different White Papers will be issued, each within 30 days after the completion of each project phase.

Each White Paper will follow the same general format. Following introductory remarks, a basic principle of ethics will be described from its philosophical roots, followed by a discussion of some practical applications of the principle. An annotated bibliography will conclude each White Paper, which is projected to be about 10 pages long. All White Papers will, of course, also be posted on our Web site in addition to being distributed to key policy-makers.

18. **Journal Articles** can be submitted to scholarly, professional, or trade journals. Which publications? What tentative article titles?

Bioethics professionals read two major journals: *The National Journal of Bioethics* and the *Bioethics Society Journal*. Each has a circulation in excess of 1,000 subscribers, consisting of theoreticians and practitioners alike. Our first submission will be to the *National Journal of Bioethics* no later than August 1, 2009. Since this journal encourages a more theoretical perspective, our tentative working title is "Theoretical Perspectives on Bioethics: The Midwest Project." In our 1,500 word article, we shall trace the ethical roots of the major decision-making principles that confront bioethicists. If accepted for publication without revision, Summer 2010 would be a reasonable publication date.

The article for the *Bioethics Society Journal* requires a slightly different approach. Since its readers are primarily practitioners and clinicians, our tentative working title is "Practical Applications of Ethical Principles: the Midwest Project." In this 1,200 word article to be submitted by October 1, 2009, we will emphasize how this project has taken basic ethical principles and applied them to complex biomedical problems. Barring major changes, a Fall 2010 publication date is expected.

19. **National Information Sources** like the National Technical Information Service can be used as a repository for reports and raw data. Can you make your data and major reports available to a nationwide information service?

Our primary source data and major project reports will be filed with the National Technical Information Service (NTIS), a branch of the U.S. Department of Commerce. This information warehouse makes federal grant data available to interested individuals. More precisely, other professionals concerned with bioethics will be able to learn the project title,

project director, information about our organization, and a detailed description of the project along with the resulting data.

We anticipate filing the NTIS documents no later than August 1, 2011. Our entry will then be included in their electronic catalog within two weeks, thereby making the project results instantly available, as opposed to waiting a year or more for an article to be published in a professional journal. Our newsletters and poster displays will direct interested professionals to NTIS for more project details. NTIS averages more than 400,000 information requests annually.

20. **Newsletters and Listservs** can be circulated to selected organizations and individuals in the field. Who are the influential decision-makers that share your concern for this project?

To disseminate the results of this project, we will publish a monthly electronic newsletter titled "Bioethics Briefings," with the tagline Tips, Ideas, and Techniques to Promote Bioethics among Health Professionals. The target audience includes central hospital administrators, all department heads and Institutional Review Board members from all participating hospitals. Feature columns include From the Editor's Desk, Practically Speaking, Ethically Speaking, Clinician's Calendar, Field Focus, and Medicolegal News. Since health professionals are very busy, it will be written for newsletter skimmers: short copy, highly practical, bolded text for emphasis, white space, and bulleted lists. Readers can skim, skip, surf and flip through the text quickly.

The newsletter will emphasize four features under the direction of Robert Hopkins, Director of Staff Communications:

1. It will tell people who we are, where they can find us, and what we can do for them.
2. It will draw people into the newsletter by showing that we can provide what the readers need and that we have expertise in the area.
3. It will give specific features and reasons why readers should follow the principles of ethical behavior.
4. It will tell the readers what action to take—attending a seminar, joining a study group, participating in a focus group, or discussing cases with colleagues.

21. **Pamphlets** describe available project products and their potential use. Do you anticipate a tangible, marketable product?

One major result of this project is the development of training materials in bioethics that are specifically targeted to Institutional Review Board members. Since IRB training is now federally mandated, an identifiable need and market exists. The budget requests $5,500 to publish and distribute a brochure that would announce the availability of the training materials.

Since our organization lacks the capacity to publish attractive but reasonably priced pamphlets and brochures, this production item will be outsourced to the Midwest Brochure Publishing Company. For a cost of 75 cents per pamphlet, they can produce and mail a three-fold, four-color document. In total, 3,000 pamphlets will be distributed nationwide. The resulting income from product sales will be used to continue the project beyond the grant period.

22. **Press Releases** can be issued to the mass media. Do you have the necessary resources to issue quality press releases?

The project staff have 84 years of cumulative experience in issuing successful press releases. Over time, the following rules of writing press releases have become clear. Press releases attract attention when they emphasize the relevant. Include all of the who-what-when-where-why-how facts. Write in simple sentences. Don't jam too much into a sentence. Make the lead paragraph strong.

Writing strong press releases is only part of the job; the other part is distributing it to the right targets. The first rule of trash-can avoidance is don't send trash. Take the time to do a good job but don't bury the recipients in a paper blizzard. The case study applications of bioethics have strong human interest appeal and will be the focus of mass media press releases.

23. **Staff Presentations** might be made at local, state, and national meetings. Can you and your staff proactively reach out to various professional forums?

Dissemination of project results is a project priority. Among the multiple dissemination strategies used in this project, key staff members will use their existing networks to make presentations at local and regional meetings. To ensure quality and uniformity of presentations, the project director will oversee the development of a PowerPoint presentation, approximately 30 minutes in length that can easily be adapted for different audiences. A minimum of one presentation per month is planned.

The content of the presentation will mirror the Manual and Training Video, namely, ethical principles, bioethical practices, and case studies. While all key staff members are experienced in making public presentations, the Chairman of the Speech Department at Midwest University will present a short in-service workshop to ensure quality field presentations.

24. **Text Messages** are a quick, easy, and quiet way to send and receive brief information. Will your target audience be responsive to this means of mass communication?

The ubiquitous cell phone offers an easy and affordable way to keep in contact with workshop participants: group text messaging. At the conclusion of the workshop, participants will have the opportunity to sign up for personalized text alerts to be sent to them monthly. Alerts will serve as a reminder to visit our Web site for announcements about upcoming workshops, recently published white papers, and new video on demand offerings. A private group chat can also be established for particular topics of interest.

Sending a group text message is quite simple: messages of up to 160 characters are typed in using the keypad and then sent to cell phone numbers or e-mail addresses. Even if a cell phone is turned off, the text message will be stored and retried for delivery for up to 72 hours. Many workshop participants can be reached with a single text message. What's more, regular messages prevent this topic from becoming "out of sight, out of mind."

WRITING TIPS FOR THE DISSEMINATION SECTION

1. Identify the specific information you wish to disseminate, e.g., interim findings, project results, project outcomes, project impacts. Your evaluation data will help pinpoint significant findings.
2. Determine your dissemination target audiences, e.g., staff members, parents, politicians, educators, policy-makers, community leaders, grantmakers, media representatives, business officials.

Project Dissemination Strategies		
Specific Information	Target Audience	Dissemination Strategy
Project Policy Implications	Local, County Politicians	Executive Summary
Final Project Report	Professional Colleagues Program Officer	Journal Article Conference Presentation
Practical Health Implications	Community Citizens	Press Release Media Presentation

TABLE DEPICTING PROJECT DISSEMINATION STRATEGIES

EXHIBIT 50

3. Select the appropriate dissemination strategies from among the options listed in Exhibit 49.
4. Consider introducing your dissemination strategies to your reviewers by use of a table, as illustrated in Exhibit 50.

Exhibit 50 presents the beginnings of a table summarizing how you might write-up your dissemination strategies. You would, of course, begin with an introductory paragraph, as modeled above. After the table, you would include the two-paragraph descriptions of each dissemination strategy, adding perhaps a sentence or two about the specific target audiences. If space is limited, some of the fuller descriptions of dissemination strategies could be included as an appendix item.

REJECTION REASONS

Some reviewer comments from rejected proposals include the following.

1. The project is unique but lacks an effective strategy for disseminating some potentially significant results.
2. This proposal contains no plans for translating the results in a highly readable form, drawing practical implications, and getting this information into a dissemination network.
3. Unfortunately, the proposal advances no mechanism to share the project results with influential policy-makers.

4. While the proposal offers some novel dissemination strategies, the costs of dissemination are not addressed in the budget.
5. The resume of the project director is silent on his technical capabilities to handle videoconferencing as a dissemination strategy. Before funding can be recommended, the project director should either document his technology expertise, especially as regards to bandwidth, or agree to hire a consultant in this area.

Clip File Action Item # 16 Dissemination

To build your Dissemination clip file, follow these suggestions:

- Each day, pick one of the dissemination strategies cited above and write a "generic version" for your organization: proper names, project titles, and dates can be inserted later. In one month, you will have a smorgasbord of dissemination strategies that can be called upon when needed.
- Garner examples of successful dissemination strategies used in other proposals.
- Enter the key words highlighted above for each of the 24 dissemination strategies into your favorite search engine to find ideas that will strengthen your clip file offerings.

CHAPTER 12
Budgets

There are no price objections, only value questions.
—Helen Feden

PURPOSE

A project budget is more than a statement of proposed expenditures. It is an alternate way to express your project, establish its credibility, and judge your project's value. Reviewers will scrutinize your budget to see how well it fits your proposed activities. Incomplete budgets are examples of sloppy preparation. Inflated budgets are signals of waste. Low budgets cast doubt on your planning ability. In essence, your budget is as much a credibility statement as your project narrative.

In addition to the size of your budget, your distribution of expenditures gives important clues about your organization's commitment to the project. For instance, with training or service grants, don't ask for all the money up front with a vague promise that you will share the costs in subsequent years. Instead, when preparing multiyear budgets, show that you will pick up an increasing amount of the costs each year. In doing this, you communicate your intent to continue the project after the sponsor's funds are gone. Further, you are developing your capacity to fund the program. In this way, you demonstrate that you will be a good steward of the sponsor's funds. Future funding is not apt to be an issue in most research grants, which may have limited time spans.

Preparing proposal budgets can be a bedeviling experience for beginning writers. The starting point is to understand the different types of costs included in budget building. Some key budget terms are discussed below, namely, direct costs, indirect costs, and cost sharing. In mathematical terms, the amount of money you request from the sponsor is the sum of your direct and indirect costs minus any cost sharing.

Direct Costs

Direct costs are explicit project expenditures listed as line items in the budget. Direct costs are usually categorized into personnel (people) and nonpersonnel (things) components. Personnel costs include such items as salaries, wages, fringe benefits, consultant fees, and contractor charges. Nonpersonnel costs include such items as equipment, supplies, travel, and publication charges. Usually, direct cost figures are easy to pinpoint. For example, grant-funded salaries are calculated as a percentage of the time and effort devoted to the project relative to one's annual salary. As another illustration, travel costs can be computed on the basis of reimbursement costs per mile or round-trip airfare, as appropriate. (For the latest federally approved reimbursement rates, visit the Internal Revenue Service Web site at www.irs.gov and search for "mileage rates.") Space and utilities may be reflected either as direct costs or included as a part of your indirect cost rate, which is described next.

Indirect Costs

Indirect costs represent other project costs not itemized as direct costs. Typically, grant budgets don't list *all* of the costs associated with a project because some costs are hard to pin down, e.g., payroll and accounting, library usage, space and equipment, and general project administration. Do you include in your proposal budget the costs associated with preparing payrolls or the time your boss spends talking with you about your project? Although you could cost out those factors, and others, with some effort, they are more difficult to quantify. At the same time, they are real project costs, e.g., someone has to write your payroll checks. Rather than calculating a strict cost accounting of these nebulous factors, many sponsors allow you to compute them as a percentage of your direct costs and add it to your budget request as an indirect cost item.

Federal Indirect Costs. Semantically, most federal agencies now use the term "facilities and administration costs (F&A)" instead of "indirect costs" to refer to these additional project operating costs. These F&A grant costs are usually calculated on a percentage figure assigned to you by the federal government as a result of an indirect cost audit. The percentage figure may be based on either the total direct costs or a percentage of the total project salaries and wages. To illustrate, assume the federal government assigned you an indirect cost rate of 45 percent of total direct costs. This means that for every dollar you receive in federal direct costs, the government would give you an additional 45 cents to administer that dollar expenditure. The government recognizes that it costs something to do business.

Organizations regularly receiving federal grants have an approved federal indirect cost rate that is included in the budgets of federal proposals; it consists of two major component categories: facilities and administration. "Facilities" is defined as depreciation and use allowances on buildings, equipment and capital improvements, interest on debt associated with certain building, equipment and capital improvements, and operations and maintenance expenses. "Administration" is defined as general administration and general expenses such as the director's office, accounting, personnel, library expenses, and all other types of expenditures not listed specifically under one of the subcategories of "Facilities."

If you plan to periodically submit federal proposals and do not have a federal indirect cost rate, your federal program officer can refer you to the appropriate federal agency to find out how you negotiate a federal indirect cost rate for your organization. Alternatively, you can get started by visiting the Office of Management and Budget Web site, www.white house.gov/omb/grants/attach.html#cost.

Foundation Indirect Costs. Foundations often use the term "administrative costs" rather than the term "indirect costs" or "F&A costs" when referring to additional project operating expenses, although the terms are interchangeable. Foundations vary considerably in their policies regarding administrative costs. Some will pay administrative costs on grants and their application guidelines specify the allowable percentage of total direct costs. For instance, one health-related foundation has a fixed administrative cost rate of 20 percent; to submit a budget, you add up all of the direct costs and add an additional 20 percent to the total to cover your operating expenses.

Other foundations will say explicitly in their application materials that they do not fund administrative costs. In those instances, you have two options: (1) absorb those operating costs within your organization's budget, or (2) itemize those operating costs as direct costs within your proposal budget and recover those costs as direct line-item costs.

For instance, if you think you will need 5 percent of your boss's time to provide updates on your project progress, include that 5 percent time as a direct proposal cost. If you choose the first option of absorbing those costs, at least show it as a cost-sharing component to your project, as discussed below. If you choose the second option of direct cost itemization, you are, in reality, taking your administrative (or indirect cost) rate apart and budgeting it as a direct cost item. Many nonprofit organizations fail to realize they can recover these operating costs if only they would ask for them. Administering a grant should not cost your organization any money.

Although some private foundations permit charging administrative costs and others don't, the majority of the foundations remain silent on this budget issue; that is, their application materials do not specify what their policy is, and yet they have administrative costs themselves. Somebody has to pay their utilities, payrolls, insurances, and other operating costs. In such instances, the preferred approach is to request of private foundations the same indirect cost rate that they are paying themselves. To do that, look at a foundation's tax returns, annual reports, or description in the Foundation Directory (see Chapter 3) and identify two figures: (1) the total amount of grants awarded, and (2) the total expenditures for the year. For instance, recall that the Ramsey Charles Foundation (from Chapter 3) spent $17,221,933 during their fiscal year, including $16,032,149 in grants. What happened to the other $1,189,784? That amount (7 percent) represented their operating costs. Accordingly, when submitting a budget to the Ramsey Charles Foundation, you might include this language:

> In addition to the direct costs of $10,000, we are requesting 7 percent or ($700) in administrative costs, the same rate that the Ramsey Charles Foundation incurred in your last fiscal year, according to your tax records. Our total project investment is $10,700.

Corporate Indirect Costs. In contrast to governments and foundations, corporations use the term "overhead" to mean the same thing as administrative, indirect, or F&A costs. As business professionals, they are accustomed to the concept of overhead and are apt to have a high overhead rate themselves.

In most instances, the corporate application materials do not specify a policy regarding the payment of overhead. Unlike foundations, you do not have access to their tax records to request a comparable corporate rate for your project but you do have three other options for determining a reasonable overhead rate to include in your proposal.

First, if they are a publicly held company, you may be able to determine their overhead rate by studying the latest annual report. Second, some corporate officials might be willing to tell you or one of your advisory members what their overhead rate is as a percentage of their total costs. Third, if you have no basis for calculating their corporate overhead, you can use your federally negotiated indirect cost rate since it is an audited figure. If none of these three options is acceptable, your fallback position is to list everything as direct cost items.

Cost Sharing

The costs that your organization will contribute to the total project costs are called "shared costs." You may contribute partial personnel costs, space, volunteer time, or other costs toward the total project expenses. Your cost sharing may be in the form of a "hard" dollar match or one of in-kind contributions—costs not requiring a cash outlay to your organization, although they would represent real dollars if you had to pay for services rendered, e.g., the value of time contributed by volunteers. Use a fair market value to calculate in-kind contributions; simply determine what it would cost you if you had to buy those volunteered services or goods outright. For example, if teens are helping you stuff envelopes as part of a direct mail campaign, you might use a minimum wage figure to show cost sharing. On the other hand, if you have a volunteer attorney giving you *pro bono* services to evaluate a new rental contract, you would use that person's hourly billing rate multiplied by the number of donated hours as a cost sharing budget item.

Because expectations about cost sharing vary considerably, check with your program officer to determine their preferences. In fact, preproposal contact (Chapter 4) is essential to determine the value that cost sharing carries in evaluating budgets. Many

sponsors still look upon cost sharing as evidence that your organization is committed to your proposed project to the extent that you are willing to absorb some of its expenses. Some sponsors will require a minimum amount of cost sharing, as indicated in their proposal guidelines. For instance, the challenge grants program at the National Endowment for the Humanities requires recipients to raise three or four times the amount of the federal funds offered. On the other hand, some sponsors don't place a high value on cost sharing, even to the extent of insisting that the cost sharing be dropped from the proposed budget as a condition of awarding a grant. For example, the National Science Foundation actively discourages cost sharing unless it is specifically requested in the application eligibility criteria. In short, sponsor attitudes towards cost sharing vary widely, so ask your program officer.

Mandatory versus Voluntary Cost Sharing. Cost sharing may be mandatory or voluntary. Mandatory cost sharing is often referred to as "matching funds"; it is required whereas voluntary cost sharing is optional. Your promise of cost sharing in a proposal budget may be a key factor in a sponsor's funding decision.

Mandatory—as one of the eligibility requirements of the grant, the sponsor requires you to share a certain percent of the total project costs. For example, "Local organizations are required to provide a local match totaling 75 percent of the requested grant funds." In this case, if a sponsor provides $20,000, you must provide an additional $15,000 toward the total project cost of $35,000.

Voluntary—you offer cost sharing in your proposal as an incentive to get the grant award. For instance, a sponsor may indicate, "Consideration will be given to organizations with in-kind contributions." In response, you may offer 20 percent cost sharing of personnel time toward the total project cost of $150,000. This means the sponsor would contribute $125,000, and you would provide $25,000 of the total project costs. However, you can cost share too much: for some agencies, higher levels of cost sharing require more administrative monitoring on their part, something program officers may wish to avoid. Accordingly, check with your project officers to see whether they have a "preferred level" of voluntary cost sharing.

Cash versus In-Kind Cost Sharing. Cost sharing may be in the form of a cash match (hard dollars) or an in-kind contribution (soft dollars).

Cash—your organization contributes so-called hard dollars toward your proposed project. Perhaps you were planning to purchase some equipment with your regular internal budget. Those dollars can be allocated toward your project. Usually, you had already planned to spend the money; now, in a tactical budget building mode, you link those planned expenditures to your proposal.

In-kind—these "soft dollars" do not require a cash outlay by your organization, yet they represent real dollars you would have to pay if the costs were not absorbed elsewhere. Personnel effort is perhaps the most common form of cost sharing, since it can include salaries, fringe benefits, and associated indirect costs. To illustrate, Ms. Ida Know, Project Director, may allocate 50 percent of her time (salary and fringe benefits) to a project grant, yet request sponsor funding for only 10 percent effort. Ms. Know's institution would cost share the remaining 40 percent of her salary and fringe benefits. As a further example, you can also cost share indirect costs. So, if your organization has a 26 percent indirect cost rate and your sponsor only allows a maximum reimbursement of 20 percent on direct costs, you can show the 6 percent difference as cost sharing.

Internal versus External Cost Sharing. Assuming you've decided to cost share on your proposed budget, the funds may come from either internal or external sources—or both.

Internally—you may allocate a portion of your direct or indirect costs to your proposed project. These shared costs may take on the form of cash or in-kind contributions. Consider this internal cost sharing example: assume you decide to cost share 20 percent of the project director's salary towards your proposed project. This means that instead of your project director receiving 100 percent of her salary from your agency personnel budget, she will now receive 80 percent from that source and the remaining 20 percent from the cost sharing account on the grant; you merely reallocate a portion of her salary; her income remains the same. The source(s) of income are changed on the bookkeeping records.

Externally—you may allocate extramural dollars from other sources to the project, as indicated in the following three examples.

- You have a matching grant from another sponsor.
- A wealthy philanthropist has given you unrestricted dollars that can be earmarked to this project.

- Revenue is generated from another fundraising activity, e.g., golf outing income can be directed to this project.

In each case, you can redirect dollars from those sources to help support the total costs of your proposed project, thereby showing your sponsor you are financially committed to supporting your proposal.

Cost Sharing Example. If your sponsor requires or strongly encourages cost sharing, then you obviously should do this. But where do you find the cost sharing dollars, particularly if your organization has a modest budget? Cost sharing is often done through a portion of salary, fringe benefits, and indirect costs. For instance, assume that a project director will spend 20 percent of her time on the project, but is requesting the sponsor to fund only 10 percent of that effort. The other 10 percent of the project director's salary can be shown as cost sharing. In addition to the cost sharing on salary dollars, additional cost sharing can be shown on the fringe benefits and indirect costs associated with the salary dollars, as Exhibit 51 shows.

In essence, this cost sharing portion of the overall budget tells your sponsor that your organization is willing to absorb one-half of the personnel costs, provided the sponsor will pay the other half. Once funded, your organization uses the grant funded salary dollars ($3,000 in this example) to pay the project director. In turn, your organization can use the deobligated salary dollars ($3,000 in agency dollars) to hire someone else part-time to do those tasks that the project director is surrendering during the course of the funded project. The project director will still receive the same salary. Instead of 100 percent of the salary coming from the organization, now 90 percent will come from the organization and 10 percent from the grant.

If your project personnel are not spending 100 percent of their time on the grant, you should identify how the remainder of their time will be spent. For example, the one-year budget shown in Exhibit 52 suggests that the project director will be spending 40 percent of her time on the grant. Among other things, that means she must "give up" doing 40 percent of her current activities in order to devote 40 percent of her time to the grant. In turn, 40 percent of her agency salary is now "deobligated" and can be used to temporarily hire someone else part-time to pick up those duties that were relinquished by the project director in order to administer the grant.

Item	Amount Requested	Cost Sharing	Total Amount
Project Director ($30,000/ yr x 1 yr x 20% effort)	$3,000	$3,000	$6,000
Fringe Benefits (28% of salary)	$840	$840	$1,680
Indirect Costs (30% of salary)	$900	$900	$1,800
Totals $	$4,740	$4,740	$9,480

SAMPLE COST SHARING

EXHIBIT 51

Exhibit 52 shows how one budget could be put together, but one size does not fit all. There are many variations in assembling meaningful grant budgets. Looking at past winning proposals and talking with your program officer will help clarify expectations. The following Web addresses will suggest other budget models that may be adapted to your situation.

- A university-based sample budget page
  http://www.indstate.edu/osp
- Grants.gov sample SF 424 R&R (Research & Related) forms
  http://apply.grants.gov/apply/FormsMenu
- National Endowment for the Humanities sample budget form
  http://www.neh.gov/grants/guidelines/pdf/ BudgetFormNew.pdf
- National Institutes of Health sample modular budget form for amounts under $250,000 annually
  http://grants2.nih.gov/grants/funding/424/ SF424R-R_PHS398_ModularBudget_Sample.pdf
- U.S. Department of Education sample budget narrative
  http://www.ed.gov/admins/grants/apply/techassist/ resource_pg8.html
- A common application form used by multiple private foundations in Rochester, NY
  http://www.grantmakers.org/common/ commonappform.html
- A common application form used by many private foundations in Milwaukee
  http://www.marquette.edu/fic/commonapp2006.doc

To look for other budget models, use the phrase "grant budget forms" in your favorite search engine.

Public and private sponsors vary within and among themselves regarding the cost categories they use on budgets. Some require more detail than others. Occasionally, a sponsor may request a list of other sponsored support or a copy of your most recent independently audited financial statement.

NIH Modular Budget. Most grant budgets require precision in their calculations, as illustrated in Exhibit 52. The NIH (National Institutes of Health) approaches budget construction differently. For grant budgets less than $250,000 annually, no detailed budget or budget justification is required. Budget requests are recorded in units of $25,000. Modular budgets save the reviewers' time and avoid the picky questions like "Could you buy that $3,000 laptop for $2,500?" Of note, application form SF 424 R&R is gradually replacing form PHS 398. An example of a NIH modular budget is available online at http:// grants.nih.gov/grants/funding/modular/modular.htm.

KEY QUESTIONS TO ANSWER

Use these key questions to prepare your next grant budget. Does your proposal do the following:

1. Follow all pertinent guidelines governing your project's budget?
2. Provide sufficient resources to carry out your project?
3. Include a budget narrative that justifies major budget categories?
4. Present the budget in the format desired by the sponsor?
5. Show sufficient detail so reviewers know how all budget items were calculated?
6. Separate direct costs from indirect costs and describe their components?
7. Specify the type and amount of any cost sharing? Relate budget items to project objectives?
8. Include any attachments or special appendixes to justify unusual requests?
9. Identify evaluation and dissemination costs?

Budget Item	Requested from Sponsor	Cost Shared by Applicant	Total
Personnel			
➢Salaries			
Jane Doe, Project Director $30,000/yr x 1 yr x 40% effort	$6,000	$6,000	$12,000
Carol Wooden, Survey Coordinator $20,000/yr x 6 mo x 50% effort	$5,000	$0	$5,000
Emily Johns, Secretary $15,000/yr x 1 yr x 25% effort	$3,750	$0	$3,750
10 Volunteers @ 100 hours each $8/hr x 100 hr x 10 volunteers	$0	$8,000	$8,000
➢Fringe Benefits			
Jane Doe, Project Director 30% of salary	$1,800	$1,800	$3,600
Carol Wooden, Survey Coordinator 25% of salary	$1,250	$0	$1,250
Emily Johns, Secretary 20% of salary	$750	$0	$750
10 Volunteers 20% of salary (entry level)	$0	$1,600	$1,600
➢Consultants			
James Ball, Project Evaluator $300/day x 5 days	$1,500	$0	$1,500
➢**Personnel Subtotal**	$20,050	$17,400	$37,450
Nonpersonnel			
➢Physical Facilities			
Space Rental $700/month x 12 month	$4,200	$4,200	$8,400
Utilities (Gas, electric) $125/month x 12 month	$1,500	$0	$1,500
➢Equipment			
Pentium IV Laptop Computer	$3,000	$0	$3,000
LaserJet 6 Plus Printer	$4,000	$0	$4,000
Annual Maintenance Contract Laptop ($300) + Printer ($400)	$0	$700	$700
➢Supplies			
Basic Office Supplies $300/person x 3 people	$900	$0	$900
Survey Printing and Mailing $1.27/survey x 1,500 surveys	$1,905	$0	$1,905
Long Distance Phone + Fax Charges $50/month x 12 month	$600	$0	$600
➢Travel			
Local Mileage: Smith (1,000 miles) + Wooden (500 miles) @ 33.5¢/mile	$502	$0	$502
Volunteers 300 miles x 33.5¢/mile x 10 volunteers	$0	$1,005	$1,005
Smith R/T Airfare ($400) + Per Diem ($125/day x 3 day)	$775	$0	$775
➢**Subtotal Nonpersonnel**	$17,382	$5,905	$23,287
Total Direct Costs (Personnel + Nonpersonnel Subtotals)	$37,432	$23,305	$60,737
Indirect Costs (30%)	$11,230	$6,692	$18,222
Total Project Costs	$48,662	$30,297	$78,959

SAMPLE ONE-YEAR COMPLETE BUDGET: FEDERAL HEALTH EDUCATION PROJECT

EXHIBIT 52

WRITING TIPS FOR THE BUDGET SECTION

These tips will help you plan and write your next budget.

1. Show the basis for your calculations: Fuzzy: Travel = $534. Specific: Local mileage for Project Director, 100 mi/mo x $0.445/mi x 12 mo = $534; if attending conventions, indicate name, location, and date.

2. Desktop supplies (pens, pencils, paper clips, and so forth) average $350 year/key person. It is not necessary to itemize these costs; just indicate that this is an estimate.

3. Tell sponsors the components of your fringe benefit rate. Indicate if it includes FICA, health, life, retirement, dental and disability insurance, and other benefits.

4. In university-originated proposals, separate graduate student stipends from tuition.

5. In multiyear budgets, allow for yearly increases; indicate annual percentage increases. Ask your program officer what percentage increases are currently being approved in multiyear budgets.

6. Include a budget narrative immediately following your budget figures to explain or justify any unusual expenditure items, even if one is not specifically requested (see Exhibit 52).

7. Include your organization's overall budget, if requested, showing how the grant budget request fits into your general operating budget.

8. If you have applied for or received other funding, say so. It will enhance your credibility, for they recognize your commitment to supporting your project.

9. Check agency regulations for indirect costs and your approved rate, if applicable.

10. Some grant budgets require cost sharing; that is, the sponsor and you must co-pay for the project. If so, distinguish between your cost sharing and the sponsor's share.

11. Itemize the budget and justify each item, such as travel, equipment, personnel, and other major expenses. Don't lump costs together. You can either round numbers to the nearest $10 or show exact numbers, as Exhibit 52 indicates, to let the sponsor know you are using "measured" numbers.

12. If the project is to occur in phases, identify the costs associated with each phase.

13. Don't overlook budget support for such things as service or maintenance contracts, insurance, shipping, or installation. If you anticipate training costs associated with the purchase of new equipment, include those costs in your budget as well. Your budget clip file should contain basic financial information needed in preparing proposal budgets, such as fringe benefit components, and indirect cost rates. Use your computer spreadsheet to draft various versions of your budget.

14. All costs must be incurred during the proposed project period. You cannot prepay someone for follow-up work that will be performed before or after the grant. All costs must be auditable.

15. Budgets should be close approximations of what you plan to spend. You do have some flexibility in the expenditure of funds and often it is possible to reallocate dollars between certain cost categories. For example, one federal agency will allow up to a 25 percent cost transfer between supplies and equipment. If you need to shift more than 25 percent of your supply budget to equipment, prior

written approval is required. Your award notice will indicate the flexibility you have in rebudgeting your grant dollars. If you are uncertain about budget flexibility, ask your program officer for a copy of their grant administration guidelines *before* you submit a proposal.

BUDGET SIZE

"How much should I ask for?" is a common question asked when preparing a grant budget. Your prospect research will reveal typical sponsor award amounts and represent one important clue in establishing your target budget, but use it only as a guide. If your organization is new to the sponsor or lacks an established track record, you may want to request something less than their average grant size. On the other hand, if your needs are well documented and you have strong credibility, you may wish to exceed the average amount awarded by the sponsor. Remember, nobody gets an "average" grant. "Average" is a mathematical concept, and organizations continually receive grant awards above or below the "average."

If you need bigger dollars than your sponsor typically awards for a grant, you may wish to take your larger project and divide or "chunk" it up into smaller but logical segments, thereby inviting the sponsor to fund a phase of your overall effort. If phase-one funding for them proves to be successful, they are reasonable candidates for phase-two funding. As another alternative, you can approach multiple sponsors, requesting each to partially fund your project. Although this can be done, frankly, it is difficult to

do because it requires an extensive amount of marketing and intersponsor coordination on your part. Experienced grant-getting organizations seek partial funding from multiple sponsors only as a last resort; their preferred alternative is to target a different sponsor, one who is capable of giving the entire amount.

SUPPLEMENT OR SUPPLANT FUNDS

Most grantmakers want to be sure that you use their money to *supplement*, not *supplant*, existing funds. In other words, they don't want to have their money used to replace—supplant—existing dollars. Said differently, they generally don't want to provide money for regular operating support. Instead, they want their money to supplement or expand projects, programs, or services. They want their money to be used as an "add-on" instead of a substitute for existing dollars. In essence, they want their funds to be used for project support, not operating support. Accordingly, you may wish to include a sentence like the following in your budget narrative, "The requested funds will be used to supplement, not replace, existing internal budgets."

ALLOWABLE BUDGET ITEMS

What can you include in your budget? Answer: usually every reasonable expense associated with the project. Unless sponsor regulations indicate otherwise, you can include such cost components as indicated in Exhibit 53.

Occasionally, a sponsor's guidelines will prohibit a specific budget item, e.g., computers or equipment.

Accounting	Indirect Costs	Renovation
Advertising	Instruments	Rent
Audiovisual instruction	Insurance	Repairs
Auditing	Legal services	Salaries and wages
Binding	Maintenance	Security
Books	Periodicals	Subcontracts
Computers	Postage	Supplies
Consultants	Publications	Telecommunications
Dues	Recruitment	Travel
Equipment	Registration fees	Tuition
Fringe benefits	Relocation	Utilities

ALLOWABLE BUDGET ITEMS

EXHIBIT 53

In such cases, show them as cost sharing items. Program officers can provide useful reactions to draft budgets.

The budget exhibit and narrative are meant to persuade the reviewer that sufficient funds are requested to achieve the project goals and objectives in a cost-effective manner. The budget in Exhibit 52 is for one year only. If it were requesting multiyear funding, it would look the same, except that three additional columns per year would be added on the right side of the ledger, namely, amount requested, cost sharing, and total. First-year funding is usually higher because of inevitable start-up costs, while subsequent funding levels decrease over time.

USING COMPUTER SPREADSHEET PROGRAMS

Spreadsheet programs, such as Excel, enable you to manipulate numbers and automatically recalculate whenever you change a budget figure. As a result, they are particularly helpful in preparing grant budgets. With a spreadsheet program, you could extend the budget over multiple years, showing what would happen as salaries rise and year one start-up costs drop. Multiyear budgets are easy to calculate. If you plan to submit a three-year budget request, you need to prepare four budgets: one for each year separately and the fourth for a cumulative total. Similarly, consortium budgets can detail figures for each strategic partner as well as a collective budget total.

Spreadsheet numbers can be sorted, extracted, or merged with other spreadsheets. You can display your values as pie charts or graphs. Consider attaching to your proposal budget a bar graph that shows the requested and cost-shared amounts each year over a multiyear grant; many sponsors will respond favorably if you can systematically increase your cost-sharing portion over time.

When reviewing grant funding histories, many sponsors report their average grant size. That "average" may be misleading for organizations like yours. Consider entering funding histories from a targeted sponsor onto a spreadsheet, sorting out the organizations that are like yours, and computing averages and ranges on this narrower information. It may give you an entirely different picture of how much to request in your proposal.

FUTURE FUNDING

Some sponsors expect you to sustain your project after the grant expires. If you have a financing plan for future funding, briefly outline it. Forecast your future budget needs for this project and indicate whether those dollars will come from internal or external support. Mention other sponsors that could become involved in your project. If government funding is unavailable, state that fact because it is especially important to corporation and foundation proposals. Other methods to raise money include, but are not limited to, the following.

Special Events

Special fundraising events should follow these basic principles:

- Be restricted to ones that your organization can effectively carry out
- Bring in significant revenue for the efforts of paid and volunteer staff
- Attract new volunteers and new money
- Provide positive community relations
- Be followed up for future volunteer/donor support
- Be evaluated each year to determine your future involvement

Among the options for special events: antique shows, auctions, balloon races, beach parties, bingo, book signings, business openings, car shows, casino nights, celebrity appearances, chili cookoffs, concerts, cooking demonstrations, costume parties, cow chip bingo, dances, dine-arounds, golf outings, home tours, pancake breakfasts, races, radiothons, raffles, runs/walks, sidewalk sales, telethons, and tournaments. The following example presents some future funding grant language, using a dinner as the special event.

> To sustain this project after the initial grant period, we plan to initiate an annual fundraising event called Dinner with the Docs. The dinner will feature local prominent physicians who support our project outcomes or other individuals who are well known in the community. The main purpose of this special event is to raise funds and heighten attention to volunteer service opportunities. Briefly, one high-profile physician will be selected as head waiter who will assist in recruiting other physician/waiters. Each waiter will personally invite their own guests to fill a 10-person table or provide a list of colleagues and friends to which invitations could be sent. Additionally, they will choose a theme to decorate their table and be in a costume to match the theme. They will entertain their guests as they wait on their tables, competing during the evening for tips.

A four-course gourmet meal will be served at a leisurely pace, allowing ample time for waiters to dream up new ways to work for their tips, e.g., serve meals in bedpans. Finally, a Master of Ceremonies will auction off the head waiter's apron autographed with the signatures of all CEO waiters.

While many special events can be a financial disaster, this one has the elements of success. The event is great fun and the volunteers love to be involved with no begging. Ticket sales are generally nonexistent; most often the waiters invite their own table guests. Decoration committees are not needed, as the waiters select their own themes and decorations. The Celebrity Waiters provide most of the entertainment for their table. The event is repeatable every year. The event stimulates natural competition between visible leaders in the community. Our past experience has shown that people are more like to donate to a cause in a competitive social event than to respond to direct, one-to-one solicitation.

Fee-for-Service

We believe it would be ethically irresponsible to initiate the important social services described in this proposal and then abruptly terminate the services at the end of the grant period. That notion flies contrary to our mission of helping people help themselves. The support requested in this proposal seeks start-up funding to establish the awareness, systems, and service delivery procedures. Once beyond the three-year implementation phase, services will be sustained on a fee-for-service basis. Even using a sliding scale fee schedule based on patient income, our business plan analysis suggests this service can be self-funded, as evidenced by the budget and expenditure projects included in the appendix. Our patient surveys reaffirm not only the need for this service but the willingness of patients to sustain it. Their bottom line message: the nearest comparable service is more than 100 miles away.

Membership Fees

Once the Biomedical Research Institute is established and fully operational within the three-year grant period, it will continue its activities by charging corporate membership fees. Within a two-hundred-mile radius

of the Institute, there are 247 different manufacturers of biomedical equipment. They will be offered different membership levels and benefits.

Basic Membership: $1,500/year

- Discounts for attending seminars and workshops
- Publications including the institute newsletter, seminar and workshop materials, and membership director

Executive Sponsors: $10,000/year

- All basic membership privileges
- Opportunity to do projects with center staff
- Participate in center program activities
- Referral of qualified personnel for internships and recruitment
- Serve on Institute Advisory Board
- Contribute to newsletter articles
- Participate in collaborative activities with other members

Corporate Sponsors: $25,000/year

- All above privileges
- List company name prominently on Institute letterhead, the banner in the center newsletter, and all press releases
- Serve as speakers in program activities
- Unlimited access to Institute-initiated project reports
- Staff presentations to sponsor clients or prospects once at no charge

Grants

For years, grants have been the lifeblood of our organization. As a result, we have established long-term relationships with major grantmakers. More than two-thirds of our annual budget over the past decade has come from grant-funded support. While one cannot run a program on grants forever, our grantmakers recognize us as a responsible steward of their funds. Once the funding for the demonstration phase of this proposed project ends, other grantmakers will be approached for implementation funding. In that sense, the demonstration funding requested in this proposal will become a magnet to attract follow-up support. Preliminary conversations with two community foundations have been encouraging; more precisely, both foundations reacted favorably to our preliminary proposal and have expressed interest in jointly funding the next project phase.

Annual Direct Mail Campaign

Our annual direct mail campaign has four main goals:

- To acquire new donors
- To encourage prior donors to increase their giving size
- To renew lapsed donors
- To bolster public relations

We are particularly interested in acquiring new donors since our experience shows that 50–80 percent will donate again.

An effective direct mail campaign involves multiple mailings. For purposes of sustaining the project after the grant funds lapse, we plan to initiate quarterly mailings during the final project year. The most crucial element in a direct mail campaign is the quality of the mailing list. Beyond mailing to prior donors, new donors will be identified by consulting with a mailing list vendor to target people who live in upper-income geographic areas, meet minimum income levels, and subscribe to magazines compatible with our overall mission. A preliminary check of individuals living in the 532XX zip code range with family income levels exceeding $75,000 and subscribing to the Strengthening Family Values Magazine identified 938 mailing targets. The Project Director will oversee the direct mail campaign, which will be crafted with the help of board member Joyce Kunkel, who is director of advertising for Zigfried and Associates, a leading advertising and public relations firm with more than 200 cumulative years of experience in direct mail advertising.

Planned Giving

Planned giving integrates personal, financial, and estate planning with the individual donor's plans for lifetime giving. Through bequests or other planned gifts, donors have the capacity of funding a charitable gift annuity with relatively small investment. Planned giving is an intricate long-term fundraising strategy that requires special training in financial planning and tax laws. Although no staff members have this type of training or expertise, we are fortunate that Attorney Terrence Case, Trust Officer at the Wells Fargo Bank, is an active member of our Board and has volunteered to lead a planning giving campaign on behalf of our organization. His interactions with

potential donors will include bequests, charitable gift annuities, charitable remainder trusts, life estate contracts, life insurance policies, and revocable trusts.

Phone-a-Thons

Telephone solicitation is a powerful fundraising strategy. While the idea of telephone solicitation does generate some negative semantic reactions—people don't like to be bothered—our experience has shown that relatively few people are annoyed by telephone solicitations from well-respected charities. Universities, for example, use phone-a-thons with great success.

Using the facilities at a local telemarketing firm, we will conduct a phone-a-thon by having volunteers call people and solicit donations. This approach enables us to reach out to people who don't give on a regular basis. Additionally we can encourage regular donors to give more. Our primary target audience will be current and past donors. The key is the training of volunteers, who will undergo a six-hour program that will consist of two parts: (1) the carefully scripted opening, and (2) the follow-up question-objection-ask sequence. Because telephone solicitations are most effective when conducted by a peer of the prospect, the volunteers will come from backgrounds that match as close as possible to those of the prospects. No paid solicitors will be used. Since the phone banks are donated for this project, no up-front money is required.

Some of these options will be appropriate for your organization, while others will not. Here are some questions to help identify some more viable options.

1. Can your organization absorb future funding in your general operating budget over the next few years?
2. Could you contract with a third party to subsidize your services to clients?
3. Could your future expenses be covered as a part of a nongrant fundraising program?
4. Do you have another profitable service or activity that can be expanded to cover costs of running your new project in the future?
5. Could the financial responsibility for your project be transferred to some other organization?

Proposal reviewers are not looking for an ironclad guarantee that you can provide future project funding.

Rather, they want specific evidence that you have a tentative plan in place. Such a plan also shows that you have an extensive project network of support, thereby enhancing your credibility. Some types of research grants may not need extensive funding beyond the grant; nevertheless, this proposal section may be used to lay the groundwork for future support requests.

Example of Future Funding Plan

Proposal seeking minority fellowship support from a national science agency.

Midwest University is committed to continuing this program after completion of agency funding. To help sustain the program, we have identified the following sources of future funding:

1. **Summer Employment in Industry.** The College of Engineering will use its strong partnership with industry to arrange summer employment for future participating students. Through such employment, students will gain practical experience and financial support.
2. **Consortium Membership Support.** As noted in Section V.B.1.b, the College of Engineering is part of the Midwest Engineering Consortium which includes the membership of several local companies and three engineering colleges. (See Appendix E.) Funds generated from membership fees will be targeted for future program participants.
3. **Training Grants.** The College of Engineering, working in close cooperation with the Development Office, will aggressively seek extramural funding from private sources, including corporations and private foundations, to continue the proposed Minority Fellowship Program.
4. **Engineering Fellowship Funds.** The College of Engineering will give future and continuing program participants first priority for fellowships from funds received each year from its Engineering Fellowship Fund. These funds average over $30,000 per year.
5. **Graduate Research and Teaching Assistantships.** The Department of Electrical and Computer Engineering will supplement support generated from the four sources above with research and teaching assistantships. Currently, the Department has 27 university-funded assistantships.
6. **Online Fundraising.** Since the department has thousands of graduates spread throughout the country, many in high-paying jobs, a Web site will be established to encourage online giving. Electronic donations will be encouraged through the College's quarterly alumni newsletter.

Together, these six sources of future funding will continue the program beyond the agency grant period. Nevertheless, agency support is needed, as detailed in the budget proposal, to establish the Minority Fellowship Program.

REJECTION REASONS

Here are some reasons why reviewers have rejected proposals based on inadequate budgets.

1. The applicants' claim that "we will continue to look for alternative sources of support" does little to inspire confidence.
2. No systematic funding plan beyond the termination date is presented.
3. The budget is too high for the expected results.
4. The principal investigator is asking the sponsor to carry costs normally borne in his institutional operating budget.
5. While full funding of this project cannot be recommended, given its highly innovative nature, pilot support should be provided.
6. The budget request is unusually excessive, not justified, and not linked to specific project objectives.
7. Without adequate justification, the proposal appears to request support for resources already in place.
8. The budget does not seem to reflect costs associated with the marketing of the newly proposed services.
9. The budget does not identify personnel full-time equivalents.
10. The budget does not identify sources or amounts of in-kind contributions.
11. Is it realistic for the project director to dedicate 50 percent effort in year one and only 20 percent effort in years two and three, especially when year two proposed to expand into new and larger communities?
12. The budget request for project evaluation seems inadequate given the magnitude of the evaluation plan.
13. The budget does not appear to include a line item for project evaluation, nor does the budget narrative identify an evaluator. Who is doing the evaluation and how much will it cost?

14. The proposal doesn't identify who will be doing the project evaluation or indicate what will be evaluated, so how do they know that the evaluation will cost 5% of the budget?

15. The budget does not identify the fringe benefit rate or its components.

16. The federal share of the project funding decreases over the five-year period, but there is no discussion of who is picking up the expense. Do partner agencies have the capacity to integrate project costs into their operating budgets?

17. The proposal narrative does not discuss a sustainability plan for this specific project.

18. The proposal narrative identifies potential sources of future private and federal government funding; however, no firm commitments of cash or in-kind funding dedicated to sustaining services exist yet.

19. The proposal's plan to secure sustainability funding is weak. Many agencies will not be able to absorb project costs to maintain efforts. A more comprehensive plan might include examples of private foundations and corporations to approach for support.

20. If they have a federally negotiated indirect cost rate, they should say so in the narrative and include a copy of it in the appendix.

Clip File Action Item # 17 Budgets

Consider these action items to build your Budget clip file:

- List all of the items included in your fringe benefit package.
- Get a copy of your current indirect cost rate.
- Include a copy of your overall organizational operating budget.
- Add a copy of your most recent audited financial statements.
- Write generic versions of the future funding options cited above, ones that are applicable to your organization.

CHAPTER 13
Appendixes

Great minds must be ready not only to take opportunities,
but also to make them.

—C.C. Coulton

PURPOSE OF APPENDIXES

Proposal appendixes are opportunities waiting to be finished. They contain supportive secondary information that will further strengthen your proposal narrative. As a writer, you may need to include appendix items such as those listed in Exhibit 54.

In essence, appendixes contain secondary supporting material for your proposal. Some grantmaking agencies do not circulate copies of appendixes when transmitting proposals to reviewers, a practice you should clarify with your program officer. Keep essential proposal information in your project narrative. Each item listed above represents a valuable addition to your clip file.

KEY QUESTIONS TO ANSWER

Ask yourself these key questions as you plan your appendixes:

1. Could reviewers evaluate the proposal without any appendix information?
2. Have strong letters of support and commitment been included?
3. Are assurances of cooperation provided in instances of interagency collaboration?
4. Are resumes included for all key project personnel and consultants?

WRITING TIPS FOR APPENDIXES

1. Judicious use of appendixes can overcome sponsor constraints on page limits.

2. Use appendixes for presentation of secondary supporting material.
3. Put long charts, graphs, tables, formulas, and other forms of visuals in the appendixes.
4. Make sure all resumes reflect expertise essential to your proposed project.

CONSORTIUM AGREEMENTS

A consortium grant is an award made to one institution (known as the lead institution) in support of a project that carries out programmatic activity in collaboration with other organizations, which are separate legal entities, administratively independent of you. Your selection of coalition partners for a consortium grant should be guided by these principles. The collaborators should be able to do the following:

1. Build on existing strengths and resources.
2. Develop and pursue concrete, attainable goals and objectives.
3. Partner on activities and evaluation.
4. Share in both processes and outcomes of the coalition.
5. Promote a learning and empowering process.
6. Disseminate findings and knowledge to all partners.
7. Foster mutual respect, understanding, and trust.

When submitting a consortium proposal to a sponsor, you should include a copy of the agreement that all agencies would sign, an agreement based on these seven principles that binds them together for a common cause. The preferred approach would be to have the agreements formally executed prior to

Agency publications	Maps of service areas	Reprints of articles
Certifications	Organizational charts	Resumes
Consortia agreements	Organizational fiscal reports	Significant case histories
Definitions of terms	Past success stories	Subcontractor data
Letters of commitment	Publicity material	Tabular data
Lists of board officials	Recent annual reports	Vendor quotes

POSSIBLE APPENDIX DOCUMENTS

EXHIBIT 54

proposal submission and to include them as an appendix item. Because that is not always possible, the fallback position is to at least include a draft of the consortium agreement in the appendix and indicate that it is the type of document all parties would sign once the grant award was made.

In consortium agreements, a separate, detailed budget for the initial and future years for each institution is submitted as well as a composite budget for all institutions. The lead institution must approve any major rebudgeting requests from collaborating institutions; additionally, the collaborators must provide the lead institution with appropriate reports (progress reports, expenditure reports, invention statements) in order to fully comply with sponsor requirements.

Following are two examples of consortium affiliation agreements often found in proposal appendixes. Exhibit 55 involves two agencies collaborating on a federal grant; Exhibit 56 involves the same two agencies collaborating on a private foundation grant. These exhibits are meant to represent common examples, but should be modified to conform to specific sponsor requirements.

In Exhibit 55, the programmatic consideration indicates how ABC and XYZ will work together to conduct the project. The fiscal considerations specify how the grant finances will be managed. The administrative considerations detail the intent to comply with existing federal regulations.

Exhibit 56 contains the same three categories of information—programmatic, fiscal, and administrative considerations—but does not require the same regulatory agency compliance details found in many government agreements.

PHANTOM COLLABORATIONS

Successful grantseekers know that true collaborations must be genuine, not phantom-based. To illustrate, a local grantmaking agency recently announced its intention to fund a health-related project, but with a catch. Only one proposal would be funded per geographic area, and all interested applicants in the county should get together, join forces, and submit a collaborative proposal. The sponsor's well-intended but conceptually flawed idea was to create a grant opportunity that would automatically guarantee interagency collaboration.

Here's what happened. The lead applicant agency asked other collaborators to submit a one-page outline of what they could contribute to the proposal. On the basis of those one-page descriptions, the lead applicant crafted a proposal and sent it in without further collaborations. The other collaborators requested meetings to talk about the content and format of the proposal. Their request for collaborative meetings was denied.

To no one's surprise, the proposal didn't get funded. The lead applicant agency didn't recognize the characteristics of successful collaborative proposals. Consider these key ideas.

1. Collaborators talk about the strategic planning process used to develop the proposal.
2. Collaborators identify the contributions of each participant and how it contributes to the "big picture."
3. Collaborations usually contain an advisory board with representation from the major participants.
4. Collaborators include a draft consortium agreement showing how they will cooperate administratively, fiscally, and programmatically.
5. Collaborators schedule progress reports that involve the major players.

This proposal had none of these characteristics. As the reviewers quickly determined, this was not a "real" proposal; rather, it was a phantom proposal. Phantom collaborations don't get funded.

Consortium Grant Agreement between Alzheimer's Basic Care Agency and XYZ Agency

This Consortium Agreement is entered into this first day of May 2008, by and between Alzheimer's Basic Care Agency (hereinafter called ABC) and XYZ Agency (henceforth XYZ).

Whereas, ABC was awarded a single grant (HRSA-09214-8421-0672) from the U.S. Department of Health and Human Services (hereinafter called "Sponsor") and this single grant involves multiple agencies; and

Whereas, XYZ proposes to provide support for this project;

Therefore, ABC and XYZ mutually agree on the following programmatic, fiscal and administrative considerations.

Programmatic Considerations

1. **Project Director.** Ms. Jane Smith is the Project Director for ABC. In the event she cannot perform in this capacity for any reason, ABC retains the right to appoint an alternative Project Director of its choice, subject to Sponsor approval.
2. **Project Co-Director.** Mr. Jon Jones will serve as Project Co-Director for XYZ. Any personnel change will require prior written approval from ABC and Sponsor.
3. **Scope of Work.** The scope of work to be conducted by Ms. Smith and Mr. Jones and project associates is described in the award titled "Evaluation of Service Delivery Models for the Frail Elderly," which is incorporated herein by reference referred to as the "Grant Award." Ms. Smith and Mr. Jones are responsible for directing and monitoring the grant effort as described in the Grant Award.
4. **Performance Standards.** XYZ will use reasonable efforts to accomplish work in the Grant Award following generally accepted standards of professional skill.

Fiscal Considerations

1. **Allowability of Costs.** ABC will determine the allowability of direct costs in accordance with applicable Sponsor policies and guidelines. If fiscal policies and practices at XYZ differ from those of ABC, the policies of the institution where the costs are generated will apply, provided any such policies are in compliance with those of the Sponsor.
2. **Facilities and Administrative Costs.** Facilities and Administrative Costs ("indirect costs") for XYZ will be 8% of the total direct costs, as specified in the Grant Award.
3. **Excess Cost Reimbursement.** Any cost reimbursement to XYZ in excess of its budget award will require prior written agreement from ABC.
4. **Billing Schedule.** ABC shall pay XYZ on a monthly basis, provided invoices and vouchers are in such form and reasonable detail to verify the allowability of costs in accordance with Sponsor grant administration guidelines.
5. **Payment Schedule.** ABC shall pay XYZ no later than thirty (30) days after the receipt of each invoice or voucher, unless Sponsor delays its funding to ABC.
6. **Rebudgeting.** XYZ can rebudget up to 10% of its Grant Awards funds at its sole discretion, provided Sponsor requirements are not violated. Rebudgeting in excess of 10% for XYZ must have prior written approval of ABC.
7. **Financial Records.** XYZ agrees to provide ABC and Sponsor access to records supporting grant-related costs upon reasonable demand. Further XYZ agrees to preserve its records for five years after the expiration of the Grant Award.

Administrative Considerations

1. **Effective Date and Duration.** This Agreement becomes effective when signed by duly authorized representatives of ABC and XYZ and ends upon the project completion of May 30, 2011, unless otherwise stipulated in writing.
2. **Inter-agency Collaborations.** ABC and XYZ agree to cooperate, communicate, and collaborate in the manner and detail described in the Grant Award.
3. **Title to Equipment.** Title to all equipment purchased with funds under this Agreement resides with ABC. However, ABC may wish to make such equipment available to XYZ for an indefinite period of time, provided Sponsor guidelines allow it and XYZ agrees to furnish ABC with reasonable and appropriate inventory control information.

CONSORTIUM AGREEMENT INVOLVING GOVERNMENT GRANT

EXHIBIT 55

4. **Project Dissemination.** ABC and XYZ shall make reasonable efforts to disseminate project results through research reports and other print and electronic distribution mechanisms.
5. **Compliance.** In accepting this Agreement, XYZ agrees to comply in all applicable federal requirements, including but not limited to citations six through eleven below, or their successors.
6. **Employment Authorization.** All project personnel must be authorized for employment as stipulated in the Immigration and Reform Control Act of 1986.
7. **Civil Rights and Equal Employment Opportunity.** XYZ affirms that they have filed assurance of compliance regarding the Civil Rights Act of 1964 and the Rehabilitation Act of 1973.
8. **Projection of Human Subjects.** Interactions with human subjects comply with 45 CFR Part 46, assuring individual rights are protected and no one is put to undue risk.
9. **Drug-Free Workplace.** XYZ will comply with regulations implementing the Drug-Free Workplace Act of 1988.
10. **Scientific Misconduct.** XYZ will comply with 42 CFR Part 50 governing reporting procedures dealing with possible misconduct in science.
11. **Patents and Inventions.** XYZ will comply with Sponsor regulations on patents and inventions. If the Sponsor declines ownership of any intellectual property arising from this Agreement, disposition of such rights will be determined by the policies of the inventor's employer.
12. **Amendments.** ABC and XYZ may amend this agreement upon written approval.
13. **Entire Agreement.** This Agreement, the Proposal, and the Grant Award constitute the entire understanding of XYZ and ABC; any oral understanding shall be without effect.

In Witness Herewith, ABC and XYZ warrant they are empowered to execute this agreement.

ABC Agency
By _____
Adam Q. Quinkleberry
President

XYZ Agency
By _____
Murgatroyd Grivlovitch
President

CONSORTIUM AGREEMENT INVOLVING GOVERNMENT GRANT

EXHIBIT 55 (Continued from page 155)

The elements of a successful collaboration include the following:

1. A clear statement of goals, objectives, and outcomes to which all partners subscribe.
2. Clear identification of each partner's roles and responsibilities.
3. Regular meetings to provide feedback and share or exchange information.
4. Concrete benchmarks to monitor progress and maintain focus.
5. Patience to survive periods of frustration and seeming lack of progress.
6. Open, effective channels of communication between partners.

STRATEGIC PARTNERING WITH ACADEMIA

Looking for a strategic partner? Consider partnering with a nearby college or university. They are place-bound and their futures depend on the social and economic vitality of their regions. Institutions of higher education are ecological connections to their local communities. No longer can academics expect to thrive by being aloof from the conditions, needs, and opportunities of their neighbors. Academia is shifting philosophically from the concept of the academy as a cloister to the academy as a public space directly linked to the life of society.

Bluntly, academia needs partnerships with nonprofit organizations. If you don't have a point of contact in a nearby academic institution, call the nearest one and asked to be connected to the Grants Office or the Development Office and explain your interest in collaboration. As a nonprofit organization you can provide opportunities to enrich the educational experiences of students, focus on areas of shared concern that offer the prospect of mutual benefit, and create a "town/gown" community that values all members. Communication is the staple of any successful partnership. You'll be borrowing their credibility that will, in turn, strengthen you next proposal and increase your likelihood of getting funded.

Consortium Grant Agreement between Alzheimer's Basic Care Agency and XYZ Agency

This Consortium Agreement is entered into this first day of May 2008, by and between Alzheimer's Basic Care Agency (hereinafter called ABC) and XYZ Agency (henceforth XYZ).

Whereas, ABC was awarded a single grant from the We Care Foundation (hereinafter called "Sponsor") and this single grant involves multiple agencies; and

Whereas, XYZ proposes to provide support for this project;

Therefore, ABC and XYZ mutually agree on the following programmatic, fiscal and administrative considerations.

Programmatic Considerations

1. **Project Director.** Ms. Jane Smith is the Project Director for ABC. In the event she cannot perform in this capacity for any reason, ABC retains the right to appoint an alternative Project Director of its choice, subject to Sponsor approval.
2. **Project Co-Director.** Mr. Jon Jones will serve as Project Co-Director for XYZ. Any personnel change will require prior written approval from ABC and Sponsor. Mr. Jones will coordinate the institution-specific functions and activities with the overall project and serve as liaison between ABC and XYZ.
3. **Scope of Work.** The scope of work to be conducted by Ms. Smith and Mr. Jones and project associates is described in the award titled "Evaluation of Service Delivery Models for the Frail Elderly," which is incorporated herein by reference referred to as the "Grant Award." Ms. Smith and Mr. Jones are responsible for directing and monitoring the grant effort as described in the Grant Award.
4. **Performance Standards.** XYZ will use reasonable efforts to accomplish work in the Grant Award following generally accepted standards of professional skill.

Fiscal Considerations

1. **Allowability of Costs.** ABC will determine the allowability of direct costs in accordance with applicable Sponsor policies and guidelines. If fiscal policies and practices at XYZ differ from those of ABC, the policies of the institution where the costs are generated will apply, provided any such policies are in compliance with those of the Sponsor.
2. **Administrative Costs.** Administrative Costs ("indirect costs") for XYZ will be 8% of the total direct costs, as specified in the Grant Award.
3. **Excess Cost Reimbursement.** Any cost reimbursement to XYZ in excess of its budget award will require prior written agreement from ABC.
4. **Billing Schedule.** ABC shall pay XYZ on a monthly basis, provided invoices and vouchers are in such form and reasonable detail to verify the allowability of costs in accordance with Sponsor grant administration guidelines.
5. **Payment Schedule.** ABC shall pay XYZ no later than thirty (30) days after the receipt of each invoice or voucher, unless Sponsor delays its funding to ABC.
6. **Rebudgeting.** XYZ can rebudget up to 10% of its Grant Awards funds at its sole discretion, provided Sponsor requirements are not violated. Rebudgeting in excess of 10% for XYZ must have prior written approval of ABC.
7. **Financial Records.** XYZ agrees to provide ABC and Sponsor access to records supporting grant-related costs upon reasonable demand. Further XYZ agrees to preserve its records for five years after the expiration of the Grant Award.

Administrative Considerations

1. **Effective Date and Duration.** This Agreement becomes effective when signed by duly authorized representatives of ABC and XYZ and ends upon project completion on May 30, 2011, unless otherwise stipulated in writing.
2. **Inter-agency Collaborations.** ABC and XYZ agree to cooperate, communicate, and collaborate in the manner and detail described in the Grant Award and include the following: (a) participate in the Evaluation Advisory Board by designating two representatives, one of whom shall be an Assistant Director; (b) work with Project Director in organizing and offering two multidisciplinary workshops of one day's duration for health professionals at ABC; and (c) designate three guest lecturers to participate in the project's Speaker's Bureau.

CONSORTIUM AGREEMENT INVOLVING PRIVATE FOUNDATION GRANT

EXHIBIT 56

3. **Title to Equipment.** Title to all equipment purchased with funds under this Agreement resides with ABC. However, ABC may wish to make such equipment available to XYZ for an indefinite period of time, provided Sponsor guidelines allow it and XYZ agrees to furnish ABC with reasonable and appropriate inventory control information.
4. **Project Dissemination.** ABC and XYZ shall make reasonable efforts to disseminate project results through research reports and other print and electronic distribution mechanisms.
5. **Amendments.** ABC and XYZ may amend this agreement upon written approval.
6. **Entire Agreement.** This Agreement, the Proposal, and the Grant Award constitute the entire understanding of XYZ and ABC; any oral understanding shall be without effect.

In Witness Herewith, ABC and XYZ warrant they are empowered to execute this agreement.

ABC Agency   XYZ Agency
By _____   By _____
Adam Q. Quinkleberry   Murgatroyd Grivlovitch
President   President

CONSORTIUM AGREEMENT INVOLVING PRIVATE FOUNDATION GRANT

EXHIBIT 56 (Continued from page 157)

LETTERS OF SUPPORT AND COMMITMENT

Letters of support are important appendix enclosures. Strong letters help establish your credibility and document that you have a solid base of support for your project. Your strong letters of support should go beyond the customary "This is a great project" endorsement, and spell out what commitment is being made to the project, e.g., personnel time, space, physical facilities, financial resources. To get a strong commitment letter, provide the targeted letter writers with a draft copy of your proposal and a draft copy of the letter you would like them to sign. They can make whatever changes they feel are warranted and have it printed on agency letterhead.

When considering letters of commitment, grant writers often wonder if they should solicit endorsements from congressional officials. Often, congressional letters are one of support, and not commitment; at best, most congressional officials can "bless" you or your project as being worthy of support but are not in a position to make a firm commitment. Although congressional officials will usually provide such letters when requested, use them sparingly; that is, save congressional "muscle" for big projects, not routine ones. For example, one hospital follows the "two-comma" policy for getting congressional support letters; that is, the requested budget must have two commas in it, i.e., be greater than one million dollars. When you judge that such a letter is appropriate, contact a staff officer, explain your situation, and request a

support letter. Offer to send background information about your organization as well as a draft of the letter you would like to receive.

A letter of commitment is usually short, less than one page. Exhibit 57 contains an example of a weak letter of commitment, the kind that you do not want to include with your proposal. It was actually included with a proposal that reviewers declined to fund.

In Exhibit 57, Dr. Eggerding only indicated that the proposed project was a good idea. She did not indicate what she would do to ensure project success. Reviewers are left wondering what specific role she might play in the project. Note the contrast provided in Exhibit 58, which does spell out precise commitments to the project.

The typical letter of commitment contains an opening paragraph, a statement of past relationship between the collaborating organization and the sponsor, a precise listing of what the collaborator will contribute to the project, and a closing paragraph. The following sample paragraphs endorse various projects. Each paragraph below came from a separate letter. Typically, these letters contain a polite opening and closing paragraph and one more substantive paragraph as exemplified below.

Commitment Letter # 1: Opening Paragraph

I am pleased to lend official support from our agency to your project. I welcome this opportunity to blend our interests with your very real

Today's Date

Mr. Peter Barnett, Project Director
Organization Name
Street Address
City/State/Zip

Dear Mr. Barnett:

I enjoyed speaking with you today and am familiar with the basic goals and methods of your proposed work towards creating HealthAlert Oregon, a statewide advocacy coalition aligned to local HealthAlert Coalitions.

I am honored to be part of such a needed and forward thinking project that will work toward expanding and extending coverage to all people in Oregon. Let me know what I can do to facilitate this important partnership endeavor.

Sincerely,

Doris Eggerding, MD
University of Oregon

EXAMPLE OF WEAK COMMITMENT LETTER

EXHIBIT 57

needs. I enthusiastically endorse the involvement of my agency. All will profit from this cross-pollination of ideas. I know from experience that multiple viewpoints are needed to traverse the milieu you face.

Commitment Letter # 2: Opening Paragraph

I have just finished reviewing your proposal. Your emphasis will certainly be of benefit to your agency and ours. Bringing together the interdisciplinary expertise you have assembled in this proposal can only augment the richness of your project. I enthusiastically endorse the involvement of our agency and will personally assure the administrative support required to reach your project objectives. We eagerly await the formal beginning of your project.

Commitment Letter # 3: Opening Paragraph

For more than a decade, our agencies have worked cooperatively on a variety of social service projects. In that context, I see your current proposal as a systematic continuation of our past joint efforts. The human and physical resources are in place—and have been for years—to achieve your desired project objectives.

Commitment Letter # 4: Opening Paragraph

Thank you for the opportunity to review your proposal. You have identified some very significant local problems. As you address these problems in your agency, I am particularly pleased that we can contribute our organizational strength: (specify). Our agency personnel have a demonstrated concern for and proven expertise in this area. In total, you have assembled an excellent interdisciplinary cadre of professionals to make this project quite promising. I want you to know that this project has the highest levels of support and commitment to success. We eagerly await active participation.

Commitment Letter # 5: Opening Paragraph

I enthusiastically support your proposal. Its interdisciplinary approach to addressing the ever-increasing challenges we face promises valuable guidance. Your leadership role provides you with unique experience and insights with which to direct this project. Your past efforts will serve as an indispensable resource to professionals and enrich the delivery of services. Your proposal has my strong support, and I will continue to allocate time for my personnel to participate in your project activities.

Today's Date

Mr. Peter Barnett, Project Director
Organization Name
Street Address
City/State/Zip

Dear Mr. Barnett:

I was pleased to learn about your project to address health literacy in Oregon, an issue that many health professionals are very concerned about. I am writing this letter of commitment that the XYZ Health System will partner with you in your grant proposal, Reducing Health Disparities by Improving Health Literacy: A Model for Collaboration.

As you know, we have a network of 128 HealthAlert centers distributed throughout the state. Collectively, we have more than 300 healthcare professionals that are affiliated with our umbrella organization. We have been serving communities statewide since 1964. Our tenure has afforded us opportunities to build a strong network of individuals who share the values reflected in this project. Your Health Literacy project represents a continuation of your decade long collaboration on various health-related projects.

We are dedicated to partnering in this project by:

1. Appointing a representative to the Health Literacy Advisory Council, which would meet semi-annually in Portland for three years to monitor and evaluation the progress of this project;
2. Provide opportunities for project partners to met with our staff to obtain input into the development of this project, as needed;
3. Work with project partners to increase awareness of health literacy in Oregon hospitals; and
4. Communicate knowledge gained and relevant products developed through this project to hospitals throughout the state.

We look forward to working with all partners on this grant and believe this is a much-needed and innovative initiative.

Sincerely,

Doris Eggerding, MD
University of Oregon

EXAMPLE OF A STRONG COMMITMENT LETTER

EXHIBIT 58

You can mix and match sentences from these five different examples to craft an opening—and closing—paragraph. The heart of the letter is, however, the specific commitments that might be made. What might your collaborator be able to bring to your project? Your answer lies in one or more of the following areas, as the following table indicates with 18 different examples in Exhibit 59. Put your letter of commitment on letterhead stationery and address it to the Proposal Project Director, not the grant Program Officer.

RESUMES

Format

Your organization should settle on a standardized format for proposal resumes so that they all look similar. The choice of formats is not as important as the fact that all of your organizational resumes match. The format you ultimately choose should emphasize the skills that are essential to conduct your proposed project. Most grant applications call for an abbreviated resume

Financial Funds	Human Resources	Professional Expertise
Cash support	Advisory council participation	Disseminate knowledge gained
In-kind support	Access to special populations	Fiscal accounting
Tuition/Scholarships	Facilitate partnership linkages	Programmatic competence
Physical space	Loan of personnel	Testing samples
Use of credit cards	Attendance at meetings	Legal counsel
Excess equipment	Graduate students/Lab technicians	Medical advice

EXAMPLES OF POSSIBLE TYPES OF COMMITMENT

EXHIBIT 59

ABBREVIATED BIOGRAPHICAL SKETCH	
NAME	CURRENT POSITION TITLE
Todd M. Randall, M.B.A.	Executive Director
POSITION TITLE IN PROJECT	PERCENT EFFORT IN PROJECT
Tuberculosis Specialist: Capacity Building	25%

EDUCATION/TRAINING			
INSTITUTION AND LOCATION	DEGREE (if applicable)	YEAR(s)	FIELD OF STUDY
Michigan State University	B.S.	1990	Chemistry
University of Illinois	M.B.A.	1992	Organizational Management

Positions and Honors
1998–2001   Assistant Director, Blood Bank, Milwaukee, WI
2001–2005   Associate Director, Blood Bank, Milwaukee, WI
2005–   Executive Director, National Health Education Center, Milwaukee, WI

Selected Peer-Reviewed Publications (X out of Y)

Research Support

Pertinent Project Management Experience

Special Skills

Collaborators

International Travels

Project Accomplishments

Relevant Experience

Professional Organizational Membership

Languages/Special Skills

BIOSKETCH FOR NONPROFIT PERSONNEL

EXHIBIT 60

or biosketch, often two to four pages. Exhibit 60 shows a partially completed biosketch of an individual working at a nonprofit organization.

Exhibit 61 shows a similar biosketch format but it is focused more on university-based personnel. Both are adapted from a form currently used at the National Institutes of Health.

TRANSMITTAL LETTER

Although the transmittal letter is not an appendix item, it often emerges as a last-minute detail when the proposal narrative and appendixes are assembled. Accordingly, it is included here because of the sequence in which proposals are assembled.

ABBREVIATED BIOGRAPHICAL SKETCH	
NAME	CURRENT POSITION TITLE
Todd M. Randall, M.D.	Associate Professor of Family Medicine
POSITION TITLE IN PROJECT	PERCENT EFFORT IN PROJECT
Malaria Specialist: Immunology	25%

EDUCATION/TRAINING			
INSTITUTION AND LOCATION	DEGREE (if applicable)	YEAR(s)	FIELD OF STUDY
Michigan State University	B.S.	1990	Chemistry
University of Illinois	M.S.	1992	Bio-Chemistry
University of Wisconsin	M.D.	1996	Medicine
Harvard University	Post-Doc	1998	Infectious Diseases

Positions and Honors
1998–2002   Assistant Professor of Chemistry, University of Pocatello, ID
2001–2006   Assistant Professor of Medicine, Northwestern University
2005–   Associate Professor of Internal Medicine, Northwestern University

Selected Peer-Reviewed Publications (X out of Y)

Research Support

Pertinent Project Management Experience

Special Skills

Collaborators

International Travels

Project Accomplishments

Relevant Experience

Professional Organizational Membership

Languages/Special Skills

BIOSKETCH FORMAT FOR ACADEMIC PERSONNEL

EXHIBIT 61

Your transmittal letter should tell who you are, what your proposal is about, how much money is requested, and the grant program to which it is targeted. You want to transmit your proposal so it is reviewed by the "right" program. If you have preproposal contact with a program officer about this project (see Chapter 4), then mention that, "This proposal culminates the preliminary discussions I have had with Dr. Jane Wingert, Program Officer in Cellular Biology."

Besides the proposal copies you send to a central receiving center, send another copy under separate cover directly to your program officer. It may take weeks between the time you send it to a central receiving station and the time it is forwarded to program officers, who usually appreciate an early review opportunity so they can begin to think about the selection of appropriate reviewers.

If you are submitting a proposal to NIH (National Institutes of Health), consider this tip. Before you submit your proposal, ask your program officer to send an internal ARA (Awaiting Receipt of Application) notice to the Center for Scientific Review, the entry point for NIH proposal review. This will flag your proposal internally at NIH so it is forwarded to the study or review section of interest to your program officer. Further indicate in your transmittal letter that, "You should have on file an Awaiting Receipt of Application (ARA) notice regarding this proposal from Dr. Kelby Merrick, Cellular Biology Program, National Cancer Institute."

Transmittal letters for proposals to private sponsors follow the same general approach but place greater emphasis on institutional support for the project, even to the point where a chief executive officer and/or board member should countersign the

---

Today's Date

Ms. Beau Tribblehorn, President
Black Foundation
19800 18th Street, N.W.
Washington, DC 20555

　　　　　Re: Proposal Title
　　　　　Your Name
　　　　　Your Institution

Dear Ms. Tribblehorn:

On behalf of Midwest Agency, California's most comprehensive health provider agency for the displaced Hmong population, I am transmitting the referenced proposal for your review and consideration.

The proposal requests $150,000 for a three-year project to improve the delivery of health care among the elderly Hmong, a population with limited choices, lost aspirations, and cultural/linguistic barriers.

Ms. Laura Bennett, Project Director, has reviewed with me in detail the proposed project plans, and I can assure you that it will receive our highest organizational priority since it is central to our institutional mission of serving worthy, deserving, and needy populations.

I invite you to contact Ms. Bennett at 619-555-1234 to answer any programmatic questions you may have. If you have any administrative questions, please call me directly at 619-555-6789.

　　　Sincerely,

　　　Your Name
　　　Your Title

PROPOSAL TRANSMITTAL LETTER

EXHIBIT 62

proposal. An example of a transmittal letter follows in Exhibit 62.

REJECTION REASONS

Although proposals are seldom rejected because of shortcomings in the appendixes, the reviewers nevertheless do expect to see certain information items properly presented. If their expectations are not met, then your proposal may be downgraded. These reviewer comments suggest weaknesses in proposal appendixes.

1. The proposal does not provide evidence of formal structures or relationships binding collaborators.
2. The proposal does not identify or describe the qualifications of the project director to lead this collaborative venture.
3. The resumes of key project personnel do not demonstrate they have the capability and experience to administer a million dollar grant award.

4. The applicants propose to enter an area of research for which they are not adequately trained.
5. The principal investigator intends to give actual responsibility for the direction of a complex project to an inexperienced coinvestigator.
6. The investigators will be required to devote too much time to teaching or other nonresearch duties.

Clip File Action Item # 18 Appendices

To build your Appendixes clip file, return to the beginning of this chapter and begin collecting as many of the tabled items as possible. Encourage others to contribute as well. One organization, for example, requires all people attending staff meetings to come with a clip file contribution in hand.

CHAPTER 14
Abstracts

No one objects to how much you say, if you say it in a few words.

—Martha Lupton

PURPOSE OF ABSTRACTS

Successful grantseekers follow Lupton's advice: say much in a few words. The abstract is usually the first read and last written section of your proposal. It provides a cogent summary of your proposed project. It should offer a quick overview of what you propose to do and a rapid understanding of the project's significance, generalizability, and potential contribution. Project outcomes should be clearly identified. Often, proposal reviewers must write up a summary of your project for presentation to a larger review panel. If you write a persuasive abstract, program officers may use it as a basis for their proposal review, thereby simplifying their job. If your abstract is poorly written, their job is more difficult and your funding chances diminish.

Components of Abstracts

A thorough yet concise abstract includes the following information elements:

- **Subject:** What is the project about?
- **Purpose:** Why is the project being done? What is the problem or need being addressed?
- **Activities:** What will be done? What methods will be used?
- **Target Population:** What special group is being studied or served?
- **Location:** Where is the work being performed?
- **Outcomes:** What types of findings will result? To whom will these be useful?

KEY QUESTIONS TO ANSWER

1. Does the abstract effectively summarize the project?
2. Does it place appropriate emphasis on the various proposal components?
3. Does it enumerate project outcomes?
4. Does it comply with length or word requirements of the sponsor?
5. Does it use key headings and subheadings to highlight proposal sections?

EXAMPLES OF ABSTRACTS

Example 1

The following is a project abstract statement for private foundation support for a parent training center. This abstract is presented twice: first as it was originally written and second as it was rewritten prior to final submission.

> At the conclusion of extensive long-range planning, the Parent Training Center has defined its priorities for the next decade. To implement its plan, the Center has undertaken a comprehensive multiyear development program to generate funding for its highest priorities and aspirations. The New Parent Training Program is one of the special programs for which support is sought. To date, a training curriculum has been created and a parent advisory board and a lending library were begun. The Program is proposing activities that

include parenting classes, a parenting clinic with further agency referral, and an annual one-day parenting convention. Six sites have been chosen for training sessions for more than 100 parents between January and April 2009. A three-year budget and explanatory narrative are attached delineating the fund-raising goal for the Program. Because the Foundation has evidenced a strong concern for families and children and because of the need for a New Parent Training Program in the metropolitan area, the Parent Training Center is requesting a $30,000 grant, payable over three years, to assist in addressing a pervasive problem in our society.

In contrast, consider this rewritten version that uses bold headings and white space to improve the readability of this abstract.

Overview. The Parent Training Center, the only nonprofit agency in the State exclusively dedicated to teaching parenting skills, is seeking $30,000 to establish a new program to train teenage parents.

Need for Training Teenage Parents. Child abuse and neglect have grown dramatically, up 18% in the four county area over the past two years. While the growth occurs across all socio-economic levels and races, the greatest rate of growth is occurring in families with teenage parents. These parents are poorly informed about child development and often favor corporal punishment as a means of managing their children.

Objectives of Teenage Parent Training Program. Program objectives are to:

- Conduct 10 parenting classes for teenage parents by January 2009.
- Establish a clinical program for serious problems by June 2009.
- Disseminate information about teenage parenting by January 2010.

Methods for Implementing Teenage Parent Training Program. A four-week series of parenting classes will be offered at sites that serve high-risk, teenage parents. Instructional techniques include discussion, videos, handouts, and parent support groups. Two clinical psychologists will conduct the Teenage Parent Training Program and, through their linkages with other appropriate agencies in the community, create a referral network.

Annually, a one-day parenting convention will present informative sessions and speakers on a variety of topics, e.g., toy safety, young children's literature, health issues. Additionally, exhibits will also show relevant community resources, e.g., hospitals, day care centers, preschools.

Outcomes for Teenage Parent Training Program. The effectiveness of the program will be measured through consumer satisfaction questionnaires and pre- and post-tests of parenting knowledge and skills to be developed. Pilot data suggest the culturally sensitive training materials will have a positive impact on parental behaviors. The one-day conference will heighten community sensitivity to this issue.

Notice how the use of headings enhances the readability of the proposal. The key sentences in each section are taken from key sentences in the actual proposal narrative, a persuasive writing technique also used in the following example, which is taken from a federal grant proposal to hold a series of regional conferences on the subject of perinatal depression.

Example 2

The following is a project abstract written by a nonprofit organization seeking funding to conduct some statewide workshops on the topic of perinatal depression.

Overview. The perinatal period, pregnancy through early life, is a developmental epoch that is critical to maternal and infant mental health. With a grant of $50,000 from the Substance Abuse and Mental Health Services Agency, the Perinatal Care Group will host seven regional conferences throughout Wisconsin to bridge the gap between knowledge and practice regarding prenatal and postpartum depression—a clinically significant diagnosis affecting more than 10,000 Wisconsin women annually, especially those representing culturally diverse backgrounds.

Problem. Depression during the prenatal and postpartum period is a major public health problem affecting 15% of all women and up to 30% of women living in poverty. Depression does not often resolve without treatment, yet many practitioners are untrained or inexperienced in identifying depression, or may lack referral sources for effective treatment. Of approximately 70,000 Wisconsin births last year, more than 10,000 mothers experienced clinically significant yet treatable depression that often remained undiagnosed. The consequences not only affect the mother-baby dyad but usually the entire family unit as well.

Solution. Prenatal and postpartum depression is identifiable and treatable. Early identification and treatment by primary care providers or mental health specialists is crucial. The goal of this proposal is to disseminate and integrate knowledge about prenatal and postpartum depression into the practice of providers throughout the state. Since research shows that best practices are more likely to be adopted when providers participate in face-to-face interactions, a series of seven regional conferences will be held. Given the ethnic and cultural diversity that exists within Wisconsin, improving cultural competence is a major thematic focus of the seven regional conferences that will reach 350 participants. The outcomes will produce nine different conference products that will be distributed verbally and visually, actively and passively to appropriate culturally diverse audiences.

Evaluation. Because the four project objectives are expressed in measurable terms, an external evaluation consultant will evaluate each one. Culturally and linguistically appropriate evaluation tools will collect participant feedback at the end of the conferences and again 30 days later with a minimum of an 80% response rate among regional conference participants.

Long-Term. The Perinatal Care Group has made a long-term commitment to reducing the knowledge-practice gap regarding prenatal and postpartum depression. The proposed regional conferences represent Phase IV in a series of initiatives to achieve this goal. Earlier activities have included public awareness campaigns (Phase I), a best practices symposium (Phase II), and a blueprint for action initiative (Phase III). The proposed Phase IV regional conferences represent a systematic continuation of prior events on this topic of prenatal and postpartum depression, which has enormous human and economic consequences for women, their families, and the health care system.

Again, notice the use of headings to highlight proposal content. The primary federal reviewer for this proposal was charged with the responsibility to write a summary of the proposal; the reviewer thought this synopsis was so accurate and succinct that he just used this instead of writing his own.

WRITING TIPS FOR PROPOSAL ABSTRACTS

1. Don't write the abstract until you have completed the proposal.
2. Unless otherwise indicated, limit your abstract section to between 250 and 500 words.
3. Include at least one sentence each on problem, objectives, methods, and outcomes.
4. Use major headings in the abstract: Need, Objectives, Methods and Outcomes.

REJECTION REASONS

Weak proposal abstracts have caused reviewers to raise the following concerns:

1. The applicant raises points in the abstract that are not explained in the proposal narrative.
2. The abstract was unclear and raised questions at the outset that were subsequently confirmed upon reading the narrative. This proposal simply is not well reasoned.
3. The applicant ignored the 100-word limitation on the abstract. In fact, the entire proposal is rather verbose.

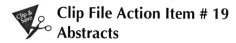

Clip File Action Item # 19 Abstracts

Following are some action items to build your Abstracts clip file:

- Gather sample abstracts of successfully funded proposals, regardless of subject matter.
- Collect examples of document design principles that will enhance your abstract: use of headings, white space, and layout.

PART IV
The Final Steps

OVERVIEW OF PART IV

At this point in the proposal development process, you have identified potential sponsors (Chapter 2 and Chapter 3) and selected one who might be interested in supporting your project (Chapter 4). It's now time to put your thoughts and ideas on paper—or the computer screen.

Establish some reasonable writing objectives. Don't try to do everything at once. Chunk it up. Whether you are writing a grant or your first novel, successful writers stress the importance of getting the first draft down on paper as quickly as possible, even if you would not want to share it with anybody. It doesn't have to be good, just down—in writing.

Successful grantseekers estimate they spend 25 percent of their time writing the first draft and 75 percent of their time editing it. Editing is a multistage process: edit for only one feature at a time. The multiple loops through the proposal ensure that all elements are presented with punch and persuasion.

Chapters 5 through 14 offer many key questions that you should be asking yourself as you write a particular proposal section. Additionally, review the examples for ideas on approaches to take and the rejection reasons for things to avoid.

In Part IV, our attention turns to the final steps. Chapter 15 focuses on creating your first draft and then doing a thorough job of editing. Once your first draft is written, you can spend the bulk of your proposal writing time polishing your document. The latter portions of Chapter 15 offer numerous editing suggestions. The key is to edit for one feature at a time, e.g., clarity of sentences, punctuation, organization, or document design. You want to edit with "tunnel vision"; that is, keep your focus on only one feature per pass through the entire draft.

Remember that no matter how many times you have cycled through the draft looking for specific linguistic glitches, you are apt to miss something. It is extremely difficult to edit your own copy; you end up reading what you intended to write instead of what is actually written. Accordingly, recruit someone with good linguistic intuitions to provide an objective, second pair of eyes on your text.

Finally, Chapter 16 discusses next steps—after your proposal has been submitted. We describe the review process, including site visits, and dealing with grant decisions. In the grants arena, there are no guarantees of funding. Recognize, however, that a "no" from a sponsor does not mean they will "never" fund you; rather, it may mean "not right now." Based on sponsor feedback, you may consider revising and resubmitting your proposal in a future cycle. Persistence pays.

CHAPTER 15
Writing and Editing Techniques

No grantsmanship will turn a bad idea into a good one, but there are many ways to disguise a good one.

—*William Raub*

PURPOSES OF PERSUASIVE PROPOSAL WRITING

As a proposal writer, you job is to "out-imagine" the reviewers.

You need to present your best ideas persuasively. There are many ways to disguise a great idea. All-too-often, proposals do just that—they cleverly mask, albeit unintentionally, a novel idea that reviewers ultimately reject. As a proposal writer, your job is to write a highly readable proposal, one that is persuasive, stylistically appropriate, and free of jargon. Your proposal should analyze a significant problem, propose an effective solution, and communicate your credibility. A well-written proposal will always have a competitive edge. Skill in proposal writing cannot compensate for a weak project, but it can provide the extra measure of quality that distinguishes a high-quality proposal from its competition.

PROPOSAL WRITING TIPS

Are you ready to start writing? Before your turn on your computer, ask yourself these questions:

1. Do I have a clearly focused and innovative idea? (Chapter 7).
2. Have I developed my idea in detail? (Chapter 7).
3. Have I had preproposal contacts with program officers, past grant winners, and prior reviewers? (Chapter 4).
4. Have I compared the application guidelines with the reviewer's evaluation form? (Chapter 10).

5. Do I have access to data that will document the frequency and severity of the problem my organization wishes to address? (Chapter 7).
6. Do I have active buy-in from project collaborators? (Chapter 13).
7. Do I have an experienced and well-credentialed project director? (Chapter 4).

If you have seven "yes" answers, then you are ready to write, but not before.

With your computer turned on, you may experience a bad case of writer's block, or grope for the perfect word or phrase. If so, insert a *** at the place where you experience trouble, and keep on going. When you have completed the first draft, activate your computer's find command and let it identify the fill-in-the-blank places.

Don't try to do all of your writing in one sitting, or in an intensive manner. You lose the benefit of two processes that are important to persuasive writing. One is the perspective that can come only with percolation time. If you back away from the project for 24 hours, you will have a clearer view when you return to it. The second process is that of testing a limited part of the project against the overall project structure. That happens when you force yourself to consider only one segment of the project at a time. Work on your idea in small pieces.

Avoid overreliance on a committee when writing. While you should seek reactions to proposal drafts from many readers, one person should be responsible for writing the proposal and have the authority to make final decisions when inevitable contradictory suggestions emerge. Further, not all committee members will share your timeline responsibilities; failure to get timely feedback demoralizes proposal writers, especially when writing under deadline. Use a committee to critique your proposals, but let it be known clearly where the "buck stops."

Successful grantseekers emphasize the importance of quickly completing the first proposal draft, so that most of their writing time is actually spent on editing—polishing the proposal. Write your first draft quickly and spend much more time on editing and revising. Experienced grant writers usually submit their ninth or tenth draft for proposal review. The difference between a good and great proposal comes in skillful editing.

GENERAL EDITING SUGGESTIONS

Put your writing aside for 24 hours before editing to give you a fresh perspective. Edit copy that is double- or triple-spaced; this format invites you to make changes. Be completely brutal with your first draft. Nothing should satisfy you. Delete. Substitute. Rearrange. Insert. Combine. Be especially critical of the first few paragraphs. You probably had not warmed up at that stage. Read aloud for content and style. When it comes to detecting errors, the ear is more efficient than the eye. Don't be the only one to proofread and edit your work. The odds of spotting errors increase with each new pair of eyes. Don't view editing as a time waster, even when time is tight. Your credibility is at stake whenever you send out a proposal.

As you begin to edit, cycle through the proposal many times, each time looking for something different. Experienced grantseekers follow a four-step editing process, which looks at content, clarity, mechanics, and design.

Content and Organization. Did you include all of the content information in the order requested in the application guidelines and on the reviewer's evaluation form?

Be sure you didn't leave out major parts that could help reviewers gain a better understanding of your proposal. Did you include a persuasive need statement, measurable objectives, process and outcome evaluation measures, table of contents, page numbers, and appropriate appendixes, including resumes? Does your proposal present a logical flow of ideas?

Clarity. Is all of the necessary content clear and persuasive?

Purge each paragraph of extraneous sentences. Weed out unnecessary words. Choose concrete words instead of abstract ones whenever possible. Make sure technical terms, jargon, and abbreviations are defined. Avoid vague adjectives. Be consistent in writing style, tone, word usage, and punctuation. Is your average sentence length about 15–20 words? Does your proposal flow smoothly with appropriate use of transitional words, sentences, and paragraphs?

Mechanics. Is your proposal structurally unblemished?

Ensure your writing is mechanically flawless by checking the following: punctuation, spelling, pronoun-antecedent agreement, verb agreement, numbers, paragraph length (1.25 inch maximum), omitted words, word choice, and passive constructions.

Design. Does your proposal look inviting to read?

Look at your proposal for appearance. Have you used adequate white space, distinctive headings and subheadings, and lists to invite skim reading? Are margins at least one inch? Have appropriate devices been used to indicate proposal structure: headings, bullets, numbers, bolding, indentations, and spacing?

Do not sacrifice proposal design in favor of including more text. Rather than reducing type size or eliminating white space, edit sentences for clarity, eliminating extra words wherever possible.

INITIAL EDITING TIPS

Below you will find a number of editing tips that are usually overlooked in the initial proposal drafting. Collectively, these suggestions can significantly strengthen your proposal.

Headings

Headings and subheadings act like a table of contents placed directly in your proposal text; that is, at a glance they reveal the main ideas and the organization of your proposal to the reader. Ask your program officer for a copy of the reviewer's evaluation form, and use those same headings and subheadings in your proposal. If a reviewer's evaluation form is not available, use headings and subheadings that are specific to your proposal. Generic headings such as "Introduction," "Background," "Materials," "Methods," "Results," "Conclusions," and "Recommendations" are not unique to your proposal. Short, specific headings such as these will have more impact on your readers:

- **The Problem: Overcoming Distance Barriers**
- **Eliminating the Shock Waves**
- **Our Credentials: 125 Years of National Experience**
- **Benefits of Youth Programming**
- **Capabilities: 75 New Volunteers**

Specific headings give reviewers an overview of your entire project, even if they are merely skimming your proposal. Note that the headings are in a different type style (Arial Boldface in the above examples) than the proposal text (Times New Roman in this paragraph).

Levels of Organization

You can use vertical and horizontal white space to create up to three levels of organizational headings. Do not use more than three levels of headings because you may lose the reader in the structural detail of your proposal. Effective use of white space sets off headings and enhances readability.

- Level one headings should be centered, sans serif typeface (e.g., Arial), all capital letters, and 12-point boldface font; double space before further text follows.
- Level two headings should be left justified, sans serif typeface (e.g., Arial), keywords capitalized, and 12-point boldface font. Single space before further text follows.
- Level three headings should be indented, serif typeface (e.g., Times New Roman), keywords capitalized, and 12-point boldface font. Punctuate and continue with paragraph copy.

Exhibit 63 is an example of all three levels of headings.

Line Length and Margin Width

Lines approximately 65 characters long are preferred from the standpoint of readability. Physiologic studies of the eye suggest this line length is comfortable to read without inducing fatigue. The line length relates to the standard one-inch margins used in proposals. While smaller margins allow more words per page, proposal narrative becomes too difficult to read.

Sentence Length

While sentence length varies, limit each sentence to 15 words or less on the average. If you have any sentences over 30 words, they are too long to track easily. Hold your draft copy in your hand and walk around the room at a fast pace while reading it aloud. If you have to fight for breath in the middle of any sentence, it is too long.

Too Long: The elastic fabric surrounding the circular frame whose successive revolutions bear you onward in space has lost its pristine roundness.

Better: You have a flat tire.

Sexist Language

Use nonsexist language to prevent excluding others. Pronoun problems with "s/he" or "his or her" can usually be avoided by shifting the entire sentence to the plural form: "they" or "them." Write with a sense of dignity, equality, and appropriateness for both sexes.

THIS IS A LEVEL ONE HEADING

The rest of the proposal would continue here.

This Is a Level Two Heading

The rest of the proposal would continue here.

This Is a Level Three Heading. The rest of the proposal would continue here.

Note the spacing between the three heading levels. This visual chunking strategy is highly readable and facilitates reviewer skimming.

LEVELS OF HEADINGS

EXHIBIT 63

Sexist:	Every participant will complete his evaluation form at the end of the program.
Nonsexist:	Participants will complete their evaluation forms at the end of the program.

Transitional Words and Phrases

Transitional expressions—words and phrases that signal connections among ideas—can help you achieve coherence in your writing. Each expression is a signal to the reader that explains how one idea is connected to the next. Business writers suggest that the use of transitions makes the difference between average and persuasive copy. Common transitional words and phrases can indicate:

- *Addition:* also, in addition, again, and, and then, too, besides, further, furthermore, equally important, what's more, next, then, finally, likewise, moreover, first, second, third, last, indeed, more precisely
- *Comparison:* similarly, likewise, in like manner, in the same way, in comparison
- *Concession:* after all, although this may be true, at the same time, even though, of course, to be sure, certainly, naturally, granted
- *Contrast:* but, yet, however, on the other hand, nevertheless, nonetheless, conversely, in contrast, on the contrary, still, at the same time, after all, although true, and yet, in spite of, notwithstanding
- *Example:* for example, for instance, thus, as an illustration, namely, specifically, in particular, incidentally, indeed, in fact, in other words, said differently, that is, to illustrate, of note
- *Location:* in the front, in the foreground, in the back, in the background, at the side, adjacent, nearby, in the distance, here, there
- *Restriction:* despite, contrary to, although, while, provided, in case, if, lest, when, occasionally, even if, never
- *Result:* therefore, thus, consequently, so, accordingly, due to this, as a result, hence, in short, otherwise, then, truly, that caused, that produced
- *Sequence:* first, firstly, second, secondly, third, thirdly, next, then, finally, afterwards, before, soon, later, during, meanwhile, subsequently, immediately, at length, eventually, in the future, currently, after a short time, as soon as, at last, at the same time, earlier, in the meantime, lately, presently, since, temporarily, thereafter, thereupon, until, when, while
- *Summary:* as a result, hence, in short, in brief, in summary, in conclusion, finally, on the whole, to conclude, to sum up, thus, therefore, as a consequence, at last

Transitional Sentences and Paragraphs

To ensure that your proposal reads smoothly and fluently, use transitional sentences and paragraphs. They blend separate proposal segments into one continuously flowing copy. Insert them wherever you are making major content shifts within your proposal. These overview paragraphs provide signals that the current ideas are shifting to something else; often they summarize what was just read and foreshadow what is coming next.

1. A transitional bridge from a problem section to a solution section in the proposal.

> In sum, a combination of school and community poverty, health disparities, and shortage of health care providers are preventing children from leading healthy lifestyles. School-based health centers can bridge these gaps in order to provide comprehensive primary and preventive health care to this medically underserved community.

This transition paragraph reminds reviewers of the problems as a prelude to discussing solutions.

2. An introductory statement to a methodology section.

> This section summarizes our plans, and is supplemented with concise statements that provide the motivation behind this plan of action.

This sentence does two things: it foreshadows for the reviewer what the upcoming proposal section is all about, and it alerts the reviewer that the rationale for selecting this particular methodology section will be explained, an important inclusion that is often overlooked.

3. A proposal section that helped establish the credibility of the project codirectors.

> One added value of the codirectors is that they have experienced the challenges of managing multifaceted projects; they know what works and doesn't work. Based on this experience, and a concern that reviewers might feel the codirectors are already "overextended," considerable thought has gone into this carefully crafted project organizational structure, which

includes strategic highly trained professionals as key support personnel.

This section tells the reviewers that the key project personnel are not only experienced project managers, but are also not over committed.

4. A proposal section that alerts the reviewer to the structure of the methodology section.

Each of these activities is written in a way that is consistent with the agency scoring system.

This sentence signals the reader that the proposal writers obtained a copy of the reviewer's evaluation form from the Program Officer and followed it in their discussion of the methods section, thereby simplifying the reviewer's task.

5. These proposal writers had a pretty good idea who their competition might be and wanted to posture themselves favorably against it.

Our plan of activities is built on a careful reading of the RFP priorities, and of activities of the existing center at the XYZ Institute. While their activities are appropriate, we believe we have the infrastructure in place that enables us to aim higher.

In a very professional manner, this section says "we're better than our competition."

Verb Choice

Use action verbs instead of forms of "be" and "have" whenever possible. Persuasive proposals typically contain no more than 25 percent of passive voice sentences. Although passive-voice verbs add variety to your sentence structure, your proposal becomes dull, weak, hard to read, and filled with useless words if you use too many passives. Passives are a form of the verb "to be" and a past-tense form of another verb.

Passive: The homeless are little appreciated by people today.

Active: Today, people don't appreciate the homeless.

Passive: By the year 2010, half of this population is projected to be 75-plus, according to the Census Bureau.

Active: The Census Bureau estimates one-half of the elderly will be over age 75 by the year 2010.

When you write in passive sentences, readers often "rewrite" the sentence into an active form, thereby slowing reader comprehension.

When editing, use your computer's find command to locate forms of "be" and "have." Convert passive to active sentences whenever possible, but do not feel guilty about using some passives.

White Space

Use white space to break up long copy. Ample white space makes your proposal appear inviting and user-friendly. In addition, white space gives readers a visual clue to the structure of your proposal. That is, on a page full of print, a block of unprinted lines or white space, stands out immediately. White space can indicate that one section is ending and another is beginning, or that an idea is so central to the proposal that it needs to be set off by itself. Judicious use of white space breaks your proposal into smaller, manageable "chunks" of information. Some grant writers recommend that up to 50 percent of each page should be white space. To open up white space in your proposal, consider these suggestions:

- Indent five spaces at the start of new paragraphs.
- Limit paragraph length to an average of eight single-spaced lines (or no longer than the distance between the first and second knuckle on your index finger).
- Insert a blank line of space between minor proposal segments.
- Insert two blank lines of space between major proposal sections.

Finally, when writing proposals, demonstrate the capability to carry out the proposed activities and stress the impact of the project on others. For example, one effective corporate proposal started out:

Fifty-one percent of the community, 58 percent of the company's future workers, and 62 percent of the firm's potential stockholders are represented by the applicant.

Needless to say, this caught the eye of the contributions committee.

USING COMPUTERS TO EDIT PROPOSALS

Line Numbering

When editing proposal drafts, experienced grant writers use the line numbering feature, whereby each line of text is numbered consecutively. That way, it is an easy matter to pinpoint where questions exist when critiquing text, thereby saving editing time.

Comparing Edited Drafts

Another useful word processing feature involves the "Track Changes" (Microsoft Word) or "Compare" (Word Perfect) command. When electronically editing a proposal draft, the track changes command enables you to strike through words that should be deleted and add new copy in a different color type. This way, it is easy to identify precisely changes that have been made between an original and edited text. Later, you can accept or reject the proposed changes, as you wish.

Using Your Computer's "Find" Command

The "find" command on most word processing programs enables you to locate any word or phase in your proposal and replace it with a substitute, if desired. This simple feature can be a very powerful "low-tech" tool to upgrade the quality of your written proposal. Use it to spot and fix the following sentence structures.

"There is" or "There are". Sentences that begin with "There is" or "There are" are often weak structures. They prevent the verb from carrying a full sentence load.

Example: There is no easy solution to this problem.

Revised: The problem is not solved easily.

Experienced grant writers often use sentence starter phrases like "there is/are" or "here is/are" to quickly generate first draft copy. However, since those structures are weak, they use the find command to strengthen the sentences during proposal editing.

Example: As we begin our fifth year, there are several problems facing our agency.

Revised: As we begin our fifth year, three problems face our agency: increasing service demand, decreasing resources, and an inadequate infrastructure.

Use your find command to hunt for "there is/are" structures and see whether they can be revised to eliminate this phrase.

Linking Verbs. Linking verbs join the subject and predicate in sentences. Although they bond the two major parts of a sentence, linking verbs also rob color, energy, and force from the sentence.

Example: Our agency has two types of clients it serves.

Revised: Our agency serves two types of clients.

Notice that linking verbs stand alone and are not joined by other verbs.

Example: Mrs. Smith is a volunteer in our Clinic.

Revised: Mrs. Smith volunteers in our Clinic.

Linking verbs are forms of "to be" (be, being, been, am, is, are, was, were) or "to have" (has, have, had). Sometimes these verb forms appear with other verbs, such as "She was applying" or "He had traveled." Used that way, they are helping verbs, not linking verbs. Limit yourself to using no more than 30 percent of linking verbs in your proposal sentences.

Sacrificing Verbs for Nouns. Many proposal writers weaken their narrative when they sacrifice verbs and bury proposal action in a noun or adjective.

Example: Parental involvement can be beneficial to implementation of the project.

Revised: If we involve parents, it helps us implement the project.

You add zest when you change a noun or an adjective to a verb.

Example: It is our expectation that we will see an improvement in productivity when the staff learns to use the new computer.

Revised: We expect the staff to produce more when they master the new computer.

Changing nouns to verbs also lets you cut excess words. Use the find command to locate words that end in *-ion*, *-ance*, *-ment*, *-ence*, and *-ing*. Such word endings often hide verbs and weaken your proposal narrative.

"Make" Verbs. A common offender of the verb phrase is the use of the word "make" (present tense) or "made" (past tense). Examples follow in Exhibit 64.

Use your find command to locate "make" and "made" verb constructions.

PROPOSAL APPEARANCE

Although you will obviously spend much time working on the content of your proposal, you should also pay attention to its appearance or design. Experienced proposal writers believe that appearance may account for as much as one-half of your overall proposal evaluation. Just as clothing is important in the business world for establishing initial impressions, so too is the appearance of your proposal as it reaches the reviewer's hands. The proposal should "look" familiar to the reader. A familiar proposal is a friendly proposal. Look at the printed materials issued by the sponsor. When appropriate, use the same type size and style, layout, white space, and headings as they do.

A good proposal design reduces the likelihood of reviewer errors and misunderstandings about the proposal. As a consequence, you will simplify the reviewer's job. A well-designed proposal makes even complex information look accessible and gives the reviewers confidence that they can master your proposal information.

Use these design tips to create visual chunks of information that can be quickly noticed and absorbed.

- Visual devices like headings and white space help reviewers see your proposal structure.
- Use white space to make difficult subjects easier to comprehend by breaking into smaller units.
- Use white space as an active design element to communicate user-friendliness to readers as opposed to a cluttered, tightly packed page that intimidates the readers.

- Major headings should normally appear at the top of a page.
- Never leave a heading on the final line of a page.
- The most effective positions for headings and captions are left-hand outside columns because the outsides of pages are noticed first.

As you learn about your reviewers and consider proposal appearance, try to anticipate which of the following reading styles the reviewer is likely to use: skimming, search reading, or critical reading. Recall that your earlier prospect research from a past reviewer or program officer identified the manner in which your proposal would most likely be reviewed. Reviewers skim proposals when they have many pages to read in a very short time. Reviewers use a search reading strategy when they are following an evaluation sheet that assigns points to specific proposal sections. Reviewers always critically read proposals, especially when the reading occurs in the time luxury of a mail review. Exhibit 65 shows some of the writing techniques that are particularly appropriate for different reading styles.

Sample Edited Proposal

A sample edited proposal is provided as Exhibit 66. Note the comments in the left-hand margin, which exemplify many of the specific document writing tips outlined previously.

THE FINAL EDIT

You're nearly ready to send the proposal to the sponsor. It's time for one last pass through all proposal details to make sure everything is complete. Double-check these major last minute items.

Instead of	Rewrite as
• make a decision	• decided
• made a modification	• modified
• make a determination	• determine
• made a revision	• revised
• make a recommendation	• recommend
• made a suggestion	• suggested
• make a judgment	• judged

CONVERTING NOUNS TO VERBS

EXHIBIT 64

Reading Style	Writing Technique
Skim reading	• White space • Headings and subheadings • Short paragraphs • Ragged right margins • Graphs and charts • Illustrations
Search reading	• Bold type • Lists and examples • Select repetition of key ideas • Table of contents • Page numbers • Appendixes
Critical reading	• Transitions • Varying length and structure of sentences • Capitalization and punctuation • Type size and style • Line spacing • Consistent formatting

READING STYLES AND WRITING TECHNIQUES

EXHIBIT 65

Binding. For small-to-medium-size proposals (less than 30 pages), staple the proposal once (using a heavy-duty stapler) along the vertical margin of the upper left-hand corner of the proposal. Do not bind serially along the left-hand margin or use "slip-on" binders. Both procedures make it difficult to open up the proposal and read the inside pages. Use a large binder clip for larger proposals, making sure that your agency name and page number is a heading on each page.

Mailing Day. Unless you have a specific deadline date, mail your proposal so it arrives on a Tuesday or a Wednesday. Most people receive less mail on those two days, so your proposal will be better noticed. If you do have a specific deadline date, check to see whether it is a receipt date or a postmark date.

Mailing Envelope. Mail the proposal in a manila envelope large enough to accommodate the proposal without having to fold or bend it, even if you have a short letter proposal. It'll be more distinctive than those with folds in the paper.

Page Numbering. Place page numbers on the top right or bottom center of the pages of your proposal. Start numbering with "2" on the second page of your proposal; do not number the first page.

Paper Size. Use the standard 8.5- by 11-inch paper unless the sponsor indicates otherwise.

Paper Color. Use white paper. Do not use colored paper for the proposal text or as a divider between proposal sections.

Paper Weight. Use a 20-weight bond paper, a moderately high quality, reasonably priced paper that will photocopy or print nicely in laser printers.

Paragraph Style. Indent your paragraphs five spaces because it increases readability.

Printer. Print your proposal on a laser or ink jet printer. It gives an excellent quality product. Those organizations lacking access to a laser printer can use one for a nominal cost in many stores that specialize in photocopying services.

Proofreading. Proofread your proposal several times in multiple readings, looking for different features on each reading. As you proofread, look at mechanics and format.

Are words spelled correctly, especially proper names? Are there any missing words? Did any words get transposed due to sloppy cutting and pasting? Are sentences grammatically correct? Are sentences punctuated properly? Is there any missing punctuation? Are words properly capitalized? Are apostrophes used appropriately? Are all numbers and computations accurate?

Know your common mistakes. Make one proofreading pass looking exclusively for your common

Today's Date

Mr. Lee K. Wallet
Executive Director
Deep Pockets Fund
P.O. Box 17971
Anytown, WI 53017

Dear Mr. Wallet:

Our House, a nonprofit community-based agency providing quality educational and recreational opportunities for Anytown's southside, invites your investment in a $25,320 project to prevent drug and gang involvement among "at-risk" youth.

Begin with a one-sentence summary of the entire project.

Our House, a recent winner of Anytown's Community Development Award, utilizes a self-help philosophy to encourage the growth and development of individuals, families, and a health community. Three years ago, Our House began participating in a federally funded program to prevent the recruitment of at-risk youth into gang and drug activity. During this time, Our House helped more than 120 misguided youth find their way back to being fully functional members of the community. However, dollar-conscious politicians have systematically reduced government funding of critical drug and gang prevention programs. More immediately, neighborhood youth centers, including Our House, face an emergency situation because the government, without notice, terminated federal support funds fourteen months ahead of schedule. Consequently, Our House must identify new and creative ways of continuing to provide quality prevention programs at minimal expense.

White space creates visual "chunks" of information. Double space between proposal sections.

Our House: Anytown's Southside Neighbor. Established in 1973, Our House is located in the heart of Anytown's southside neighborhood. Unquestionably, Our House is in one of the most ethnically diverse areas in Anytown. Neighborhood demographics consist of:

Headings are specific to the proposal and help readers to skim or search for details.

- 54% Hispanic
- 23% Caucasian
- 14% African American
- 5% Native American
- 4% Asian

In addition to being one of Anytown's most diverse neighborhoods, it is one of Anytown's most desperate. The southside neighborhood accounts for over one-quarter of all county AFDC cases, nearly one-third of all General Assistance cases, and over one-fifth of all Children's Court referrals for abuse, neglect, and teen births.

For over one-quarter of a century, Our House has provided healthy alternative activities for Anytown's southside youth. However, Our House can attend to only a limited number. With more than 100 children per square block, it is virtually impossible to provide quality education and recreational opportunities for everyone. Consequently, Our House is currently focusing its efforts on Anytown's "at-risk" youth population.

Sample Edited Letter Proposal

EXHIBIT 66

Problem: Prevalence of Gangs and Drugs. Without a doubt, Anytown has it share of gangs. In fact, gang membership currently averages 4,000 participants operating in 20–30 gangs. Furthermore, studies indicate:

- Gang members are 15 years old, on average
- 52% of gang members used alcohol in the preceding month
- 72% of gang members have an average g.p.a. of 1.73, "D"

In addition, law enforcement agencies witness that there is a significant link between gangs, drugs, and violence. But perhaps the most revealing assessment of gang activity in Anytown was made by the Juvenile Court Assistant District Attorneys when they asserted that membership in gangs was a way of identifying oneself.

At Our House, we recognize this need to "fit in." Furthermore, we recognize that many adolescents turn to gangs, drugs, and violence as a means of combating boredom and loneliness. Our House provides adolescents with healthy alternatives to gang life. More importantly, the youth who participate in Our House's programs report increased levels of respect, self-esteem, positive peer involvement, and more positive attitudes and behaviors. In other words, at Our House they find a real sense of purpose and belonging.

Solution: Youth Programs. Our House currently services over 120 "at-risk" youth and adolescents between ages of 10–16. These "at-risk" youth include those failing in school, in children's court on minor offenses, causing neighborhood disturbances, or having trouble socializing at home.

Our House, together with a local consortium of churches and residential leaders, has designed a Neighborhood Strategic Plan (NSP) to improve the overall quality and safety of the southside neighborhood community. NSP addresses the particular strengths and weaknesses of the community and outlines policies and procedures for social improvement. Our House has taken a leading role in this project by establishing a safe haven where youth and adolescents can get away from the stresses and pressures of street gang life and actively cultivate personal growth through specific programming.

- Educational: after-school and ESL tutoring
- Cultural: computer programming, drawing, painting, field trips
- Recreational: basketball, volleyball, pool, Ping-Pong
- Employment: summer work opportunities

More importantly, because students are involved in educational and recreational activities, they gain a new sense of personal identity; consequently, they no longer turn to gangs, drugs, and violence for identification and recreational purposes.

Capabilities: Encouraging Responsible Life Decisions. Last year alone, there were over 11,500 youth participant visits to Our House's educational and recreational facilities. That averages out to over 200 participant visits each week. In the past three years, Our House has had many distinguishing educational and recreational successes.

Our House's educational programs have had remarkable participation. In three years, 71 students have earned GED certification – more than any other community-based program in Anytown!

Arial type style headings match those used in the sponsor's printed material.

Times Roman type style matches that used in the sponsor's printed material.

Bulleted list conveys information simply and quickly. List is set off with extra white space above and below.

SAMPLE EDITED LETTER PROPOSAL

EXHIBIT 66 (Continued from page 179)

Bold type creates emphasis. Use sparingly to stress what is truly important.

Participation in Our House's recreational programs has more than tripled since its inception three years ago. Specifically, youth and adolescents are active in at least one of three unique Rec Center Programs:

- **The Hang Tough Club**—a drug and alcohol prevention club for teens
- **Girls in the House**—a special club for addressing the needs of girls and young women
- **Youth Opportunities Initiative**—a teenage gang prevention club

12- point type size matches use in the sponsor's publications.

The goal of each of these programs is to provide youth and adolescents with the skills, foresight, and habits necessary for them to make responsible life decisions. More concretely, as a result of obtaining a more positive self-image, youth and adolescents attend school more regularly, earn better grades, and employ more effective coping strategies in their lives.

Since this project is still in its formative years, Our House will continue to track the progress and success of these programs to evaluate their effectiveness. Specifically, we will calculate the number and frequency of youth participating in these programs; we will also gather program improvement suggestions from youth and adolescents, their educational and religious leaders, and private consultants. These suggestions will be used to implement any necessary changes in youth programming and determine the feasibility of expanding our services to include other at-risk adolescents.

Ragged right margins are easier to read than right justified margins.

Budget Request: $25,320. With the demonstrated concern that the Deep Pockets Fund has shown for community revitalization programs, Our House requests a grant in the amount of $25,320. Quite frankly, without fiscal government support, this project extends beyond Our House's financial boundaries. Accordingly, we must now reach out for assistance in what surely is a vital service to Anytown's southside community. In effect, by investing 72¢/day in each of the 120 adolescents who participate in Our House's at-risk youth programs, you will be empowering many youth and families to better combat the issues of gangs, drugs, and violence.

Standard one-inch margins throughout the proposal.

Your support really will make a significant difference. The Deep Pockets Fund will be directly aiding hundreds of children and adolescents who are in desperate need of quality educational and life-skill opportunities, and at the same time, you will be making a significant contribution to gang and drug prevention in Anytown. Please contact Lindy Ross, Development Coordinator at Our House, at (414) 867-5309 to answer questions or provide additional information.

Sincerely,

Karen Tilly
Executive Director

P.S. Please come visit Our House and see this important project yourself!

Enclosures
    Attachment A: Budget
    Attachment B: IRS 501(c)(3) Certification

SAMPLE EDITED LETTER PROPOSAL

EXHIBIT 66 (Continued from page 180)

errors, e.g., pronoun-antecedent agreement. Have three different people proofread, including at least one reader who has not been involved with the writing of the proposal.

Use your computer spell-checker but recognize it will not pick up certain types of errors, e.g., misuse of "there" for "their," "assure" for "ensure," or "principle" for "principal." Existing grammar checkers are of some value but are still in their linguistic infancy.

To proofread word by word, start from the end of the proposal and read backwards. By doing this you are not influenced by the syntax; you must read each word independent of the others.

To spot the extra spaces sometimes accidentally inserted between two words, turn the proposal upside down and read the spaces; spacing errors quickly reveal themselves. You can also use your computer's find command: search for instances of two spaces together.

Increase the size of your proofreading copy on your computer or photocopy machine; mistakes show up more easily in larger print. Do your proofreading from doubled-spaced copy.

Title. Select an interesting, descriptive title: 10 words or less. Avoid cutesy titles or tricky acronyms on the cover page.

Poor: Extinguishing Apollo's Flame

Better: Expanding Fire Protection Services in Dallas

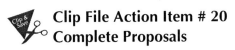

Clip File Action Item # 20
Complete Proposals

While each suggestion in this chapter represents a potential clip file action item, perhaps the starting point is to have on-hand complete examples of successful proposals. They become important reference points as you consider such things as organization, structure, and level of detail. While you can conduct a keyword search for "sample grant proposals" in your favorite search engine, recognize that "sample" proposals are not necessarily "model" proposals. The best way to obtain copies of successful proposals is to swap with past grant winners.

CHAPTER 16
Grant Review and Funding Decisions

The way to avoid criticism is to do nothing.

—Steve Ross

OVERVIEW

This final chapter discusses what happens to your proposals once they are submitted. More precisely, you will learn the following:

- The value of submitting your proposal to more than one sponsor at the same time.
- The different ways in which your proposal might be reviewed.
- What to do if you should be selected for a site visit.

Finally, this chapter suggests follow-up actions you should take, whether or not your proposal is funded. The review and constructive criticism of your proposal—not you—can only strengthen your idea. Beginning grantseekers with eggshell egos can take the advice of a Fortune 500 CEO, Steve Ross, and do nothing, but, obviously, that won't get you funded.

MULTIPLE SUBMISSIONS

Your completed proposal represents an important piece of intellectual property. To receive full value from your efforts, you should submit your proposal to multiple sponsors. This will increase your chances of getting funded.

Beginning grantseekers sometimes wonder if it is ethical to submit a proposal to more than one sponsor at the same time. Our answer is "Yes, it is ethical, provided you advise all grantmakers of your actions." Failure to let sponsors know of your actions would be deceitful—and that is unethical.

Implications

"Will making multiple submissions hurt your chances of getting funded?" ask beginning grantseekers. While the question is understandable, in practice, making multiple submissions will not jeopardize the likelihood of getting your proposal funded. In fact, it could help because sponsors with similar interests often form close communications networks among themselves. Grantmakers with similar interests talk to each other. Cofunding is not uncommon in some cases; that is, several sponsors may contribute partially to the total project cost. Furthermore, engaging in multiple submissions communicates to sponsors that you are seriously committed to your project and that you are willing to exert considerable effort to secure funding.

When submitting multiple proposals, present similar but not identical versions; that is, each version should be tailored to meet the varying interests of sponsors as determined by feedback from your preproposal contacts (Chapter 4). Sponsors expect you will submit similar proposals to other grant makers. You should name the other sponsors in your transmittal letter. For example, your transmittal letter might include a sentence like this:

> A similar version of this proposal is currently under consideration by the Pain Management Foundation; Mr. Guillermo Sainz, 414-234-6789, is the point of contact.

or

> A similar version of this proposal will be will be submitted to the Pain Management Foundation within the next month; preliminary

communications have been held with Mr. Guillermo Sainz, 414-234-6789.

Budget Considerations

If you submit multiple proposals, how much money should you request? The total amount you need from multiple sponsors? Partial amounts from each of several sponsors? For example, assume you identified five potential sponsors and want to request support for a $50,000 project. It would be very difficult to get all five sponsors to agree to contribute $10,000. Getting five sponsors to collaboratively support your project is akin to trying to herd cats. Rather, ask all five sponsors for $50,000 each. Funding from any one of them could support your project.

On rare occasions, you may have an "embarrassment of riches" problem whereby several sponsors want to fully fund the same project. To solve this problem, you have two main options. First, you may accept both awards and increase the size or scope of your project, assuming you can handle such a project increase and if both sponsors agree. If you expand the project size, you should keep the budgets separate and not comingle the funds. Second, you may delay the start date from the second sponsor in order to increase the length of the project period; each sponsor will therefore profit from the funds of the other sponsor. In essence, consider making your project bigger or longer before rejecting offered grant dollars. Usually, sponsors will be flexible in implementing your project, once they decide it merits funding.

REVIEW MECHANISMS

Your preproposal contact revealed how your proposal will be reviewed. The review process varies considerably. Your proposal may be reviewed internally by existing staff members or referred externally for evaluation. The external review may either be done by mail (print or electronic) or panel meetings. You need to know how your proposal will be reviewed and by what type of individual because your proposal should be written to the level of expertise of the reviewer. This audience analysis will help you determine the amount of detail you need to include in your proposal. For instance, if your proposal will undergo mail review by a technical specialist in your field, you will need considerable detail and documentation in your proposal.

On the other hand, if your proposal will be reviewed by generalists who are also reading 15 other proposals in a three-hour panel review (where they might be able to spend a maximum of 20 seconds per page reviewing your proposal), you would write with all the organizational and skimming mechanisms at your disposal. With an electronic review, your proposal may lose some special features like boldface or italics; as a result, document design considerations (Chapter 15) become critical.

The National Institutes of Health is an example of a federal agency that relies on outside specialists to conduct panel review meetings. In fact, they use a two-tier approach to the proposal review process. The first level of review has specialists evaluate the content or merit of the proposal. The second level of review examines the proposal's relevance to the agency mission. The National Institutes of Health two-tier approach is illustrated in Exhibit 67.

Of note, for informational purposes only, NIH publishes a roster of the individuals who serve as reviewers for the various study sections: www.csr.nih.gov/committees/rosterindex.asp. While it would create a conflict of interest scenario if you contacted these individuals directly, you should conduct prospect research on these individuals to get a better understanding of their values glasses. This will help you to write more persuasively. For instance, your literature review (or methodological approach) may reflect best practices in the field and include strategic citations, as appropriate, of articles published by members of the review committee. In other words, by recognizing reviewers' expertise in research-based approaches to advancing health, you enhance the credibility of your own project.

The job of reviewers is to ask questions about your proposal. Regardless of whether your proposal is being reviewed by a public or private agency, five basic areas are covered, at a minimum:

1. Scope of work
2. Personnel
3. Facilities
4. Track record
5. Budget information

Experienced proposal writers often conduct proposal review sessions within their organizations prior to formal submission.

Although reviewers look for many elements when reviewing proposals, one predominant feature in evaluating service delivery proposals is how many people will be reached by the proposed project. More precisely, reviewers are often asked, "How many people in the target population will be affected by this project? All? Most? Many? Some?" Proposal writers should use interim summary statements in their proposal sections to highlight how many people will be impacted. Reviewers will be looking for this information. Make their job easier by drawing their attention to things that will boost your proposal ratings.

KEY QUESTIONS TO ANSWER

Does the proposal do the following:

1. Show sufficient understanding of sponsor guidelines and priorities?
2. Address well-documented problems in need of solution?
3. Show a good approach to the problem?
4. Have an efficient time schedule?
5. Indicate probable outcomes?
6. Identify key personnel and their assignments?
7. Provide sufficient information to evaluate key personnel?
8. Deal with all clearance requirements?
9. Propose a reasonable budget?
10. Identify the probable project impact?

SITE VISITS

Occasionally, the sponsor may wish to conduct a site visit as a part of the evaluation process. This visit is a good sign that you are on their "short list" of potential grantees. The purpose of the site visit is to see first-hand your organization, its environment and people. Site visits are held when reviewers feel they need

information available only at the proposed project site. The information gathered in a single day by a team of reviewers can decide the fate of an application that may have taken months to prepare. Think of a site visit as a "quality control" measure for the sponsor, a way for the sponsor to run a credibility check on you, your organization, and your idea.

Site Visit Survival Strategies

If you are involved in a site visit, you should prepare properly. First, bring all potential project personnel together and review in detail the components of your proposal. Ask the sponsors if they have a particular agenda they wish to follow or if they want to see any special background documents. Arrange a private room for them to meet in and conduct interviews. Your job is to show them, not snow them, that your idea and organization are indeed credible.

Site visits represent a double-edged sword. A poor showing on your part may doom the application. On the other hand, site visits give you a golden opportunity to make up for weaknesses in an application and meet with specialists in the field.

To survive a site visit, follow the three "Rs."

• **Review.** Have everyone reread the proposal, understand, and be able to articulate their contributions, both to your organization and the project.
• **Rehearse.** Conduct practice site visits. The most common mistake in a site visit is for project team members to be unfamiliar with proposal details. It is for this reason that a "dress rehearsal" is

crucial, even to the extent of asking outside colleagues to come in and hold a practice site visit.

- **Respond.** Follow the established agenda. Stay on schedule. Don't bombard reviewers with lots of new information. Do provide copies of any specific documents that are requested. Do provide plenty of time to answer reviewers' questions. Give reviewers a "Take Away" folder that includes the agenda, proposal abstract, contact information for all key participants, any requested documents, written answers to any specific questions raised, and a list of other related projects.

Site Visit Example

Successfully managing site visits is, in large part, a matter of paying attention to many details. The following nuts-and-bolts example came from a recent full-day site visit from a national foundation. A proposal had received favorable initial reviews, and now four site visitors wanted to see the applicant organization firsthand and discuss in greater detail some aspects of the proposed project.

The sponsor provided three weeks advanced notice of the site visit date. They asked the applicant to develop an agenda for the day, which would include a short presentation of the proposal, answers to specific follow-up questions, and time for questions and answers with the project's collaborative partners. A great deal of preparation was done behind the scenes to ensure that the site visit went smoothly. Here's an outline of what happened—and when.

Two Weeks before the Visit.

- Review the sponsor's specific follow-up questions
- Identify key participants—internal staff and collaborative partners
- Confirm participant availability
- Have all participants review the original proposal
- Reserve a conference room for the presentation
- Begin to develop the presentation
- Begin to develop the agenda for the day
- Offer to coordinate hotel and travel accommodations for out-of-town site visitors

One Week before the Visit.

- Finalize the agenda
- Send the agenda to the sponsor and participants
- Send a map and driving directions to the sponsor and participants

- Contact the sponsor and participants to identify any special dietary restrictions
- Share the presentation with key participants for critique and input
- Discuss participants' roles and responsibilities during the presentation
- Practice

One Day before the Visit.

- Print name tags
- Hang up signs directing site visitors and participants to the conference room
- Order continental breakfast, box lunches, and afternoon snacks
- Copy handouts: (1) agenda, (2) participant list, (3) PowerPoint presentation slides, and (4) answers to specific follow-up questions
- Check technology—laptop, data projector, Internet, PowerPoint
- Make sure the conference room is clean and has an adequate number of chairs
- Have a final dress rehearsal for the presentation
- Get plenty of sleep

During the Visit.

- Look good. Feel good. Think good. Do good.
- Smile

One Day after the Visit.

- Send a thank you note to the sponsor
- Send a thank you note to key participants

During the actual site visit, the reviewers asked questions to assess project leadership, accountability, involvement, and communication. Some of their actual questions follow.

- Could you describe your vision for this project?
- Have you secured buy-in from project personnel?
- Do you anticipate ongoing evaluation and feedback during the project: With project participants? With project personnel? With collaborating institutions?
- Do you anticipate that labor shortages will be a problem for staffing this project?
- Have you had difficulties with staff turnover?
- Who will be responsible for data entry?
- Are project personnel familiar with technology, e.g., laptops, palm pilots, Internet?
- Can data systems communicate across partnering institutions?
- How do you deal with language and cultural issues?

Since the project under review involved multiple institutions, the site visitors asked questions of project partners about the nature of the collaborative relationships. These questions get at intangible characteristics such as energy, passion, trust, commitment, and ownership.

- How does this project fit in with the work that you do?
- How often do you interface with the project director and lead applicant institution?
- Have there been previous alliances among your institutions?
- Could you describe the planning process: Who was involved? Why does it work so well? What would you do differently?
- Do you see any barriers or challenges to this collaboration that need to be addressed?
- Do you feel the need for formalized administrative and management structures?

The preparation and attention to detail paid off: the proposal was funded.

DEALING WITH GRANT DECISIONS

Plan Ahead

Planned reactions become planned options. How do you plan to behave if your proposal is funded? Rejected? What are your options? When you have a powerful itch, it is almost unbearable waiting to get it scratched! Having to wait to get what you want demands patience and tolerance—unless you have planned options. Patient people turn to other activities to meet other needs while they are waiting for grant decisions. These activities keep them strong and in control. Strong people wait a lot. It may take many months before the decision on your proposal is made.

Sometimes while you are waiting for a funding decision, you may be asked to supply further information or respond to specific questions from your potential sponsor. Do this in a timely manner, for it means your proposal is under active consideration. Your clip file may be able to provide the requested information.

If You Were Funded

At some point, you will find out if your proposal was successful. Whether your proposal was funded or not, you should do some follow-up work. For example, if you were successful with a proposal, you should

request a copy of the reviewer comments, if allowed by the sponsor. Ask the program officer about common mistakes others make in implementing a grant so you don't fall into the same trap. Inquire how you can be a good steward of their money. Ask your sponsors what attracted them to your proposal. The answer provides insights about your organizational uniqueness. Add those uniqueness statements to your clip file and use them in your next grant proposal. Clarify the submission deadlines for technical and financial reports; you can keep your program officer very happy if you submit your reports on time. Invite your program officers to visit you. Add them to your organizational public relations list for news releases about your agency.

If You Were Not Funded

If you were not funded, don't take it personally. Many factors can cause a proposal to be rejected: amount of competition, available budget, geographic distribution, and closeness of match to priorities. Often, these factors are beyond your control. If the sponsor declined your proposal, thank them for reading the proposal and ask what can be done to improve it. Request verbatim written reviewer comments, not summary comments, which are less specific. If you can't get reviewer comments, then request a "debriefing" to go over your proposal over the phone or in person. Learn how your proposal could be more competitive. Ask if you should reapply next year. Use this as an opportunity to build bridges with the sponsor for the next submission cycle. Periodically send them a photocopy of articles or publicity with the "Thought you might not have seen this and might be interested" approach. Invite them to your agency to get to know you better. Avoid the "You only love me at submission time" syndrome.

If You Were Approved but Not funded

It's a rather inglorious message when you learn that you were "approved, but not funded," a reality in grantseeking. This letter of disappointment often uses these words:

> Your application was sufficiently meritorious to warrant a recommendation for approval, but in terms of available funds and the competition for them, it did not receive a priority score high enough to be funded.

This "close-but-no-cigar" communication amounts to a near miss. Usually, it is "good news" information, for it suggests that the reviewers were attracted to your proposal but were concerned about some procedural issues, as opposed to finding the proposal inherently flawed. To leverage this situation to your advantage, ask the program officer for "verbatim reviewer comments," not just summary remarks. Once you learn what the precise issues of concern were to the reviewers, you need to decide whether you should revise and resubmit your proposal to this sponsor or seek another funding source. To make this decision, you need three pieces of information: probability estimates, proposal weaknesses, and time frames.

- **Probability Estimates.** Call the program officer and find out where you are on the "alternate" list: first, tenth, or whatever? Ask how far down the "pay list" the agency has gone in past competitions? Ask about their probability estimate of you getting funded: 10 percent, 50 percent, or 80 percent?
- **Proposal Weaknesses.** Ask for the program officer's reactions to the written reviewer comments; of the weaknesses cited, which ones were the most significant? Are they easily fixable?
- **Time Frames.** Find out when the next review cycle is. Are you better off to withdraw the proposal, revise and resubmit it as opposed to leaving it in the "hopper?" How soon will the program officer know if additional grant funds might become available?

If you decide to revise and resubmit, your revision should cite the concerns of previous reviews, itemizing them one-by-one and offering appropriate responses, whether you have made changes to accommodate their concerns or rejected their concerns for solid reasons, which you spell out.

THE LANGUAGE OF REJECTION LETTERS

Rejection letters from government agencies usually include comments about concerns raised by the reviewers. You are entitled to this feedback and should request it, if it does not accompany your rejection letter. Private foundations, on the other hand, vary in the extent of their communications. To illustrate, one private foundation provides you with a successful proposal when they turn down yours. Another private foundation commonly provides a funding source book to help you identify alternative sponsors when they reject you. A few private foundations will write detailed rejection letters, spelling out the reason for turndown.

The most common experience for private foundations is to get the "form letter" rebuff. The rejection language in four typical foundation letters reads as follows:

- We regret that we will be unable to contribute as the funds available to us are, unfortunately, not sufficient to assist all the worthy organizations which come to us for support.
- Due to numerous requests for gifts and grants and limited funds, we regret we are not in a position to be of assistance to you. We were pleased to have the opportunity of reviewing the proposal, and only regret we will not be able to provide support for your organization.
- We regret to inform you that the Foundation is not in a position to provide a grant for your program.
- We have received your request to our Foundation. In reviewing your proposal, it appears your project is beneficial to certain segments of the community. However, in view of the numerous requests we receive, our limited funds, and the direction in which Foundation funds are applied, it appears we cannot be of assistance.

Occasionally, a reasonable amount of time elapses and you don't hear anything from a foundation: no funded or declined feedback. This is probably due to the fact that most foundations lack a support staff to handle such communications; at best, they can only communicate with their grantees. When faced with this situation, you should first attempt to call and see when funding decisions can be expected. If you cannot connect via phone, successful grantseekers usually wait a maximum of one year before sending a letter requesting that their proposal be withdrawn from further consideration. The language of that letter might include something like the following example.

> On February 2, 2007, we submitted a proposal to you entitled, "STAR Parent Training Program." Though a fortunate combination of circumstances, we now have the necessary resources to carry-out this project. Accordingly, we ask that you withdraw this proposal from further consideration. Since you value the importance of parent training, we will keep you posted on our major project outcomes. Perhaps, some future occasion will warrant submission of a different proposal to you.

In most cases, corporations decline grants in a manner similar to foundations; that is, they usually send some short letter announcing their decision without any elaboration of key reasons. A follow-up telephone call may provide further insights. If no response is forthcoming after a reasonable time frame, then you may wish to submit a withdrawal letter, like noted above.

Response to Rejection Letters

Getting rejected is the first step to getting funded. Rejection letters present an opportunity to build good will with a future potential sponsor. Consider sending them a letter like the following in those instances when your proposal is declined. This letter contains model paragraphs for use with corporations or foundations.

> Thank you for your letter informing us of your decision regarding our request for support the STAR Parent Training Program. We are, of course, disappointed that the Healthy Baby Foundation cannot support the project. We recognize, however, that there are always more requests than funds and we are sympathetic with the difficult responsibilities of Foundation officers.
>
> As I reflect on the many achievements of our organization and on the challenges yet to be addressed, I am hopeful that the Foundation will be able to give future consideration to support for us if we submit a different proposal. As a nonprofit organization, we must rely on the generosity of those who value our mission.
>
> We appreciate your consideration of our request. You and your colleagues of the Foundation have our cordial good wishes and our esteem for the conscientious work you do.

In contrast with foundations and corporations, it is not necessary to respond to rejection letters from government agencies for two reasons. First, government funding is more dependent on the merit of the idea and less on their relationship with you. Second, many government agencies are mandated to respond to any communication received from citizens; your letter to them means they must write back to you. In essence, responding to their initial rejection letter simply makes more work for them, instead of building a relationship.

Persistence Pays

Like so many things in life, the first "no" is not necessarily the final "no." With federal grants, it is often possible to obtain reviewer comments, revise your proposal, and resubmit. Your funding chances usually improve with resubmissions. In fact, many successful federal proposals are rejected the first time they are submitted. Accordingly, initially declined proposals are revised on the basis of reviewer feedback and resubmitted with a greater likelihood of funding. Lack of prior success is not a solid reason for not trying again.

At the National Institutes of Health, records show that over one-half of those who apply eventually get funded, if they are persistent and obtain rewrite suggestions from their program officers. Another federal agency reports that the mathematical odds of getting first-time funding are one chance in six. Those who are initially rejected but then revise their proposal resubmit it to improved odds: one chance in three for funding. If the second submission is rejected, the odds improve to one chance in 1.5 for a third, revised submission—decent funding chances. Most successful grantseekers switch to a different sponsor after the third declination.

In the world of grantseeking there are no guarantees. Even resubmitting a revised proposal a second or third time is not an assurance of funding. Why? Because review panels change personnel and perspectives. A proposal feature acceptable to one review panel may be unacceptable to another. In reality, this is beyond your control. Successful grantseekers minimize the possibility of changing standards by flagging those components in the revised proposal that respond to concerns of a previous review panel. In this way, you let the current review panel know you have taken previous concerns seriously and attempted to follow through on them.

Rejection Reasons

Some years ago, the federal government studied 353 research proposals that had been rejected in order to identify some common proposal mistakes. Their review of the rejected proposals yielded the following findings:

- 18% failed to number the pages
- 73% provided no table of contents
- 81% had no abstract
- 92% didn't provide resumes of proposed consultants
- 25% had no resume for the principal investigator
- 66% included no project evaluation plan
- 17% failed to name the project director
- 20% provided no list of objectives

These are easily correctable mistakes, pitfalls you should avoid. Some people may make these mistakes out of ignorance about the proposal writing process. Probably more people make these mistakes out of time pressure and haste. As you write your proposal, you should allow sufficient time to attend to these format issues as well as to your proposal content. Both content and format are important. Collectively, they speak to your overall credibility.

GETTING GRANTS: THE LONG-TERM VIEW

In this book you have been introduced to the basic reference tools for identifying funding sources. From these potential suspects, you have seen the importance of engaging in preproposal contact in order to maximize the "fit" between your idea and the sponsor's interests. You have read the clip file suggestions that will help you establish your own grants system for developing proposals while saving valuable time. You have dissected the components of public and private proposals. You have seen in this chapter the importance of being persistent; if you get turned down the first time, revise and resubmit your proposal based on feedback from your reviewer.

We conclude with one final tip: become a grant reviewer yourself. The "inside look" is very helpful later when you are ready to prepare your next grant. For instance, in addition to experiencing the peer review process firsthand, you will be exposed to persuasive writing strategies and common proposal mistakes, meet and develop relationships with program officers, and serve with professionals who may become future project collaborators. As a grant reviewer, you are acting as the conscience of the community, providing sponsors with vital information to ensure that their funds are invested wisely.

How do you get to be a federal grant reviewer? It's usually a self-nomination process. Once you identify a grant program for which you'd like to become a reviewer, tweak your resume to show related skills and experiences and send it to the program officer, along with a cover letter expressing interest. It might look like this.

> You and I share something in common—
> an interest in serving multiply handicapped children.
>   I'm writing now because depending on how you are reviewing your grant proposals, there is

a possibility my expertise and experience may be of value to you.
    As you review the enclosed resume, you will note the following:

- Six years of experience in the delivery of rehabilitation services to multiply handicapped children.
- Hands-on experience with children who have two or more of the following disabilities: hearing, vision, speech, intellectual, emotion, and motor control.
- Extensive interactions with diverse rehabilitation professionals.
- A bachelor's degree in special education.

    I'll call you in two weeks to see if you'd like more information or have special application forms to fill out.

Most federal agencies actively seek reviewers and welcome your volunteer efforts. For instance, at the National Institutes of Health Web site (www.nih.gov) you can search for "How Scientists Are Selected For Study Section Service" and the Center for Scientific Review will explain selection criteria and the nomination process. Occasionally, sponsors will respond with a simple form you will need to fill out so they can enter demographic information in their reviewer database. A few federal agencies allow you to register online directly:

- National Endowment for the Humanities
  http://grants.neh.gov/prism
- National Science Foundation—Chemical, Bioengineering, Environmental and Transport Systems Division
  http://www.nsf.gov/eng/cbet/reviewer
- U.S. Department of Education—Office of Postsecondary Education
  http://opeweb.ed.gov/edfrs

Sometimes the *Federal Register* will announce an agency's interest in finding new reviewers. A scan through its search engine will identify such opportunities. It is usually not necessary to have a Ph.D. and publish 20 books to become a reviewer. More importantly, your resume should show you understand the target problem.

The process in becoming a reviewer for a private foundation is not standardized. We suggest you contact the program officer and ask whether they use external reviewers. If so, volunteer by sending your customized resume.

Clip File Action Item # 21
Grant Review and Funding Decisions

Build your Grant Review and Funding Decisions clip file by including the following items:

- Sample letters to program officers requesting verbatim reviewer comments, whether your proposal was funded or rejected.

- Sample letters to program officers acknowledging their declination notice.
- Lists of grant programs where you could serve as a reviewer.

You have hundreds of tips on successful grantseeking and efficient, time-saving suggestions to implement them.

Now, go write your best grant ever!

Bibliography

Anderson, Cynthia. *Write Grants, Get Money*. Columbus, OH: Linworth Publishing, 2002.

Avery, Caroline D. *The Guide to Successful Small Grants Programs When a Little Goes a Long Way: Feature Case Studies of Foundation Programs*. Washington, DC: Council on Foundations, 2003.

Barbato, Joseph. *How to Write Knockout Proposals: What You Must Know (and Say) to Win Funding Every Time*. Medfield, MA: Emerson & Church Publishers, 2004.

Barber, Daniel M. *Finding Funding: The Comprehensive Guide to Grant Writing*. Long Beach, CA: Bond Street Publishers, 2002.

Bauer, David G. *The "How To" Grants Manual: Successful Grantseeking Techniques for Obtaining Public and Private Grants*. Westport, CT: Praeger Publishers, 2003.

Bishop, Wendy, and David Starkey. *Keywords in Creative Writing*. Logan, UT: Utah State University Press, 2006.

Boess, Marilyn M., ed. *Arizona Guide to Grants & Giving*. Glendale, AZ: Arizona Human Services, 2003.

Brewer, Ernest W. *Finding Funding: Grantwriting from Start to Finish, Including Project Management and Internet Use*. Thousand Oaks, CA: Corwin Press, 2001.

Brinkerhoff, Robert O., Dale M. Brethower, Terry Hluchyj, and Jeri Ridings-Nowakowski. *Program Evaluation: A Practitioner's Guide for Trainers and Educators*. Boston: Kluwer-Nijhoff, 1983.

Brophy, Sarah S. *Is Your Museum Grant Ready?: Assessing Your Organization's Potential for Funding*. Lanham, MD: AltaMira Press, 2005.

Brown, Larissa G. *Demystifying Grant Seeking: What You Really Need to Do to Get Grants*. San Francisco, CA: Jossey-Bass, 2001.

Browning, Beverly A. *Grant Writing for Dummies*. New York: Hungry Minds, 2001.

———. *Grant Writing for Educators: Practical Strategies for Teachers, Administrators, and Staff*. Bloomington, IN: National Education Service, 2005.

———. *How to Become a Grant Writing Consultant: Start-up Guide for Your Home-based Business*. Chandler, AZ: Bev Browning & Associates, 2001.

Burke, Jim, and Carol Ann Prater. *I'll Grant You That: A Step-by-Step Guide to Finding Funds, Designing Winning Projects, and Writing Powerful Grant Proposals*. Portsmouth, NH: Heinemann, 2000.

Burke, MaryAnn. *Simplified Grantwriting*. Thousand Oaks, CA: Corwin Press, 2002.

Burke Smith, Nancy, and E. Gabriel Works. *Complete Book of Grant Writing*. Naperville, IL: Sourcebooks, Inc., 2006.

Carlson, Mim. *Winning Grants Step by Step: The Complete Workbook for Planning, Developing, and Writing Successful Proposals*. San Francisco: Jossey-Bass, 2002.

Catalog of Federal Domestic Assistance. Available at www.cfda.gov, updated semiannually.

Chronicle of Philanthropy. Available at www.philanthropy.com, published biweekly.

Clarke, Cheryl A. *Storytelling for Grantseekers: The Guide to Creative Nonprofit Fundraising*. San Francisco, CA: Jossey-Bass, 2001.

Clarke, Cheryl A., and Susan P. Fox. *Grant Proposal Makeover: Transform Your Request from No to Yes*. San Francisco, CA: Jossey-Bass, 2006.

Coley, Soraya M., and Cynthia A. Scheinberg. *Proposal Writing*. Thousand Oaks, CA: Sage Publications, Inc., 2000.

———. *Proposal Writing: Effective Grantsmanship*. Thousand Oaks, CA: Sage Publications, Inc., 2007.

Crum, Nina, ed. *Grant Funding for Elderly Health Services*. Manasquan, NJ: Health Resources Publishers, 2003.

Directory of Corporate Affiliations. Available at www.lexisnexis.com/dca.

Dove, Kent E., Alan M. Spears, and Thomas W. Herbert. *Conducting a Successful Major Gifts and Planned Giving Program: A Comprehensive Guide and Resource*. San Francisco: Jossey-Bass, 2002.

DuBose, Mike, Martha Davis, and Anne Black. *Developing Successful Grants: How to Turn Your Ideas into Reality*. Columbia, SC: Research Associates, 2005.

D&B Million Dollar Directory. Bethlehem, PA: Dun & Bradstreet, Inc., 2006.

Edles, L. Peter. *Fundraising: Hands-on Tactics for Nonprofit Groups.* New York: McGraw-Hill, 2006.

Federal Register. Available at www.gpoaccess.gov/fr/index.html, published weekdays.

Fortune 500 Companies. Available at www.hoovers.com.

Foundation 1000. New York: Foundation Center, 2007.

Foundation Center's Guide to Grantseeking on the Web. New York: Foundation Center, 2003.

Foundation Center's Guide to Winning Proposals. New York: Foundation Center, 2003.

Foundation Directory. New York: Foundation Center, 2006.

Foundation Directory Part II. New York: Foundation Center, 2006.

Foundation Directory Supplement. New York: Foundation Center, 2006.

Foundation Grants to Individuals. New York: Foundation Center, 2006.

Freeman, David F., John A. Edie, and Jane Nober. *The Handbook on Private Foundations.* Washington, DC: Council on Foundations, 2005.

Friedland, Andrew J., and Carol L. Folt. *Writing Successful Science Proposals.* Cumberland, RI: Yale University Press, 2000.

Fund Raiser's Guide to Religious Philanthropy. Washington, DC: Taft Group, 2000.

Geever, Jane C. *Foundation Center's Guide to Proposal Writing.* New York: Foundation Center, 2004.

———. *Foundation Center's Guide to Proposal Writing.* New York: Foundation Center, 2007.

Gerin, William. *Writing the NIH Grant Proposal: A Step-by-Step Guide.* Thousand Oaks, CA: Sage Publications, Inc., 2006.

Gitlin, Laura N., and Kevin J. Lyons. *Successful Grant Writing: Strategies for Health and Human Service Professionals.* New York: Springer Publishing Company, 2003.

Glass, Sandra A., ed. *Approaching Foundations: Suggestions and Insights for Fundraisers.* San Francisco, CA: Jossey-Bass, 2000.

Grants for At-risk Youth. Gaithersburg, MD: Aspen Publishers, 2002.

Grants Register. Chicago, IL: St. James Press, 2007.

Grantseekers Guide to Faith-based Funding. Silver Spring, MD: CD Publications, 2003.

Guide to Community Foundations. Antwerp, OH: Freeman & Costello Press, 2002.

Guide to Funding for International and Foreign Programs. New York: Foundation Center, 2006.

Guide to Minnesota Grantmakers. Minneapolis, MN: Minnesota Council on Foundations, 2004.

Guide to U.S. Foundations, Their Trustees, Officers, and Donors. New York: Foundation Center, 2006.

Guyer, Mark. *A Concise Guide to Getting Grants for Nonprofit Organizations.* New York: Kroshka Books, 2002.

Hale, Phale D., and Deborah Ward. *Writing Grant Proposals That Win.* Boston, MA: Jones & Bartlett Publishers, Inc., 2005.

Hall, Mary S., and Susan Howlett. *Getting Funded: The Complete Guide to Writing Grant Proposals.* Portland, OR: Continuing Education Press, 2003.

Hall-Ellis, Sylvia D., and Ann Jerabek. *Grants for School Libraries.* Westport, CT: Libraries Unlimited, 2003.

Health Funds Grants Resource Yearbook. Wall Township, NJ: Health Resources Publications, 2004.

Henson, Kenneth T. *Grant Writing in Higher Education: A Step-by-Step Guide.* Boston, MA: Pearson/Allyn and Bacon, 2004.

Johnson-Sheehan, Richard. *Writing Proposals: Rhetoric for Managing Change.* New York: Longman, 2001.

Jones, Francine, ed. *Corporate Foundation Profiles.* New York: Foundation Center, 2002.

———. *Corporate Giving Directory.* Washington, DC: Taft Group, 2006.

Karsh, Ellen, and Arlen Sue Fox. *The Only Grant-Writing Book You'll Ever Need: Top Grant Writers and Grant Givers Share Their Secrets.* New York: Carroll & Graf, 2006.

Kenner, Carole, and Marlene Walden. *Grant Writing Tips for Nurses and Other Health Professionals.* Washington, DC: American Nurses Association, 2001.

Klein, Kim. *Fundraising for Social Change.* Oakland, CA: Chardon Press, 2001.

Knowles, Cynthia. *The First-Time Grantwriter's Guide to Success.* Thousand Oaks, CA: Corwin Press, 2002.

Lansdowne, David. *The Relentlessly Practical Guide to Raising Serious Money: Proven Strategies for Nonprofit Organizations.* Medfield, MA: Emerson & Church Publishers, 2005.

Levenson, Stanley. *How to Get Grants and Gifts for the Public Schools.* Boston, MA: Allyn & Bacon, 2001.

Liberatori, Ellen. *Guide to Getting Arts Grants.* New York: Allworth Press, 2006.

Martorana, Janet, and Sherry DeDecker. *RFP and Grant Writing Resources.* March 2002. Available at www.library.ucsb.edu/guides/rfps.html.

McGrath, James M., and Laura Adler, eds. *Grant Seeker's Guide: Foundations That Support Social & Economic Justice.* Kingston, RI: Moyer Bell, 2005.

McNabb, David E. *Research Methods in Public Administration and Nonprofit Management: Quantitative and Qualitative Approaches.* Armonk, NY: M.E. Sharpe, 2002.

Mikelonis, Victoria M., Signe T. Betsinger, and Constance E. Kampf. *Grant Seeking in an Electronic Age.* New York: Longman, 2003.

Miner, Jeremy T., and Lynn E. Miner. *Models of Proposal Planning and Writing.* Westport, CT: Praeger Publishers, 2005.

Miner, Lynn E., Jeremy T. Miner, and Jerry Griffith. "Best—and Worst—Practices in Research Administration." *Research Management Review* 13, no. 1 (Winter/Spring 2003), available online at www.ncura.edu/content/news/rmr/docs/v13n1.pdf.

Mudd, Mollie, ed. *Grants for K-12 Schools.* Gaithersburg, MD: Aspen Publishers, 2001.

National Directory of Corporate Giving. New York: Foundation Center, 2006.

National Guide to Funding for Libraries and Information Services. New York: Foundation Center, 2005.

National Guide to Funding for the Environment and Animal Welfare. New York: Foundation Center, 2004.

National Guide to Funding in AIDS. New York: Foundation Center, 2005.

National Guide to Funding in Arts and Culture. New York: Foundation Center, 2004.

New, Cheryl Carter, and James A. Quick. *How to Write a Grant Proposal.* Hoboken, NJ: John Wiley, 2003.

Nober, Jane C. *Grants to Individuals by Community Foundations.* Washington, DC: Council on Foundations, 2004.

Orosz, Joel J. *The Insider's Guide to Grantmaking: How Foundations Find, Fund, and Manage Effective Programs.* San Francisco, CA: Jossey-Bass, 2000.

Paprocki, Steven L. *Grants: Corporate Grantmaking for Racial and Ethic Communities.* Wakefield, RI: Moyer Bell, 2000.

Patterson Porter, Deborah. *Successful School Grants: Fulfilling the Promise of School Improvement.* Pittsburg, TX: D & R Publishing, 2003.

Peters, Abby Day. *Winning Research Funding.* Aldershot, NH: Gower, 2003.

Peterson, Susan L. *The Grantwriter's Internet Companion: A Resource for Educators and Others Seeking Grants and Funding.* Thousand Oaks, CA: Corwin Press, 2001.

Quick, James A., and Cheryl Carter New. *Grant Seeker's Budget Toolkit.* New York: John Wiley, 2001.

———. *Grant Winner's Toolkit: Project Management and Evaluation.* New York: John Wiley, 2000.

Reif-Lehrer, Liane. *Grant Application Writer's Handbook.* Sudbury, MA: Jones and Bartlett Publishers, 2005.

Robinson, Andy. *Grassroots Grants: An Activist's Guide to Grantseeking.* San Francisco, CA: Jossey-Bass, 2004.

Setterberg, Fred, Rushworth M. Kidder, and Colburn S. Wilbur. *Grantmaking Basics II: A Field Guide for Funders.* Washington, DC: Council on Foundations, 2004.

Solla, Laura A. *The Guide to Analyzing Wealth and Assets: Corporations, Foundations, Individuals.* Freeport, PA: L.A. Solla, 2001.

———. *The Guide to Prospect Research & Prospect Management: Corporations, Foundations, Individuals.* Freeport, PA: L.A. Solla, 2007.

Swan, James. *Fundraising for Libraries: 25 Proven Ways to Get More Money for Your Library.* New York: Neal-Schuman Publishers, 2002.

Teitel, Martin. *Thank You for Submitting Your Proposal: A Foundation Director Reveals What Happens Next.* Medfield, MA: Emerson & Church, 2006.

Thompson, Waddy. *The Complete Idiot's Guide to Grant Writing.* New York: Penguin Group, 2004.

Tremore, Judy, and Nancy Burke Smith. *The Everything Grant Writing Book: Create the Perfect Proposal to Raise the Funds You Need.* Cincinnati, OH: Adams Media Corporation, 2003.

Ward, Deborah. *Writing Grant Proposals That Win.* Boston, MA: Jones & Bartlett, 2006.

Wason, Sara D. *Webster's New World Grant Writing Handbook.* San Francisco, CA: Jossey-Bass, 2004.

Weinstein, Stanley. *Capital Campaigns from the Ground up: How Nonprofits Can Have the Building of Their Dreams.* Hoboken, NJ: John Wiley, 2004.

Wells, Michael K. *Grantwriting Beyond the Basics.* Portland, OR: Continuing Education Press, 2005.

Wholey, Joseph S., Harry P. Hatry, and Kathryn E. Newcomer, eds. *Handbook of Practical Program Evaluation.* San Francisco, CA: Jossey-Bass, 2004.

Yang, Otto O. *Guide to Effective Grant Writing: How to Write a Successful NIH Grant Application.* New York: Springer, 2005.

Yuen, Fancis K., and Kenneth L. Terao. *Practical Grant Writing and Program Evaluation.* Pacific Grove, CA: Brooks/Cole Thomson Learning, 2003.

Zils, Michael. *World Guide to Foundations.* München: K.G. Saur, 2001.

Zimmerman, Robert M. *Grantseeking: A Step-by-Step Approach.* San Francisco, CA: Zimmerman-Lehman, 2001.

Index

190–91; Persistence and, 189; Planned reactions to, 187; Rejection letters, 188–89

Grant ideas, 5–7

Grantmakers, 1, 5, 8, 24, 53, 55–56, 89, 120, 128–29, 146, 183

Grant myths, 4

Grant review and funding decisions, 183–91; Electronic proposal review, 184; Key questions, 185; Long-term view, 190; Multiple submissions, 183–84; Overview of, 183; Rejection letters, 188–89; Rejection reasons, 189–90; Review mechanisms, 184–85; Site visits, 185–87

Grant reviewers, 1, 5, 19, 39–42, 46–48, 50, 52–53, 87, 90, 108–9, 139, 147, 153–54, 165, 171, 177, 184–90. *See also* Past grant reviewers

Grantseeking: Attitudes about, 3–5; Getting started, 5; Individual attitudes, 3–4; Introduction to, 3–9; Organizational attitudes, 4; Sponsor attitudes, 5

Grant systems and procedures. *See* Clip files

Grant winners, 29, 42–45, 182. *See also* Past grant winners

Grants.gov, 11–14, 18, 20; Authorized Organizational Representative, 14; Central Contractor Registry (CCR), 13–14; DUNS Number, 13–14; E-Business Point of Contact, 14; Operational Research Consultants (ORC), 14

Grants Register, 27–28

Greater Milwaukee Foundation, 30

Guidestar, 29

Hall Family Foundation, 31

Headings, 172–73

Hewlett (William and Flora) Foundation, 31

Houston Endowment, 30

Illinois Research Information System (IRIS), 18, 34–35

Impact evaluation, 122

Indirect costs, 139–41; Corporate, 141; Federal, 140; Foundation, 140

In-kind cost sharing, 141–42

Internal Revenue Service (IRS), 28–29, 139; IRS 990-AR, 29; IRS 990-PF, 29; IRS nonprofit certification, 67, 72, 80, 181

Internal versus external cost sharing, 142

Johnson (Robert Wood) Foundation, 31–32

Kaiser (Henry J.) Family Foundation, 31

Kellogg (W.K.) Foundation, 30, 119, 126

Legislative officials, 21

Letter of inquiry, 55–57

Letter of intent, 55–56, 58, 87

Letter proposal, 53–86; Appeal, 59–60; Budget, 64–65; Capabilities, 63–64; Closing, 65; Complete examples, 66–67, 70–85; Elements of, 56; Examples of elements, 57–65; Overview of, 55, 69; Problem, 60–62; Solution, 62–63; Summary, 57–59

Letter proposal template, 55–68

Letters of support and commitment, 158–60

Lilly Endowment, 30

List of Cumulative Organizations, 28–29

Logic models, 126–28

MacArthur (John D. and Catherine T.) Foundation, 30

Mandatory versus voluntary cost sharing, 141

Marin Community Foundation, 30

McDonald (Ronald) House Charities, 32

Mellon (Andrew W.) Foundation, 30

Membership fees, 148, 150

Methods, 105–17; Data collection, 108; Examples of, 113–16; Justification of methods, 108; Key personnel, 105–8; Key questions, 105; Objectives-methods relationship, 108–9; Project activities, 108–9; Project collaborators, 107–8; Project management, 111–13; Project staff, 105–6; Project subjects, 107; Project timelines, 109–11; Purpose of, 105; Rejection reasons, 116–17; Start-up steps, 113; Time and task charts, 109–11; Writing tips for, 116

Mission statement, 8, 21, 24, 57

Multiple submissions, 183–84

National Center for Education Statistics, 96

National Center for Health Statistics, 96

National Directory of Corporate Giving, 36

National Endowment for the Arts, 19

National Endowment for Democracy, 19

National Endowment for the Humanities, 19–20, 141, 143, 190

National foundations, 23, 29–30

National Historical Publications and Records Commission, 19

National Institutes of Health, 19–20, 102, 143, 160–63, 184, 189–90; Awaiting Receipt of Application (ARA), 163; Modular budget, 143

National Science Foundation, 19–20, 102, 126, 141, 190

National Technical Information Service, 95, 135

Need statement. *See* Problem statement

New York Community Trust, 30

Objectives, 97–103; As evaluable, 97–98; Examples of, 99–103; As immediate, 97–98; Key questions, 98; As logical, 97–98; As measurable, 97–98; As practical, 97–98; Purpose of, 97–98; Rejection reasons, 103; As specific, 97–98; Writing tips for, 103

Office of Management and Budget, 19, 122, 140

Operating support, 4, 29, 69–72, 89–90, 146

Operational Research Consultants (ORC), 14

Orfalea Family Foundation, 31

Organizational: Attitudes, 4; Barriers, 4; Benefits, 4; Motivating others, 4

Outcome evaluation, 121–22

Outcomes, 51, 57, 97–103, 119–28; Examples of, 99–103, 123–28; Key questions, 99, 123; Outcome, 98–99, 119–22; Outcome indicators, 121–22; Process, 98–99; Purpose, 98–99; Rejection reasons, 103, 128; Writing tips, 103, 116

Overhead, 141

Toyota USA Foundation, 33

Training support, 69, 78–80

Transitions: Sentences and paragraphs, 174–75; Words and phrases, 174

Transmittal letter, 69, 82–83, 85, 162–64, 183–84

Uniqueness, 8, 57–59, 187

Unsolicited proposals, 51, 56

U.S. Department of Education, 12, 19, 98, 102–3, 119, 143, 190

U.S. Department of Health and Human Services, 12, 19, 145

U.S. Department of Justice, 19

U.S. Department of Transportation, 19, 21

U.S. Department of Treasury, 28

U.S. General Services Administration, 17, 19

U.S. Office of Management and Budget, 19, 122, 140

U.S. Patent and Trademark Office, 35

Verb choice, 175

Verizon Foundation, 33

Voluntary cost sharing, 141

Wal-Mart Foundation, 33

Walton Family Foundation, 31

WebCrawler, 28

White House, 19, 140

"White paper," 85

White space, 175

Writing and editing techniques, 171–82; Binding, 178; Clarity, 172; Comparing edited drafts, 176; Content and organization, 172; Critical reading, 177–78; Design, 172; Editing tips, 172–82; Find command, 176; Headings, 172–73; Levels of organization, 173; Line length and margin width, 173; Line numbering, 175–76; Mailing day, 178; Mailing envelope, 178; Mechanics, 172; Page numbering, 178; Paper color, 178; Paper size, 178; Paper weight, 178; Paragraph style, 178; Printer, 178; Proofreading, 178, 182; Proposal appearance, 177; Purpose of persuasive proposal writing, 171; Reading style/writing technique, 177–78; Sample edited proposal, 177, 179–81; Search reading, 177–78; Sentence length, 173; Sexist language, 173–74; Skim reading, 177–78; Title, 182; Transitional sentences and paragraphs, 174–75; Transitional words and phrases, 174; Verb choice, 175; White space, 175; Writing tips, 171–72

Yahoo!, 28

About the Authors

Jeremy T. Miner, M.A., is Director of Sponsored Programs and Director of Development for Strategic Initiatives at St. Norbert College, De Pere, Wisconsin. In addition to developing and administering proposals to public and private grantmakers as well as individual philanthropists, he has served as a reviewer for federal grant programs and helped private foundations streamline their grant application guidelines. Miner is a member of the National Council of University Research Administrators (NCURA) and the Council for Advancement and Support of Education (CASE). He is a principal in Miner and Associates, Inc., a grant consulting firm with offices in Green Bay and Milwaukee, Wisconsin, and Knoxville, Tennessee, and has presented grantseeking workshops nationally and internationally to thousands of grant-getters. His successful grant writing techniques have generated millions of grant dollars for many nonprofit education, health care, and social service agencies.

Lynn E. Miner, Ph.D., is founder and a principal in Miner and Associates, Inc. a leading nationwide grants consulting group that specializes in training successful grantseekers. He has been an active grantseeker in academic, health care, and other nonprofit environments for the past three decades. He has been affiliated with hospitals and public and private universities as a professor and research administrator as well as holding deanships in the Graduate School and in Engineering. Along with Jeremy Miner, he authored *Models of Proposal Planning & Writing* (Praeger Publishers) and coedits *Grantseeker Tips*, a free biweekly electronic newsletter on successful grantseeking, available through www.MinerAndAssociates.com.

Public Grant Web Sites

Web addresses for 50 major public grant information sources.

Name	Web Address
Electronic Funding Information Sources	
Catalog of Federal Domestic Assistance	www.cfda.gov
Congressional Record	www.gpoaccess.gov/crecord/index.html
Faith-Based and Community Initiatives	www.whitehouse.gov/government/fbci
Federal Acquisition Regulations	www.arnet.gov/far
Federal Business Opportunities	www.fedbizopps.gov
Federal Register	www.gpoaccess.gov/fr/index.html
Federal Research in Progress	www.ntis.gov
Grants.gov	www.grants.gov
Grantsnet	www.grantsnet.org
Grantmaking Agencies	
Administration for Children and Families	www.acf.dhhs.gov
Administration on Aging	www.aoa.dhhs.gov
Advanced Research Projects Agency	www.arpa.gov
Air Force Office of Scientific Research	www.wpafb.af.mil/AFRL/afosr/
Army Research Office	www.aro.army.mil
Bureau of Health Professions	bhpr.hrsa.gov
Centers for Disease Control and Prevention	www.cdc.gov
Centers for Medicare and Medicaid Services	www.cms.hhs.gov
Civilian Research & Development Foundation	www.crdf.org
Corporation for National & Community Service	www.cns.gov
Department of Agriculture	www.usda.gov
Department of Commerce	www.commerce.gov
Department of Education	www.ed.gov
Department of Energy	www.energy.gov
Department of Health and Human Services	www.dhhs.gov
Department of Homeland Security	www.dhs.gov
Department of Housing & Urban Development	www.hud.gov
Department of Justice	www.usdoj.gov
Department of Labor	www.dol.gov
Department of State	www.state.gov
Department of Transportation	www.dot.gov
Environmental Projection Agency	www.epa.gov
Food and Drug Administration	www.fda.gov
Institute of International Education	www.iie.org
National Academic of Science	www.nas.edu
National Aeronautics & Space Administration	www.nasa.gov
National Endowment for Democracy	www.ned.org
National Endowment for the Arts	arts.endow.gov
National Endowment for the Humanities	www.neh.gov
National Gallery of Art	www.nga.gov
National Historical Publics & Records Commission	www.archives.gov
National Institute of Standards & Technology	www.nist.gov
National Institutes of Health	www.nih.gov
National Science Foundation	www.nsf.gov
Office of Naval Research	www.onr.navy.mil
Smithsonian Institution	www.si.edu
State & Local Government Agencies	www.statelocalgov.net
U.S. Agency for International Development	www.usaid.gov
U.S. Information Agency	usinfo.state.gov
U.S. Institute of Peace	www.usip.org
U.S. Small Business Administration	www.sba.gov

CPSIA information can be obtained at www.ICGtesting.com
Printed in the USA
LVOW09s0635180214

374157LV00005B/17/P

9 780313 356742